THE PRODUCTIVITY DILEMMA

THE PRODUCTIVITY DILEMMA

**ROADBLOCK TO INNOVATION
IN THE AUTOMOBILE
INDUSTRY**

WILLIAM J. ABERNATHY

THE JOHNS HOPKINS UNIVERSITY PRESS / BALTIMORE AND LONDON

The Johns Hopkins University Press, Baltimore, Maryland 21218
The Johns Hopkins Press Ltd., London
Library of Congress Catalog Card Number 78–1034
ISBN 0–8018–2081–2

Library of Congress Cataloging in Publication data will be found on the last printed
page of this book.

CONTENTS

ILLUSTRATIONS

TABLES

PREFACE

This book is about innovation, productivity, and process change within a firm. It shows how innovation shapes the course of industrial progress but is, in turn, directed and then subdued by the competitive pressures within a firm. A general, if unorthodox, view of innovation is argued and then illustrated with very specific evidence about innovation, productivity, and process change in the automobile industry and the pressures that have brought that change about. This point of view is decidedly that of the general manager or strategic planner within a firm, but analysts and policymakers within government who wish to understand the pressures that affect technological change in industry also find merit in the concepts. While there are many good special studies of innovation and how it occurs, few books have considered how innovation does or does not fit into the mainstream of a corporation's competitive plans—why some firms seem to emphasize innovation in their competitive actions whereas others rely more on marketing or financial strategies or price competition.

At a time when there are many signs that industrial innovation is declining in the United States, relative to other nations, it is too easy simply to say that innovation and productivity improvement are often neglected by management and should receive greater emphasis; innovation cannot be pursued obsessively at the expense of other competitive considerations. The problem, and the focus of this book, is to understand how technological policy within a firm fits with other policies, which are based on different considerations. The basic features of past innovations offer important guidelines for making future judgments. They trace out a recurring pattern, or a "descriptive model," which embraces an array of management questions. For example, how should a firm's policy to encourage innovation tie in with its other traditional administrative functions and goals, such as selecting a type of organization or a competitive emphasis in marketing, new product introduction, automation, or labor policy? What are the relationships between innovative capabilities and the more traditional objectives of reduced production costs, tighter organizational control, and diversification in the line of products that are produced and marketed?

A clear challenge has been put to managers in government, as in industry, for greater effectiveness in managing technology—but the challenge is much clearer than the solution. Proposals include investing more money in research and development, reducing government intervention in industry, providing incentives for more entrepreneurial diversification by established firms, and restructuring large established firms that seem sluggish in their response. But would larger R&D investments really do much to stimulate important innovation? How does government regulation influence the incentives for innovation? Does it affect both established and innovative firms and product lines in a like manner? We do not have the answers to these questions. The situation cries out for a better understanding of our own heritage and of how management has successfully directed technological change in the past.

If innovation and technological change are to be well managed by a firm and wisely considered by government policymakers, these relationships need to be understood. My purpose in writing this book is to offer some ideas, formed into what I call a descriptive model, to clarify linkages between administrative action and the goals of innovation, between productivity and production process change. My descriptive model does not offer invariant rules; rather, it represents central tendencies that are apparent in historical perspective from the behavior of industrial innovation. In these relationships, however, we see contemporary management concepts that are also historically derived—the experience (or learning) curve, manufacturing organization insights or technological forecasting, the international product lifecycle—as elements of the same industrial behavior. While the ideas are presented and supported in some detail through historical analysis of change in the U.S. automobile industry, the substantial job of verification remains. I am gratified, however, by the practical affirmation of these ideas that I have personally received in presenting them before scholars and seasoned senior executives from many different industries. In this setting the ideas seem to meet an important first test; they have proved to be thought provoking, realistically capturing competitive considerations that are faced by senior executives in a variety of technology-based industries. This form of confirmation has been most important to me in the initial phase of the research.

ACKNOWLEDGMENTS

I wish to express my appreciation to the many individuals and organizations whose contributions made this book possible. Professors Richard R. Rosenbloom and Alfred D. Chandler of Harvard University have generously offered their valuable advice, guidance, and encouragement throughout the entire project. Drs. Andrew Pettifor and Alden Bean, of the National Science Foundation have also made valuable contributions in both the overall direction of the study as well as in specific detail. In particular, the substantial contribution of Dr. James M. Utterback of MIT is gratefully acknowledged, not only as my coauthor in Chapter 4 but also as a close colleague who helped in shaping the ideas of other chapters as well.

Throughout the study I was most encouraged by the interest and willingness of managers in various firms throughout the industry to contribute freely and openly to the study. Without their insight and data the book could certainly not have been completed. Managers in General Motors, Chrysler, from several suppliers, and from industry associations devoted many hours of their own time to share their knowledge with me. Much of the burden in this respect fell disproportionately upon the Ford Motor Company, since it is a central figure throughout the study. The basic support that men like Harold Bogart of Ford offered for the conceptual notions underlying the study was particularly helpful in the early stages. In execution I was most encouraged by Ford's willingness to make data available without attempting in any way to shape the nature of my conclusions. The professional staff at The Henry Ford Museum and Ford Archives, Greenfield Village, were also most helpful throughout the study in providing data as well as in sharing their own knowledge.

In addition to the above, I wish to acknowledge the great assistance provided by the individuals at Harvard who actually did the work on the project. Several graduate students made significant contributions. William H. Rodgers, Harvard Business School graduate student, carried out much of the research on the twenty innovations that are abstracted in Appendix 1 and discussed in Chapter 3. Other graduate students, including Kenneth

Wayne, Titus Adegoye, and William Berger, also contributed to various aspects of the research. Their contributions are much appreciated.

The research was supported by the Harvard Business School, Division of Research, and by a grant from the National Science Foundation, Office of National R&D Assessment NSF-DA-20571. The conclusions, however, are strictly my own and do not reflect the viewpoint of these or other organizations that have contributed so generously to the study.

THE PRODUCTIVITY DILEMMA

1 INNOVATION VERSUS PRODUCTIVITY: A FUNDAMENTAL DILEMMA

Innovation in the United States automobile industry has visibly waned over years of mass production and concentration on productivity. In 1964, Donald Frey, vice-president of the Ford Motor Company, stated publicly that the last significant innovation in the auto industry was the automatic transmission, which went into mass production in the late 1930s.[1] The giant strides in productivity taken by the industry since its beginnings are not questioned by critics, but since the 1960s, concern has been voiced on many fronts over the slow pace of significant technological change.

In the early years, rapid technological progress was spurred by fierce competition among many companies, each championing its own unique contrivance, like the Stanley Steamer or Pope's electric car. Over the years, however, radical innovation has given way to standardization and to the efficiency of highly complex mass-production methods. The question is why? Is it the age of the industry? Or its commitment to mass production? What are the management processes or historical events that have led to this change? Have long-term gains in productivity exhausted the ability to innovate? Can, or should, this trend be reversed, and what might the consequences be? For so important an industry something more than an emotional response is needed! A careful historical analysis of technological change in the automobile industry helps to provide important insight about the forces that cause industrial changes. Beyond the particulars of the automobile industry, however, such analysis helps to indicate whether the same course of events can or should be avoided in other industries where increased productivity is also urgently sought.

THE MODEL IN BRIEF

Technological change, as Joseph Schumpeter has said, has proved to be a "gale of creative destruction," wrecking industrial lethargy and leading to improvements in productivity for the benefit of society.[2] But in many cases, lo! as productivity increased, significant technological change became more difficult to achieve. In the refining of gasoline or the making of

3

steel, as well as in the production of automobiles, we see that many years of high rates of productivity have come at a cost—a declining capacity for major innovation.

Major innovations change the functions of the product in application or the basic way it is made. Such innovations are prevalent in the early stages of development of a product. Progress in this mode gives way to incremental change as the means of improvement, however, in the later stages of development.

This fact of industrial life deserves closer examination than it has usually received. The subject is full of unanswered questions, despite many good studies of particular aspects of technology. We need an integrative framework—a model—that can help to clarify the relationships of technological progress to changes in other factors: productivity, innovation, production organization, work-force skills, advances in production equipment, and new material sources. If it is to be well handled by business managers and properly encouraged by governments, technological change must be acknowledged as more than merely a matter of scientific and engineering interest.

My purpose in this book is to present a model and to illustrate and refine it through an account of technological change in the automobile industry. I developed the main ideas, largely as presented in Chapter 4, before this study was begun. Refinements and extensions of the model, as detailed in subsequent chapters, came later as I did the historical research and gained insights about the actual course of technological developments.

The model captures important milestones of change in the development of a product and its manufacturing process, from inception to maturity, over an economic life cycle, as it were. A common pattern seems to be evident in important instances for different products, firms, and industries. As the product and the manufacturing process develop over time, costs decrease, product designs become more standardized, and change becomes less fluid. At the same time, production processes, designed increasingly for efficiency, offer higher levels of productivity, but they also become mechanistic, rigid, less reliant on skilled workers, and more dependent on elaborate and specialized equipment. Perhaps of greater importance, the nature and sources of technological innovation shift with these structural changes in product and process. Innovation becomes more incremental. Major innovations, with potential to reshape the product or greatly improve productivity, originate more frequently outside the firm and the industry. Development in productivity continues until the industry reaches stagnation. Stated generally, to achieve gains in productivity, there must be attendant losses in innovative capability; or, conversely, the conditions needed for rapid innovative change are much different from those that support high levels of production efficiency.

In this book the model is developed in application to the automobile industry. But it represents a much more general pattern of change, focusing on the nature of innovation in industrial organizations, but with respect to questions that have not often been addressed in other research.

> Can innovations be well understood as an independent event or do they interact with one another and with other characteristics of the business unit in which they occur so that interactions need to be jointly considered?
>
> Does the unit of analysis make a difference? Are the traits of the firm or the industry or of individual incidents of innovation most important in systematically analyzing innovation? Would some other unit of analysis yield new insight?
>
> Is innovation a good indicator of technological progress within the firm or business unit where it occurs? How does innovation tie in with such other aspects of technological change, as the maturity of a technology, productivity improvement, the movement toward mass production, experience (learning) curve concepts, or systematic technology improvement trends? Does change in one of these encourage or retard improvement along another dimension?
>
> How does innovation relate to competition in a particular product? Why are organizations that stand out as most successful in a competitive sense often less innovative than their competitors?

THE BACKDROP OF PRIOR RESEARCH

A growing body of knowledge about technological innovation and industry characteristics is now emerging in several fields. As evidence accumulates, there is increased confidence that many findings represent common phenomena rather than isolated occurrences. As might be expected, the lines of inquiry in different disciplines have focused on different issues and offer different insights, as suggested by the following four areas that provide an underpinning for the present study.

Industry Differences

One perspective on the innovation process is provided by economists' studies of research and development (R&D) investment and industry structure.[3] When industries that support a high rate of major product innovation are contrasted with others, interesting variations become apparent, suggesting that totally different environments may support innovation. At the forefront of the innovative category are industrial segments like scientific instruments, electronics, pharmaceuticals, and chemicals. In these so-called "science-based industries," product technologies are rooted in active scientific fields, production processes tend to be labor- rather than capital-intensive, employees include a high ratio of engineers and scientists, and there is a high rate of new business creation based on new products that offer improved performance. Basic mass-production industries like steel, nonferrous metal production, railroads, and oil refining are in an opposing category. Here product innovation is typically incremental in nature. Firms are capital-, rather than labor-intensive, the technology is well established or "mature," and competition frequently hinges on price, economies of scale, and evolutionary advances in production processes. Studies of major innovaton in such industries suggest that they frequently originate from without the industry and diffuse slowly in established firms.[4]

Intrafirm Environment

Descriptive studies of major innovations offer consistent findings about particular conditions within the firm that support innovations, such as the organizational setting,[5] the traits of individual contributors,[6] and types of information linkages. Whereas large, highly structured organizations with well-developed lines of authority and control may be needed to amass and direct resources for large research and development programs, evidence suggests that they do not offer the right environment for radical innovation. Major innovations would seem to occur more frequently in loosely structured "organic" organizations with an entrepreneurial environment that provides large incentives to champions of successful innovation.

Process of Innovation

Historical analyses of the chain of events from scientific advance to invention, to innovation, and ultimately to broad commercialization, reveal the delays in the entire linear sequence from science to commercialization. The vast majority of scientific advances are in place long before the innovation occurs—in one study 90 percent came as early as ten years before the innovation.[7] They are typically drawn by market incentives into an industrial application that was usually unforeseen at the time of the scientific advance. The potential economic benefit to the nation as a whole from accelerating the time lags in the linked sequence is emphasized by this perspective.

Perfecting Innovations and Cost Reduction

A common picture of technological change in established products and production processes is one of evolutionary progress through a stream of incremental innovations and minor improvements. Independent studies of products as diverse as rocket engines,[8] computers,[9] and electric light bulbs[10] show that the cumulative effects of minor changes can be as important as radical innovation in reducing costs and improving product performance.[11] The same picture emerges for production processes. Progress in this mode is apparently related to the "experience" or "learning curve" phenomenon, frequently used in business planning. This phenomenon anticipates a rate of improvement proportional to the cumulative manufacturing volume of a given product—the more volume, the greater the improvement.

Central tendencies and systematic variations in the innovative process are shown by the wealth of prior studies in particular areas like the four briefly outlined here. However, they offer no higher-level explanation of why these tendencies or variations are observed or how one relates to another.[12] How, for example, does the knowledge about organizational conditions for major innovations relate to findings about experience-curve phenomenon or the environment for such systematic progress in established products? Specifically, will an organizational climate that is right for creating radical innovation also sustain high rates of productivity improvement? Can the rate of innovation be increased by applying insight gained from studying industry differences—say by breaking up large firms in concentrated, mature industries so that industry characteristics better match the profile for the innovative case? Why is the R&D investment rate higher in large firms within concentrated industries even though innovation arises more frequently from without such established firms? An explanation of differences is needed, especially one focused on characteristics of the innovative process, which is malleable or can be manipulated by decision makers. The present model of technological progress within the firm is a step in this direction. It offers a view of technological innovation that is consistent with many prior findings, but that at the same time leads to different interpretations and implications.

My approach departs from other studies in several ways. Productivity improvement has traditionally been favored as wholly beneficial, to be pursued without constraint or concern. My proposed model views productivity improvement as a phenomenon that has costs as well as benefits. It is beneficial when losses in innovative capability are recognized and balanced against potential gains. Similarly, a rapid rate of novel change has attendant costs in lost productivity. These distinctions about innovation and productivity lead to the second point of departure. Since both innovation in the product and cost ramifications are of interest, a special unit of analysis (called a "productive unit") is applied, encompassing both product and manufacturing characteristics. In this respect the model departs from product life-cycle studies[13] and learning-curve studies,[14] where either product or process may be of concern, but not both.

A course of industrial development that will lead to stagnation need not be followed to its ultimate conclusion. The purpose in studying a normal course of development is to understand how it might be altered or reversed when further advance is not desirable. In industries producing automobiles or steel or some appliances, development may have gone too far. In these cases, managers or government policy makers would benefit by understanding how development might be better directed in future. In other instances development has not yet been achieved, but is desired. In home construction, for example, the benefits of productivity gains would be welcomed by many buyers even though product variety was somewhat reduced. In these cases, a model that promises to clarify barriers to development would be helpful to those planning to encourage development.

The means whereby the course of technological development can be identified and intentionally controlled through government regulation or by the managers of firms are suggested in subsequent chapters by the findings about the automobile industry. The forces at play are complex, and great foresight is needed to direct technological progress in a competitive industry. For, under highly competitive conditions and pressures for productivity improvement, the course of progress leads naturally toward an extreme state of development. The analysis of technological change within the automobile industry suggests that development may be altered or reversed. Managers may have the means to control and renew their technologies by supporting and channeling their research and development programs in paths that promise significant technological innovations. Through programs that seek long-run technological advances, the forces of efficiency that drive an industry toward maturity can be kept in balance. The recent experience of the industry with massive government regulation would suggest, however, that this form of intervention has had the most direct influence on innovation. But the increased rate of innovation has not been realized without attendant cost increases and implications for industry structure.

APPLICATION IN THE AUTOMOBILE INDUSTRY

Technological change in the automobile industry deserves close study on three counts.

First, this industry plays a major role in the economy. One job in six within the private sector relates to automobiles.

Second, right or wrong, the lessons learned from the automobile industry are an important part of United States industrial culture. Past lessons still subtly shape attitudes and even current policy. For example, the basic concept of mass production—that great productivity gains can be realized by standardizing a custom product and then mass producing it—is accepted as an article of faith, partly because Henry Ford did it a long time ago. Since World War II, repeated attempts to apply this concept in building construction have failed. In his book on construction, Richard Bender concludes: "We have seen that much of the problem of industrializing the building industry has grown out of the mistaken image of the automobile industry as a model."[15]

Third, and of primary importance to me, the industry affords an unparalleled opportunity to study technological change over the full range of its development. Few products other than the automobile have left such a highly visible record of their development through a complete course from birth to apparent maturity. Two of the surviving major firms, Ford and General Motors, have been the major participants over most of this period. Because they have been essentially single-product firms, whose characteristics are uniquely associated with automobile production, technological change in the industry as a whole can be studied by analyzing these two.

From the standpoint of analysis, the Ford Motor Company is the most useful. Ford has the longest and best-documented history of the surviving automobile firms. Incorporated in 1903, it virtually created the U.S. automobile industry and has been a major figure ever since. For these reasons, disproportionate attention is given to Ford in the material that follows. The disadvantages of this bias are more than offset by the benefits. In a study of technological change it is more useful to have continuity in tracing changes in one major firm than to piece together a fragmented overview of the entire industry.

My method of study takes full advantage of the industry's size and diversity by comparatively analyzing two very different products and processes that coexist in each major firm: the automotive engine plant and the assembly plant. The engine plant is the most highly automated and advanced manufacturing process in any U.S. industry that makes products as complex as engines. But in reaching this state of development the industry lost the ability to accommodate change, as recent controversies over pollution control and fuel economy vividly illustrate. On the other hand, the automobile assembly plant has developed quite differently. Options for product change have been maintained in the assembly plant, where half of the labor used in making a car is employed. Flexibility is provided by the use of manual labor, light-process equipment, and an organizational orientation that anticipates change. A comparative analysis of these two types of plants, in terms of the model, reveals much about technological change in general and the automobile industry in particular.

2 TECHNOLOGICAL CHANGE IN THE U.S. AUTOMOBILE INDUSTRY: A HISTORICAL OVERVIEW

The United States automobile industry was born in Springfield, Massachusetts, in 1896, when J. Frank Duryea made thirteen cars from the same plans. This was the first time in the United States that two cars were made from the same design and the first time that cars were produced for sale.[1]

During the next ten years, developments were typical of an emerging industry. A great diversity of products appeared on the market. Each automobile was produced in very limited quantities, often to consumer order, and each model was rapidly made obsolete by succeeding models. Most models were built by entrepreneur-tinkers in their own back yards or in local machine shops, using equipment that was rudimentary, even at that time. At the turn of the century, the Stanley brothers designed and built their own steam-driven automobile and drove it to the top of Pikes Peak; electric, gasoline, and steam cars were built in many eastern and midwestern cities; and Henry Ford, who had already built one car in his spare time, was beginning to build a second.[2] By 1909, there were sixty-nine manufacturing firms in the industry, each committed to its own design. But technological change was rapid, and only half of these firms survived for even seven years.[3]

Today there is little real diversity among the various U.S. automobile designs. The 350 models of U.S. manufacturers offer options in respect to size, price, horsepower, and fuel economy, but in basic design features they are all very similar. Today, basic design changes very slowly, and the changes that do occur no longer spring from competition among technological entrepreneurs in the industry. The most important impetus for radical change now comes from pressures outside the industry—the Arab oil crisis, Environmental Protection Agency action, competition from foreign car manufacturers. Major components of the automobile are manufactured in highly specialized and automated production plants; the scale and capabilities of these facilities are now critically important in determining the types of changes that can be made in the product.

Innovation has given way to standardization as a competitive tool;

10

product diversity has given way to economies of scale; and external pressure on the industry has replaced entrepreneurial action as the major stimulant of technological change. The number of firms has decreased from around seventy to four, and the economic role of the industry has changed from producing an irrelevant luxury for the upper class to providing a vital source of national employment and transportation.

THE PERSPECTIVE

That these changes have come about is a matter of general public knowledge. There is broad agreement that the rate of major innovation has slowed, but there is no consensus about how serious a problem this is or what the causes are.

Explanations tend to reflect the particular viewpoint of the authority at hand. Ralph Nader claimed in his testimony before Congress that the slow rate of real innovation was due to lack of competition in the industry.[4] A U.S. Department of Commerce report claimed that the relatively low rate of innovation among firms in the automobile and steel industries was due to lack of "management ability." The study says: "We find the major barrier is one of attitude and environment. It is a problem of education—not of antitrust, taxation or capital availability."[5] The late Senator Philip A. Hart of Michigan attributed most of the problem to concentration among the firms in an industry: "New technology should be taking us in another direction—toward deconcentration, [and] greater efficiency in smaller units. But its natural thrust has been distorted—new technology has been used to rationalize the very theory it has proved to be a lie—that bigness is inevitable in a technology-oriented economy."[6] Senator Hart's statement nicely focuses the question: What is the "natural" direction of technological change and what causes it?

PRODUCT ADVANCES

Emerging consumer needs, not new technological capabilities, triggered the rapid development of the U.S. automobile industry at the turn of the century. A practical steam-powered car could have been produced twenty years earlier.[7] Allan Nevins observes that the industry was born from the consumer's desire for a light personal transportation vehicle, a desire stimulated by the bicycle boom of the 1890s. Hitherto, the motor-powered vehicle had been envisioned as a product for the commercial transportation industry, not the consumer. The firms that had the technology to produce steam engines were oriented toward railroads, shipping, and industrial application.[8]

Men with experience in the bicycle industry were the first to see the possibilities of the automobile as a means of personal transportation. Their technological orientation led them to improve the automobile's performance through lightweight designs, high-strength materials, and low-friction ball bearings rather than increased motor power. This orientation toward a lightweight vehicle suited to personal transportation was important in shaping the development of the U.S. automobile industry. It helps to explain why new firms were more successful in this new industry than the established transportation-equipment manufacturers of the nineteenth century.

The Fundamental Engine Choice

Competition among electric, steam, and gasoline engines at the turn of the century started the long sequence of market-determined design decisions that set the characteristics of the present-day U.S. automobile. The choice of an engine was the pinnacle in a hierarchy of design choices that established constraints for other choices in components. The choice has only recently been reversed.

The internal-combustion gasoline engine was initially a poor third choice among the three alternatives, but it developed rapidly. Before 1900 both steam and electric cars were more successful and reliable. Steam cars won the local and national races, and many electric cars were produced for consumer as well as commercial uses. In 1900 a gasoline-powered car defeated electric and steam cars for the first time in a free-for-all race at Washington Park racetrack in Chicago and, after this, improvements and market acceptance came rapidly.[9] Races played major roles in stimulating advanced designs, as experimental proving grounds, and as advertising. When Barney Oldfield won his first major automobile race in the 999, its builder, Henry Ford, received broad recognition that was helpful in founding the Ford Motor Company.[10]

The dominance of the gasoline engine was largely established by 1902, when the Olds Motor Works (predecessor of Oldsmobile) produced and sold twenty-five hundred small two-cylinder cars. By designing a light car, introducing mass production, and pricing the car at only $650, a 30 percent share of the U.S. market was gained, and for the first time competition was focused on one large market segment.[11] The Olds Motor Works was recognized as the world's first company to mass produce cars, and its success in the low-priced end of the market foreshadowed the competitive pattern the industry would follow for the next quarter of a century.

In rapid succession, the engine and "power-train" features of today's car were perfected and introduced.* Buick relocated the engine in the front

---

* The power train includes the engine, transmission, clutch, drive-shaft differential, and axle. The term refers to the mechanical components that generate power and transmit it to the driving wheels.

of the car in 1903; the now-familiar four-position transmission, with positions in the shape of an H, was patented by Packard in 1904,[12] and the Ford Motor Company introduced a series of models from A to R that advanced progressively toward a moderately priced four-cylinder car. The earlier photographs showing six of these models, in Plate 1, help convey the rapid rate of change in this period.

In steps and stages Ford made the engine and the rest of the power train to the wheels more reliable, cheaper to produce, and easier to maintain. Initially, the block and head for each of the engine's cylinders were cast together as one unit. Ford redesigned the block and cylinder as two separate parts that could be cast and machined with fewer difficulties. The engine was mounted longitudinally with the car, as is current practice, instead of transversely, or across the car. The earlier bicyclelike chain coupling between the engine and transmission and the wheels was replaced with a direct drive shaft to the rear wheels using the "torque-tube" principle; and the steering wheel was located on the left-hand side of the car.[13] By 1907 many of the features that distinguish the overall characteristics of today's car were in use, but they were not all used on the same car, and there was no clear indication of the best combinations.

The Fundamental Chassis Design

The Model T, which Ford introduced in 1908 at a price less than $1,000, was a spectacular success. It established the essentials of a dominant design at a higher level of component aggregation—the chassis.† The Model T chassis embodied an innovative synthesis of the industry's major advances up to that point, plus a few Ford innovations. Ford used a high-strength vanadium steel alloy in critical chassis components to reduce the overall weight by as much as one-half that of comparable cars. In past cars, the engine was often rigidly secured to the frame, and frequently even the cylinder blocks were twisted in half by the enormous strain that resulted when the car hit a rut or hole. Instead of strengthening the frame, the Model T introduced a three-point motor suspension that isolated the engine from the twisting forces that the frame absorbed. The ignition was powered by a magnet, so the traditional dry-cell batteries were no longer needed. Other new features included tough, flexible construction, high road clearances, and other mechanical dimensions suited to the rough roads and the essentially rural market the car was designed to serve.

For eighteen years the design of the Model T chassis was not significantly changed. During this period the industry's production of passenger

---

† The chassis is the whole car, except for the body. The chassis includes the frame, engine, transmission, brakes, wheels, radiator, and other mechanical components except the passenger enclosure (body) and its appointments.

EVOLUTION OF CARS IN MASS PRODUCTION

Comparing the 1908 and 1926 Model Ts shows that the design changed significantly in response to Henry Ford's policy of product standardization. Among the changes were the substitution of electric for acetylene lights, the use of a steel body instead of a wooden one, and the introduction of demountable wheels to facilitate tire repair. In addition, the 1926 version included an electric starter and a bumper. But with improvements also came efficiency-oriented losses; the magnificent brass radiator, brass fittings, and leather upholstery of 1908 had given way to austerity by 1926.

As a comparison of Ford cars manufactured between 1931 and 1942 will show, this was probably the period of the most rapid evolution in body styling. The car became more streamlined, headlights were absorbed into the fenders, and running boards were systematically eliminated in a series of changes that took place over ten years.

THE IMPRINT OF PREDECESSOR INDUSTRIES

Plate 1 shows the confluence of both the carriage and bicycle technologies in the early models. The footboard, seating, steering, and brake configuration in Ford's first car reflected the conventions of horse-drawn vehicles. The wire wheels and tires, however, showed the imprint of the bicycle industry. These features persisted in the Model C but evolved toward a unique automotive design in subsequent models.

THE RAPID PACE OF EARLY PRODUCT DESIGN

The rapid pace of design improvement in the early models can be discerned by comparing the step-by-step changes within the series of models A, C, and R, which were produced for the lower-price segment of the market. Notice that with progressive designs the engine was moved forward. In the Model A, power was applied to the rear wheels by a chain that was connected to a gasoline engine under the driver's seat. (The chain can be detected through the rear-wheel spokes, Plate 1b.) The Model C shows a clever styling response to a rapid shift in market preference for a front-mounted engine. The body was cut off at the footboardlike front end and replaced with a simulated engine housing. The engine's actual location remained under the driver's seat. Concurrently, the chassis was lowered, running boards appeared, and fenders began to take form over the wheels. In the later Model R the engine was front-mounted, behind the radiator, and the chain was replaced by the now traditional drive shaft. The pictures indicate that right-hand steering was used through Model R; not until production of the Model T did left-hand steering become firmly established.

EARLY MODEL DESIGNATIONS

The model numbers are indicative of the change and variety in the automobile industry's infancy. The Ford Motor Company was incorporated in 1903, and its first car model was designated the Model A, although Henry Ford had apparently first designed and built the car before incorporation. Numerous models were designed, built, and introduced over the next five years, addressing different markets, with model designations A through T. Only seven of these early models are shown here. All previous models were discontinued once the Model T proved to be successful. When the production of Model Ts was finally halted in 1926, after a phenomenal production record, Ford decided to retire the old model designation series and begin anew. So in 1927, twenty-five years after Ford had produced the first Model A, a second car also bore this model designation. Shortly after a second-generation Model B was introduced in 1932 alphabetic model designations were discontinued in advertising Ford cars; the policy of annual model changes had been adopted.

14

PLATE 1. *a*, Henry Ford's first car, 1896—a hobbyist's creation; *b*, Ford Model A, 1901–1903—Ford Motor Company's first car, list price $800; *c*, Ford Model B, 1904–1905—Touring Car body, list price $2000; *d*, Ford Model C, 1904—Touring Car body, list price $1000; *e*, Ford Model K, 1906–1907—Touring Car body, list price $2800; *f*, Ford Model R, 1906–1908—Runabout body, list price $750. (Photographs courtesy of the Ford Motor Company.)

15

PLATE 2. *a*, Early Ford Model T, 1908–1909—Touring Car body, list price $850; *b*, Ford Model T, 1926, the last production year—Steel Touring Car body, list price $380; *c*, Ford Model A, 1927–1931—Tudor Sedan body, list price $500; *d*, Ford V-8, 1932—Sport Coupe with rumble seat, list price $535; *e*, Ford, 1933—Tudor sedan, list price $550; *f*, Ford, 1936—Tudor Sedan, list price $565. (Photographs courtesy of the Ford Motor Company.)

PLATE 3. *a*, Ford Coupe, 1938—list price $685; *b*, Ford Fordor Sedan, 1939—list price $765; *c*, Ford Fordor Sedan, 1941—list price $775; *d*, Ford Coupe, 1942—basic model produced after World War II and until 1949; *e*, Ford Fordor Sedan, 1949—the new postwar model; *f*, Ford Granada, 1978. (Photographs courtesy of the Ford Motor Company.)

17

TABLE 2.1. Passenger Car Sales in Selected Years from U.S. Plants

1899	2,500	1910	181,000	1921	1,468,067	1932	1,103,557
1900	4,192	1911	199,319	1922	2,274,185	1935	3,273,874
1901	7,000	1912	356,000	1923	3,624,717	1940	8,717,385
1902	9,000	1913	461,500	1924	3,184,881	1945	69,532
1903	11,235	1914	548,139	1925	3,735,171	1950	6,665,863
1904	22,130	1915	895,930	1926	3,692,317	1955	7,920,186
1905	24,250	1916	1,525,578	1927	2,936,533	1960	6,674,796
1906	33,200	1917	1,745,792	1928	3,775,417	1965	9,305,561
1907	43,000	1918	943,436	1929	4,455,178	1970	6,546,817
1908	63,500	1919	1,651,625	1930	2,787,456	1975	7,050,120
1909	123,900	1920	1,905,560	1931	1,948,164		

SOURCES: Automobile Manufacturers Association, *Automobiles of America* and *Automotive Industries*, Annual Statistical Issue, respective years.

cars increased nearly sixtyfold, from 63,500 cars annually to 3,700,000, as shown in Table 2.1. Ford maintained about a 50 percent market share through 1924.

Ford's strategy caused an inverse product-adoption pattern in the United States that is unparalleled in any other high-cost consumer product. The wave of product adoption moved from remote areas toward the city. The mass market first developed in small towns, rural settings, and farms.[14] Above all else, Model T buyers needed basic transportation. This and the fact that there were initially no competitors in the low-priced market segment explains why Ford was able to dominate the U.S. market for so long with one unchanged model.

Through its success, the Model T had the effect of establishing many design features. These features include the water-cooled front engine with drive shaft and rear-wheel drive, left-hand steering, independent chassis and body construction (the body is manufactured separately and installed on the chassis), front and rear bumpers, and the essential driver controls of today's car.

Closed Steel Bodies

The very concept of the automobile was changed for the consumer by an early technological advance in body design. The introduction of closed steel bodies during the 1920s raised a whole new set of criteria for automotive design—passenger comfort, room, heating and ventilation, and quietness of ride.

As late as 1920 about 85 percent of the U.S. passenger vehicle bodies were constructed of wood. They were open; that is, they did not have solid sides and tops for the passenger compartment.[15] A closed wooden body was not widely used because it was expensive and did not stand up well on rough roads. Open bodies had been available in many varied styles, and in most cases the bodies were not produced by the company that manufactured the chassis. Ford, for example, produced few of its bodies before 1925.

In 1921, Hudson offered its Essex with an enclosed steel (that is, steel-clad wood) coach body for $1,245. The significance of this price is shown by comparison with the traditionally designed closed Hudson body, which alone cost about $1,100.[16] The closed steel body was very successful, and by 1926 over 70 percent of passenger cars were of closed construction. The premium price charged for closed bodies over open ones dropped from about 50 percent in 1922 to 5 percent in 1926. This conversion to closed steel construction was largely achieved in six years.

The closed steel body greatly increased investments by the manufacturers, for it required expensive sheet metal-forming equipment. Many firms were forced out of the industry, and by 1925 only forty-nine U.S. passenger-car manufacturers remained. There was a corresponding reduction in the body options available to the customer.

The early closed steel body resembled a rectangular rolling box, but it introduced the basic concepts of today's car. It established sheet steel as the basic construction material and the problem of effective passenger and luggage space containment as a major competitive criterion in automobile design.

Streamlined bodies evolved through incremental changes in the earlier steel bodies. The Chrysler air-flow design and the Studebaker Land Cruiser were pioneering designs that started the trend. Studebaker innovated in replacing wooden structural members. Sections of sheet-metal body components were formed to provide reinforcement so that the body shell and its reinforcing members were integral. The streamlined body and the ability to mass produce deeply contoured sheet-metal parts developed hand in hand. The last body part replaced by sheet steel was the fabric insert in the center of the top. It was not until the steel industry developed wide widths in rolled sheet steel that a one-piece steel turret top was introduced to eliminate this insert. Fisher Body of General Motors was the first to introduce the turret top in late 1934.[17] By 1940 virtually all major designs had streamlined bodies, fenders and running boards had been absorbed into the bodies, and headlights were recessed into fenders. Many of these changes are illustrated by the year-to-year differences in Ford models during these years as shown earlier in Plates 1 and 2.

The Universal Automobile Design

The new post–World War II models were introduced by all major U.S. manufacturers around 1948. They were innovative in the sense that they offered better-designed bodies and optimized the overall design of the automobiles to serve emerging postwar demands. The major innovation was the automatic transmission, which General Motors first introduced in mass production just before World War II.

This era was a plateau. The necessary technology for the major components of the car had been established during the prewar years and, for the first time, the market's attention was not predominantly drawn to rapid change in any one particular area. It is true that the automatic transmission and high-compression engines were still "in the wings," so to speak, since they had not yet diffused broadly. In general terms, however, the overall design was most important competitively. On this plateau, Nash, Packard, Hudson, Kaiser, Studebaker, Crosley, and Willys lost market share and were ultimately forced to merge or drop out. The major manufacturers excelled. Chrysler, Ford, and General Motors captured most of the market, and, in a functional sense, the designs of their major lines represented a virtually universal car for the U.S. market. They all produced six-cylinder and V-8 engines that offered ample reserves of power. All models offered durability and comparable mileage, and they were reasonably comfortable, quiet, and well heated or ventilated. Designs for different market segments were dissimilar only in degree.

The major model change introduced in postwar cars was the last one to move designs in the same direction. For the first fifty years of automobile production, through 1950, there was a sense of common direction. At any time, rapid advances in one component, such as the body or engine, provided a focus for technological competition. The resulting advances created a standardized design. The process of standardization followed a hierarchy: first came the propulsion choice, then the overall chassis configuration, and then major components were advanced. Finally, once technological change in the components subsided, the overall design of the automobile was optimized. This trend ended in the 1960s.

The horsepower race started in the middle 1950s, and the trend toward larger size continued into the 1960s. These two trends differed from earlier advances, however, for they did not have the same functional utility in the market. Later, size as well as horsepower increases were canceled by other product changes.

Diverging Design Changes

Large, general-purpose road cruisers continued to dominate the major U.S. automobile markets in the 1960s, but an underlying increase in diversity became evident. General Motors' 1960 model Corvair was radical for the U.S. market and even more so for General Motors. Its aluminum, rear, air-cooled engine, the "unitized" method of body construction, the suspension, and the fact that it did not include an integral heating system were a departure from many conventions of the market leader. Front-wheel drive was introduced in the Oldsmobile in 1966. Ford and General Motors began to diverge from the long tradition of separate frame and body construction. Unitized body construction* was introduced in some cars in the line, but not all, beginning in the late 1950s. Unitized construction saved weight. It found its major application in small cars and had the effect of increasing diversity in automobile designs. The Ford Pinto and General Motors Vega, introduced around 1970, departed extensively from conventional body designs in their size and power; number of body parts was reduced by 30 percent. The variety of engines increased greatly during the 1960s and 1970s, and by 1976 many different engines—such as V-6, overhead cam valve 4-cylinder, and slant 6—complemented the pure lines of V-8 and six-cylinder engines that had propelled cars for the preceding two decades.

The industry also demonstrated an ability to achieve technological progress in performance through incremental change. For example, under recent competitive pressures for higher fuel economies in American-made cars, mile-per-gallon ratings for some models have doubled without increasing the rate of major new model introductions.

The Logic of Design Trends

The preceding summary provides one interpretation of the trends that accompanied major changes in the principal components of U.S.-produced cars. For much of its history, the U.S. automobile evolved through a hierarchy of standardization to a highly standardized design, almost as if there were a natural logic to standardization. In the extreme state of standardization, change occurs only through adaptation and substitution of minor components.

The recent reversal in standardization has produced changes in the same manner but in backward order. For example, the response to the initial foreign-import surge of the late 1950s was generally to scale down existing designs. The Corvair would seem to be an exception, but in perspective it was not, for it finally was discontinued and did not have a lasting effect on General Motors' line of cars. Pollution regulations were first met with add-on components and modifications of existing components. Similarly, initial gains in fuel economies were realized by changes in components and not in basic design. As problems with imports and environmental regulations have persisted and have been compounded by higher fuel prices, however, the chain of ramifications has extended further up the design hierarchy to affect the basic configuration of the car. Separate frames and bodies in smaller cars have been replaced with a rationalized design combining the two in unitized construction. Body designs have been changed to reduce the number of parts. Changes that strike at more basic relationships among components are reportedly planned for post-1976

* With unit body construction the frame and body are the same unit. In effect there is no separate frame, and the body provides structural support.

model cars. These include more space-efficient transverse-mounted engines, new drive configurations to obtain more passenger space with less weight, and even more radical departures in basic designs for some cars.

It would seem that long-term trends in design and product-line development do exist, and these may be related to what is sometimes called the maturity of an industry. It would also seem that these trends may reverse themselves in changed competitive environments.

THE DEVELOPMENT OF MASS PRODUCTION

As a measure of productivity, home building and car manufacturing can be compared. Automobile manufacturers in the 1910s used roughly the same number of employee labor hours per car that a home builder uses in constructing a modest dwelling today. An early study provides data on two typical but anonymous firms in 1912. In one company that produced small cars, 1,260 man-hours were required per vehicle;[18] another firm that built a larger car used 4,664 man-hours per vehicle. Today the number of direct labor hours per car would be around 50 for a company whose material and component purchases amount to 60 percent of the car's price to dealers. If all company employees were included, the rate would be around 100 hours per car. The important role of production advances in this transformation is inescapable, but, as will be seen, these changes have also had side effects.

Early Formative Events

By most popular accounts, the early production innovations began with the moving assembly line that Henry Ford introduced in 1914. In my view, this famous innovation is not actually the proper starting point, for it is neither the most important of the process innovations that Henry Ford introduced nor the essential formative innovation in the mass production of automobiles. Some of the industry's basic contributions in mass production preceded the moving assembly line by more than a decade.

High-volume, low-cost production of automobiles rests on two basic concepts: precision-made interchangeable parts and mass production. Both of these concepts were widely applied in the bicycle industry before 1900, and the early producers of automobiles were familiar with them. Of the early firms, Cadillac was recognized for its expertise in precision-machined, interchangeable parts, and, as noted earlier, the Olds Motor Works was mass producing cars in 1901, before the Ford Motor Company was founded.

The automobile producers contributed innovations in production planning and control. The concept of interchangeable parts and the precision-machining capability needed to implement it were already in hand, but early manufacturing practices left the craftsman virtually in control of production. No one knew how to manage the total production of such a complex product. The early manufacturers had to develop new concepts to manage the massive quality-control problems, inventories, large work forces, and equipment investments involved in manufacturing something composed of tens of thousands of complex and costly parts. The problems and risks were somewhat similar to those that a mass-production home-building contractor would face today, except that house designs are not subject to rapid design obsolescence. Effective concepts for dealing with the problems of automobile manufacture came quickly. Today many of these seem obvious, but at the time they were highly imaginative and innovative.

A disaster first led firms in the industry to organize their manufacturing for large-scale mass production. A fire in the Olds Motor Works in late 1901, when mass production was just beginning, destroyed the Olds shops. Consequently, a final assembly operation was organized for the first time, and parts were subcontracted out to suppliers.[19] Historians of this era claim that this change established the idea that final assembly of parts could be set up and managed as a separate operation. More generally, it demonstrated, perhaps for the first time anywhere, that a major production process could be organized as a series of separate specialized plants.

A second important step in production organization was taken in October 1910, when Henry Ford established the first decentralized branch assembly plant in Kansas City, Missouri, to carry out the final assembly of cars.[20] This may well have been the first time in any U.S. industry that a company established specialized plants in different geographic areas as units of a common manufacturing process.

The implications of these two steps were significant. They segregated production along lines that gave opportunities for extensive mechanization and recognized the need to accommodate technological change and labor utilization rates. The component-manufacturing operations, centralized near Detroit, afforded opportunities for economies of scale through mechanization, specialization, and other process advances. The assembly operations that required many workers and a close matching of product output rates to regional sales rates were located close to the regional markets they would serve. Taken jointly, these moves recognized and probably encouraged the development of economies of scale in component manufacturing, while they minimized the employment impact in any one region. These choices in the aggregate structure of the manufacturing process were a major innovation for the automobile industry, and they provided a model for other manufacturing industries.

Moving Assembly

The moving final assembly line and other process innovations, for which Henry Ford has been credited, developed rapidly after the groundwork had been laid. Between 1911 and 1913 the specialization of labor at Ford was greatly increased, and by 1912 the moving assembly concept, without mechanized lines, was successfully applied in the manufacture of engines, radiators, and electrical parts. Finally, the famous mechanized line for the final assembly of the chassis was adopted in early 1914. H. L. Arnold and F. L. Faurote's early study of Ford production shows that with the introduction of the moving assembly line the number of labor hours required in the final assembly process for a chassis decreased by an 8 to 1 factor: from 12 hours and 28 minutes in September 1913 to 1 hour and 33 minutes in March 1914.[21]

The moving assembly line was important as one of a number of changes introduced in automobile manufacturing, but it may not be as important as these numbers suggest. The 8 to 1 improvement factor as developed by Arnold and Faurote has always been cited to demonstrate the importance of this innovation. Although the facts were carefully developed by these two independent, nationally recognized engineers and authors of the era, the improvements seem now not to be solely attributable to the moving assembly line. Ford made a second important change while the moving assembly line was being installed. In January 1914, Ford set a national precedent by introducing the eight-hour workday and by doubling wages to $5 per day. According to historians, the work environment changed overnight. Whereas previously the labor turnover rate had approached 60 percent per month, the change brought efficient tranquillity to Ford's operations.[22] Arnold and Faurote's analysis captured the benefits of this change as well as the moving assembly line innovation, since both occurred at the same time.

Thus the moving assembly line was certainly important in its own right, but its contribution may have been overstated. Productivity gains came from a series of changes, like those in length of the workday and in wages. These changes in scale, mechanization, work-force organization, process organization, and product standardization were dependent on one another, and it would seem that these trends may be reversing in the present market environment.

Mass-Produced Car Bodies

At the quarter-century point in the industry's history, the mid-1920s, techniques for mass producing car bodies were being rapidly developed, and the major automobile manufacturers frantically began their own steel body production. The mass production of bodies went hand in hand with the rapidly rising popularity of closed steel bodies, as discussed earlier, but it also depended upon advances in the widths and surface finish of rolled steel, the development of welding technology and, particularly, new paints and painting methods.

There were compelling reasons behind Henry Ford's original decision

TABLE 2.2. Cost Data for Three Model T Bodies, December 1913 (in dollars)

	Chassis Assembly				Body Assembly					
Model	Material	Labor	Overhead	Subtotal	Material (Body Cost)	Labor	Overhead	Subtotal	Total	Retail Price
Touring Car	122.23	17.034	22.65	161.92	62.55	0.362	0.48	63.00	225.32	550
Torpedo Car	122.23	17.034	22.65	161.92	43.97	0.323	0.43	44.72	206.64	590
Town Car	117.63	17.034	22.65	157.314	246.51	0.407	0.541	247.46	404.74	750

SOURCE: "Model T Cost Books," Ford Archives, Henry Ford Museum, Greenfield Village, Dearborn, Michigan.
NOTE: Chassis costs are the fully allocated total costs of producing the entire car up to and including chassis assembly. Body assembly labor is for the body only. Bodies were purchased already finished.

to offer the Model T in only a black finish. Colored finishes could not be economically mass produced on both the exposed metal chassis parts and wooden bodies. Wooden bodies could not be satisfactorily baked to dry and harden finishes. A satisfactory colored finish required sanding, rubbing, and polishing operations between repeated coat applications and long drying periods. By one estimate, 106 days were required to produce a colored body. Of this time, most was spent drying; 25 percent was spent in the paint shop where paint was applied in twenty-four successive operations.[23]

Du Pont introduced pyroxylin paint (DUCO) in 1923. This paint reduced painting time to three days. Steel bodies made baking feasible, and this further reduced production time.

Mass-production techniques could not be applied successfully as long as wooden construction materials were used. Table 2.2 shows how the cost in body construction varied by type of body. This table breaks down body and chassis costs of the Model T cars for three different bodies. All three were wooden bodies that Ford purchased already painted from suppliers. The purchase price to Ford is shown as a material cost in the "Body Assembly" side of the figure. Only the town car was a closed body.

Notice that at this time the closed body cost 150 percent more than the Model T chassis alone. Recall that the chassis included the full cost of producing all of the mechanics of the car. The closed body also cost almost five times more than the other bodies.

The mass-production technology for closed steel bodies had to be developed fresh, so to speak. It hinged on methods of sheet-metal forming with presses and welding technology. The primary production technology of the major firms before this time had been machining or metal removal and assembly, not sheet-metal forming. Moving-assembly techniques were ultimately to be developed in this area, too, but they were not of major importance until the late 1930s. Nevertheless, mass production came about, and by 1928 a closed steel body cost only 5 percent more than an open body.

Streamlined body designs became competitively important in the mid-1930s, as new ways to contour sheet steel body parts were developed. The large presses and dies for metal forming assumed a prominent role in mass production. This new technology increased the cost of model change and increased the sales volume that was needed to sustain a separate car model. Many firms, such as Graham-Paige and Reo, were forced out of production, even after the recovery from the depression had begun. Although failure to keep up with changing market trends was the market analyst's frequent explanation for many firms' misfortunes, the escalating cost of keeping abreast of body changes was an underlying cause.

Automation

The excitement of automation and systems analysis swept the automobile industry and the nation in the 1950s. The very term "automation" was developed and popularized in Detroit.[24] Transfer lines were coupled with automatic machine tools to create long machinery lines that could produce engine parts, such as the cylinder block, virtually without operator intervention. In body-parts manufacturing, automatic-feed mechanisms were coupled with high-speed stamping presses to increase productivity in sheet-metal forming. In many other areas where designs were relatively stable, such as radiator production, entire automated lines replaced manual operations. The assembly plant stood out as the one area that was largely untouched.

The influx of automation at this half-century point in the industry's history was acclaimed by the press as a revolution. The effect of these changes, however, was very similar to that of the moving assembly line. They were innovations in process organization and control, and they acted to make product and process design more interdependent rather than independent. With transfer lines, any significant change in engine design had to be accompanied by extensive retooling. As with stamping presses, these changes raised the cost of change.

Automated Assembly

The assembly plants stands out as the last major production area that has not been extensively mechanized and that still uses large amounts of direct labor. Since 1970 both General Motors and Ford have applied robots and in-line transfer concepts in some assembly plants. The more notable cases are the Lordstown, Ohio, plant for General Motors' Vega and Ford's Econoline plant at Lorain, Ohio. Volkswagen and other foreign small-car plants have probably gone even further toward mechanization in assembly. At the industry's seventy-five-year mark, extensive automated assembly seems the most likely potential area for change in mass production. A move to automated assembly also seems the logical sequel in the historical pattern of mass production. The assembly plant accounts for about half the direct labor that is now required to produce a car. The pressure on prices from foreign producers and rising wage rates make further assembly automation attractive.

Some Implications

The evolution of mass production has influenced much more than just the cost of the automobile. The industry could not have developed, of course, without the manufacturing advances that brought the cost of the car down within the economic means of the consumer. But while the course of development in mass production helped create the industry, it has also introduced a set of constraints. The moving assembly line, steel bodies, automation, and many other advances have made change and product innovation more expensive. Large-scale production processes in which the direct labor costs are low but indirect costs are high create strong economic forces to reduce real product variety.

Ford's program to develop a small car in the 1930s, the Model 92A, nicely illustrates the economic forces at play.

Ford's Small-Car Program—Model 92A

During the late 1920s and early 1930s, General Motors, with a broad product line, gained the lead in market share over Ford and by 1925 held approximately 40 percent of the market versus Ford's 25 percent and Chrysler's 22 percent. The high-volume Chevrolet (the lowest-priced GM car) emphasized product appointments and luxury over price, and it was particularly troublesome to Ford. The differential between the Chevrolet and Ford in 1926 is typical of product differentials in weight and size over many years:

	Price	Weight
1926 Chevrolet	$ 510	1,875-pound Touring
	645	2,130-pound Coach
1926 Ford	$ 310	1,607-pound Touring
	520	1,961-pound Sedan (Tudor)

Ford had been essentially a single-product company, and to compete with General Motors, Ford increased the size and price of its cars. By 1936, no major producer was selling to the low-price market that had been served by the Model T. Ford undertook the development of the 92A to supply this market. Eugene Farkas of Ford's engine development group engineered the project.

The car was to use the small, 136-cubic-inch displacement version of the V-8 engine, first introduced to the market in 1937, and a scaled-down version of the Ford frame and body. The project was a technical success but an economic failure. The reasons are discussed in Nevins's account of the project:

> Farkas engineered the model. He used the smaller V-8 engine, and the 92A, as the car was called, emerged narrower and shorter than the regular Ford, and 600 pounds lighter. The first completed model, as Farkas recalls, was a "sweet-running job." But difficulties arose. The small motor cost but $3.00 less to manufacture than the larger one. The remainder of the car was also cheaper only as it used less material, for practically all the essential elements were common to both the 92A and the V-8. Wibel calculated the possible savings in each case at a mere $36. Since the 92A would have to compete with year-old larger used cars, this was not enough . . . so by mid-April the project was abandoned, signifying that the company would not expand the range of its models downward.[25]

The implications of an integrated manufacturing process for product design changes are clearly illustrated by this example.

Several constraints placed by integrated production facilities on product design and market policy were evident. In the first place, most of the cost was apparently fixed and depended only on the number of units produced and not the specifics of model. Thus there was little incentive to produce a small car that might replace or "cannibalize" the sale of a larger car with a higher profit margin. In the second place, one would suspect that the 92A was a scaled-down version of a larger model because it could be produced in existing facilities. Otherwise, new duplicate facilities would have been required at a time when the company was operating well below capacity.

COMPETITION

Competition in the automobile industry has always been a conflict among giant firms. In terms of effective market power, there has not been a significant change in the degree of fragmentation, or division of the total market, in the industry since the early 1900s. The market-share comparison in Table 2.3 for eight major firms in 1923 and 1967 illustrates the point. The table shows unit sales and market shares and illustrates the use of the Herfindahl Index to indicate the "equivalent number of major firms." The number of equivalent firms in the industry is defined as follows:

$$\text{Equivalent Firms}^* = \frac{(\text{Sum of [Market Shares]})^2}{\text{Sum of [Market Share]}^2}$$

It can be roughly interpreted as the number of firms that would populate the industry if all had the same market share as the larger firms. For

---

* This measure is essentially the reciprocal of the so-called Herfindahl Index, which has been used by economists to define concentration of producers in a given market (see note with Figure 2.1, which follows).

purposes of comparison, the third column in the table presents a hypothetical example in which eight firms have equal market shares. For this case, then, there are eight equivalent firms. The equivalent number of firms is a single number that usefully indicates effective fragmentation. Although only four firms existed in 1967 compared to seventy in 1923, in both years about 70 percent of the market was controlled by only three firms. The number of equivalent firms, 3.4 for 1923 and 3.1 for 1967, offers a better indication of actual fragmentation than does the total number of firms.

Trends in industry fragmentation are shown in Figure 2.1, where the number of equivalent firms is shown as a graph and the actual number of firms for various years is given in parentheses at the bottom. The two initial sharp dips in equivalent firms coincide with the onset of mass production by the Olds Motor Works and the success of Ford's Model T. Since these very early events, the industry has been controlled by large firms, and trends have been stable and remarkably even.

Many small firms were forced out of the industry by the Great Depression but, surprisingly, this had only a minor effect on the number of equivalent firms. The major deflection in the trend was caused by the backlogged demand for cars and the surge of new firms that entered the market after World War II. Contrary to some popular notions, technological and market developments in the automobile industry have come about in a surprisingly consistent competitive environment as far as market fragmentation is concerned.

TABLE 2.3. Illustrative Market Share Statistics

	1923		1967		Hypothetical Example	
	Unit Sales	Market Share M (percent)	Unit Sales	Market Share M (percent)	Unit Sales	M (percent)
Total cars sold in U.S.	3,625,000	100	8,361,900	100	8,000,000	100
General Motors	754,700	20.8	4,142,900	49.5	1,000,000	12.5
Ford	1,825,800	50.4	1,853,300	22.2	1,000,000	12.5
Chrysler (Maxwell)	69,000	1.9	1,342,500	16.0	1,000,000	12.5
American Motors			234,100	2.8	1,000,000	12.5
Studebaker	145,200	4.0	—	—	1,000,000	12.5
Hudson	88,200	2.4	—	—	1,000,000	12.5
Packard	18,900	0.5	—	—	1,000,000	12.5
Nash	75,000	2.1	—	—	1,000,000	12.5
Subtotal	2,976,800	82.1	7,572,800	90.5	8,000,000	100
Other	648,200	17.9	8,600	0.1		
Foreign	—	—	780,500	9.4		
Equivalent number of major firms $\dfrac{(\text{Sum of } [M/100])^2}{\text{Sum of } [M/100]^2}$	3.4		3.1		8.0	
Actual number of firms	70		4		—	

SOURCE: Same as Figure 2.1.
NOTE: Percentages may not total to 100 due to rounding error.

Initial Competitive Strategies

During the early years of the industry, it was not unusual for firms to rely heavily on technological innovation as their competitive edge. Cadillac's early success and reputation, for example, has been attributed to its precision machining capabilities, 1/10,000 of an inch or better. In 1904, Buick's chief asset was claimed to be its patented valve-in-head engine design.[26] Since 1915, when the mass automotive market emerged, firms have not been successful in gaining a lasting advantage through radical technological innovations. Counted among the casualties are the 1915 Haynes car with an electric gear shift, the Franklin with an air-cooled engine, and the Cord with front-wheel drive. The Model T was a turning point. It blended technological innovation with a very insightful production and marketing strategy.

FIGURE 2.1. Trends in Market Fragmentation

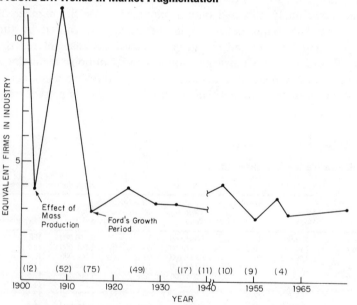

SOURCES: U.S. FTC, *Report of the Motor Vehicle Industry*; L. J. White, *The Automobile Industry since 1945* (Cambridge, Mass.: Harvard University Press, 1971), Appendix.

NOTE: The equivalent number of firms, as used here, is essentially the reciprocal of the Herfindahl Index. The reciprocal is used because it is more easily interpreted than the basic index. It provides a convenient measure of industry concentration when both the number of producers and inequalities of size affect real market power. F. M. Scherer, *Industrial Market Structure and Economic Performance* (Chicago: Rand McNally and Co., 1970), p. 51.

* Figures in parentheses are the actual number of U.S. firms manufacturing passenger cars.

Creating a Giant Industry

Henry Ford's enormous success with the Model T was not blind luck; his innovations were directed by a broad strategic plan. The essential outline of his strategy, or bragging as some called it then, is suggested by an advertisement Ford placed more than two years before the Model T was introduced: The "idea is to build a high grade, practical automobile that can be maintained as near $450 as it is possible to make it, thus raising the automobile out of the list of luxuries and bringing it to the point where the average American citizen may own and enjoy his own automobile— the question is not 'how much can we get for the car?' but 'how low can we sell it and make a small margin on each one?' "[27] Another account stated: "The Ford Company—was trying to make low-cost cars as reliable and as well supplied with good, cheap spare parts as a Singer Sewing Machine or the McCormick Reaper."[28]

The strategy was provocative, but the technology was not then at hand to carry it out. Ford's manufacturing capabilities were not as advanced as those of other firms in the industry. The vanadium steel on which the Model T's light, tough construction was claimed to depend had not yet been perfected, and automobiles that approximated this vision of performance cost around $2,800.

The impetus for implementing the strategy came from a technological innovation in steel making:

In 1905 [Henry Ford] saw a French automobile wrecked in a smash-up. Looking after the wreck, he picked up a valve stem, very light and tough—it proved to be a French steel with vanadium alloy. Ford found that none could duplicate the metal—[he] found a small steel company in Canton, Ohio [and] offered to guarantee them against loss. The first heat was a failure—the second time the steel came through. Until then [Ford] had been forced to be satisfied with steel running between 60,000 and 70,000 pounds tensile strength. With vanadium steel, the strength went to 170,000 pounds.[29]

Charles Sorensen, who helped design the Model T and was later Ford's senior production executive, reported Henry Ford's reaction to test data on the new alloy: "Charlie," he said, "this means entirely new design requirements and we can get a better, lighter, and cheaper car as a result of it." Sorensen reports further: "The vanadium steel development, which without question furnished the real impetus for abandoning the sensational success of Model N for the evolution of the Model T and ultimate realization of Henry Ford's dream of a car for the masses—this demonstration of vanadium steel was the deciding point for him to begin the experimental work that resulted in Model T."[30]

So, on the basis of a new technological development, vanadium steel, new design goals were established, and the Model T was designed. This chassis was reported to be less expensive than that of any vehicle of comparable quality and only half as heavy. Ironically, vanadium steel turned out not to be well suited to automobiles. It proved brittle, many part failures were experienced, and after a few years in production all vanadium steel in the Model T was replaced with other available steels.[31]

Thus, in retrospect, it was not really the technological advance in vanadium steel that brought about the Model T. The moving factor was the expectation aroused by this advance. After this came the policy of product standardization and Ford's later innovations in process methods and decentralized assembly plants, with mass production and distribution to provide control of markets in an era of slow communications. To summarize, it was Ford's *strategy*—bringing together appropriate product design, production, distribution, and marketing—that stands out as the most important factor in competitive success.

The expansion of market and production capacity and the pricing sequence that followed are shown in Figure 2.2. The graphs display four operating statistics of the Ford Motor Company. The graphs are extended to 1973 because they also provide a useful point of reference for interpreting interactions among alternative competitive strategies in later periods. The top two curves show changes in the median retail list price of the Ford line of cars, in 1958 dollars. The solid curve is the price of the car, and the dotted line is the price per pound of the car. Below the solid line is an index of labor utilization. It is an approximation of the number of employee hours that Ford used over the years per thousand pounds of car produced. The other graph is Ford's U.S. (North American after 1965) production in thousands of motor vehicles.

The dramatic price reduction and market expansion sequence that unfolded between 1908 and 1926 today would be called a "learning curve" or "experience curve." Very large gains in productivity were made, as suggested by the index of man-hours per thousand pounds of car produced. The full extent of labor productivity gains is masked by these graphs, however, for after 1912, Ford made unprecedented extensions in backward-integration* moves into iron and glass production, lumbering, and mining. In 1922–23 a peak production of two million Model T cars and trucks was achieved.

By early in 1920, the Model T was an aging design, however, and even though Ford added a starter and a closed steel body, there was no change in basic design. To retain market share Ford dropped the price to $290 (or $890 in terms of constant 1958 dollars), but General Motors still gained market share rapidly. Ford closed down completely in 1926 for

---

* Backward integration refers to a move by the producer, Ford, to manufacture parts or materials hitherto purchased, an expansion backward along supply channels, as it were. Forward integration would imply an expansion forward toward the market.

FIGURE 2.2. Operating Trends, Ford Motor Company: North American Operations

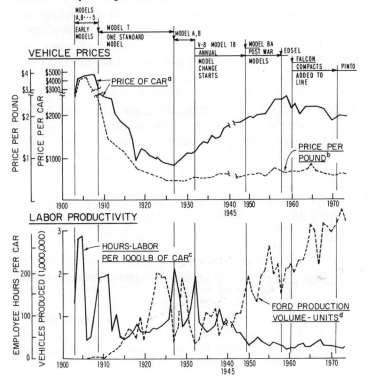

SOURCES: Corporate Reports; Ford Archives; *Automotive Industries* Statistical Issue, various years; and U.S. Bureau of Labor Statistics

a Retail price for median priced car in 1958 dollars
b Price per pound of car for curve (a)
c Ford employee hours (non salaried) per 1000 lbs of vehicles produced
d Unit production volume for North American operations—Ford

nine months to design and change over to a new model. General Motors, with a broad product line of cars, took over the leadership position in the industry.

In 1927, with unchanging strategy, Ford introduced its second-generation car for the low-price market, the new Model A. Although Ford briefly regained its prior market share, the old competitive strategy of low price, standardized design, and mass production did not work for long. After three years, Ford's market share dropped below 25 percent. In 1932, in the depths of the depression, the V-8 engine was introduced and product standardization was abandoned.

Alfred Sloan of General Motors criticized Ford's strategy as follows: "Mr. Ford had unusual vision, imagination and foresight—[his] basic conception of one car in one utility model at an ever lower price was what the market, especially the farm market, needed at the time. . . . [His] concept of the American market did not adequately fit the realities after 1923. Mr. Ford failed to realize that it was not necessary for new cars to meet the need for basic transportation. . . . Used cars at much lower prices dropped down to fill the demand. . . . The old master had failed to master change."[32]

Ford's strategy can be described as brilliant but static. A market need was identified; the product and the manufacturing, marketing, and distribution facilities to meet the need optimally were then developed and implemented. But Ford's strategy recognized neither the dynamics of market development nor the counteractions of competitors.

General Motors

General Motors' invulnerable competitive policies were carefully evolved from experience with both success and failure in the contest with Ford, according to Alfred Sloan:

In 1921 . . . no conceivable amount of money, short of the United States Treasury could have sustained the losses required to take volume away from [Ford] at his own game. The strategy we devised was to take a bite from the top of his position—and in this way build up Chevrolet volume on a profitable base.

Nevertheless—the K Model Chevrolet—was still too far from the Ford Model T in price for the gravitational pull we hoped to exert in Mr. Ford's area of the market. It was our intention to continue adding improvements and over a period of time to move down in price on the Model T as our position justified it.

We first said that the corporation should produce a line of cars in each price area, from the lowest to one for the strictly high-grade quality-production car. . . . We proposed in general that General Motors should place its cars at the top of each price range and make them of such quality that they would attract sales from below that price. . . . This amounted to quality competition against cars above a given price tag and price competition against cars above that price tag. . . . The policy we said was valid if our cars were at least equal in design to the best of our competitors' grade, so that it was not necessary *to lead in design* or run the risk of untried experiment.

The same idea held for production—it was not essential that for any particular car, production be more efficient than that of its best competitor—coordinated operation of our plants would result in great efficiency—the same could be said for engineering and other functions.[33]

Thus there were three essential elements in General Motors' strategy. (1) Product design was conceived as a dynamic process that would lead to an ultimate target through incremental change. Design was not a once-and-for-all optimization as it had been with Ford. This process later became the annual model-change policy of General Motors. (2) Market needs would be met through the product-line policy rather than independent designs.

(3) Radical product innovations were to be avoided. Sloan says it was "not necessary to . . . run the risk of untried experiment."

General Motors had learned to avoid the risk of radical innovation from its experiences from 1920 to 1923 with an experimental air-cooled engine it called the copper-cooled engine. The copper-cooled engine program was begun in 1919 by an independent company under Charles F. Kettering's direction. By acquiring this company and securing Kettering's full-time participation to develop the air-cooled engine, General Motors first instituted a formal research and development group within the corporation.

The copper-cooled engine program failed for a variety of reasons, both technical and organizational. There were many technical problems with the high-conductivity alloys used in its manufacture, and attempts to mass produce the engine failed. The central problem may have been that the engine was championed by top management and Kettering and was forced upon the Chevrolet and Oakland divisions over their resistance. All of the one hundred cars that went to retail customers were recalled by 1923. Lessons learned from the "engineering dream," as Sloan once described it, substantially influenced General Motors' policy regarding advanced development:

We were . . . more committed to a particular engineering design than to the broad aims of the enterprise, and we were in the position of supporting a research position against the judgment of the division men who would, in the end, have to produce and sell the new cars. Meanwhile, obsolescence was overtaking our conventional water-cooled models. . . . The problem was one of conflict between the top management of the corporation and the producing organizations and of a parallel conflict between the top management of the corporation and divisional management. . . . It showed the need to make an effective distinction between divisional and corporate functions in engineering and also between advanced product engineering and long-range research.[34]

In describing the new policy that emerged, Sloan further stated: "Divisions . . . can [now] go ahead about their business in their own way as they have very big problems to work out to maintain their present positions for the future."[35]

These new policies in effect changed the method of introducing major new technological features. Instead of being pushed into application as they were developed, they came to be used only as desired, or pulled into application by operating executives. While the policy spawned by this technological failure helped to protect the operating divisions against the uncertainties of technological change, it also isolated mass-produced cars from the influence of advanced technology.

The broad competitive strategy that General Motors hammered out in specific decisions, like those following the failure of the copper-cooled engine, was to prove unbeatable. The company gained a dominant position in the U.S. market in the 1920s and has held it to the present. Under General Motors' market leadership, the automobile grew in size, price, and economic importance into the 1960s. The influence of General Motors' leadership may be seen in product-price trends at Ford (see Figure 2.2). The price and weight of the Ford line rose steadily from 1927 until 1960, as is evident from the difference between the trends in price per vehicle and price per pound of vehicle.

Apparently, productivity improvement was not neglected by General Motors, even though direct price competition was shunned. When new management took control at Ford after World War II, it found that the manufacturing cost of a Chevrolet was actually lower than that of a comparable Ford.[36] Even though Ford had spent millions in the thirties on new manufacturing facilities to integrate backward fully into iron and steel production as well as other areas, and even though Ford had sought direct price competition through lower retail price until 1946, General Motors had still achieved a cost advantage.

Little change in the essentials of General Motors' strategy has been apparent over the long period since the 1920s. Increased centralization among operating divisions, less difference in technological characteristics of various cars in the product line, and greater sharing of common components have tended to make the different car lines more like a single product. In general terms, however, the strategy seems to remain intact.

The Corvair program in the early 1960s is one exception; and, ironically, it parallels the copper-cooled engine in respect to organizational implications, technology, and ultimate outcome. According to industry sources, the Corvair was introduced to combat small imports at the insistence of top corporate management and over the opposition of Chevrolet's divisional management. The slow death the Corvair suffered in the market suggests that many of the problems encountered in the copper-cooled engine in transferring a radical technology to an operating division are generic to a strong, decentralized organizational structure.

Other Strategies

Other firms followed General Motors' lead and adopted a similar competitive structure. Several important variations emerged, however, in both Chrysler's and Ford's strategies.

The Chrysler Corporation seized a foothold in the market when Ford faltered in the Model T program and shut down for nine months. Chrysler offered four basic car lines in 1929: Chrysler, DeSoto, Dodge, and Plymouth. Unlike General Motors, however, production for all product lines was centralized, and Chrysler apparently did not integrate vertically backward as extensively as either General Motors or Ford.[37] Although only spotty data on vertical integration are available for the prewar period,

TABLE 2.4. Vertical Integration Comparisons

Value Added/Sales

Year	GM	Ford	Chrysler
1947	.470	.370	.288
1950	.515	.384	.306
1955	.500	.413	.353
1960	.486	.471	.319
1965	.522	.404	.373

SOURCE: Robert W. Crandall, "Vertical Integration in the U.S. Automobile Industry" (Ph.D. dissertation, Northwestern University, 1968), p. 82.

the relative positions of the three companies are suggested for the postwar period in Table 2.4. This table provides data on "value added/sales value" ratios for selected years. This ratio of "value added/sales value" can be interpreted as the fraction of the final product's economic value (price to buyer) that is made up of work done by the producer rather than purchased from suppliers.*

Because Chrysler produced fewer of its own components, it was less constrained in adopting advanced innovative components. Thus Chrysler could seek competitive advantages through flexibility in product engineering and in styling. Chrysler pioneered in high-compression engines in 1925, frame designs permitting a low center of gravity in the 1930s, and the experimental introduction of disc brakes in 1949, power steering in 1951, and the alternator† in 1960.

This strategy of design flexibility and shallow vertical integration proved very successful in the prewar period, when the rate of technological change in the product was rapid. As product designs stabilized after the war, however, other factors, like the strength of dealerships and customer service, became more important. Chrysler's market share followed a downward trend after World War II. Cost control was difficult during times of inflation, when cost increases could not be passed on to the consumer. This aspect was particularly troublesome after 1970. Inflation, government price control, and the consumer's loss of real purchasing power have squeezed margins and capital at the very time when resources have been

* The concept of "value added" is used to identify the economic contribution of different firms or producers that do work along the line in making a final product. For example, steel mills, rubber goods producers, electronics firms, etc., all contribute value to the car. The so-called "value added" by the final producer is usually computed by substracting the cost of purchased materials and components from the final sales price of the product. Thus the ratio of "value added/sales" can be roughly interpreted as the fraction of the final product's price that the company makes rather than buys from suppliers.

† The alternator replaced the traditional d.c. generator that was standard on all U.S. cars. The alternator produces a.c. current and then a.c. is converted to d.c. for recharging storage batteries. The alternator is much more efficient and leads to better electrical performance of the car. See case abstract on "Electronic Ignition" in Appendix 1.

needed to develop and introduce smaller, more efficient cars. A competitive strategy emphasizing flexibility in product design was well suited to prewar conditions. As with Ford's early policies, however, it would seem that the development of the industry changed the necessary conditions for success.

Under new management after World War II, Ford rapidly adopted a new strategy. Independent divisions, each having its own product lines and production facilities, were envisioned. Separate engine and assembly plants for Lincoln-Mercury and Ford divisions were introduced, but the market failure of the Edsel thwarted the planned development of three separate car divisions. After 1960 all North American production facilities were consolidated under a centralized functional organization; that is, many of the same production and engineering functions serve all product lines.[38]

In describing competitive policies, Lawrence J. White concludes that Ford has been a follower in styling, but a leader in seeking out market niches.[39] New models like the Mustang, Maverick, Pinto, and a combination car and truck called the Ranchero seem to confirm this characterization. Despite these successes, Ford has not been able to excel in head-on competition with General Motors across the full product line. Since 1960, Ford has maintained about a 25 percent market share.

The Foreign Invasion

Successful market penetration by small foreign imports has had important competitive consequences since 1958. The first invasion by imports began to build up in the late 1950s. A number of European producers introduced small cars, and the market share of imports rose from 1 percent in 1955 to 10 percent in 1959. The Big Three firms did not seem to take small imports seriously at first. The American car buyer had shown little interest in small cars ten years earlier, when the Henry J. and the Willys had been forced out of the market. Both Ford and General Motors had aborted the new small-car programs they undertook after World War II.

The Big Three's compact-sized cars, introduced for 1960, checked the first foreign invasion, and by 1962 the market share for all imports fell to less than 5 percent. The second import invasion was more serious. The smallest-sized cars of the Big Three were again increased in size after 1960. This is reflected in the short-term rise from 1961 to 1965 in Ford car prices (Figure 2.2). With Volkswagen in the lead, the market share of imports started back up in 1964, reaching 9 percent of the market by 1967. Despite the introduction of subcompacts like the Vega and Pinto in the early 1970s, the tide was not halted. During the oil embargo, foreign imports achieved a 16 percent market share, with Japanese cars leading the trend. And in some California markets, which historically have been leading indicators of national automobile sales, foreign cars gained 40 percent of the market.

The successes and failures of imports in penetrating the U.S. market reveal fundamental changes in competitive conditions. Sustained inroads into major U.S. markets have been made by the foreign imports like Volkswagen, Datsun, and Toyota, all of which developed strong dealerships. Foreign firms with less thorough dealer development, like Renault, have not been able to sustain initial successes.[40]

Successful foreign cars have offered a comparative advantage in a few objective, tangible performance characteristics the consumer can assess. Preferences in different market segments seem to have diverged more widely since 1973. Initial purchase price, full-tank driving range, fuel economy, and weight-efficient passenger-space capacity have risen in competitive importance within different market segments as forces of inflation, recession, the oil embargo, and increased gasoline prices have battered the car buyer. The common denominator seems to be an increased reliance on tangible criteria by the consumer in making purchasing decisions. The more uncertain and intangible advantages of novelty, status, styling, or even safety, which might be provided by Mazda's rotary engine, for example, or Volvo's claimed extra safety features, seem to have had uncertain appeal in most market segments.

The explanation for these changes in the market may be the sequence of events since 1958 that has sharpened and channeled the consumer's focus on objective criteria. Congress enacted legislation in 1958 that required the list price to be posted on all new cars, so that dealers could not obscure real price comparisons through complex deals. The reputation of the U.S. firms as a favorable factor in purchase decisions was undoubtedly altered in the minds of some consumers by the controversy over safety and pollution controls in the late 1960s. The posting of mileage ratings by the Environmental Safety Agency, the disruptions in gasoline supplies, doubled gasoline prices, and the loss of real consumer purchasing power in 1974 have raised the importance of price and fuel economy. In addition, the long-term increase in two- and three-car families has meant that the consumer can more frequently "segment his own needs" and buy at least one small, specialized car rather than rely on a single, large, general-purpose automobile.

Because of these changes, it is not surprising that more purchasers have recently favored the small, less costly, and fuel-efficient or space-efficient cars. Once adopted, however, it is unlikely that the consumer will now turn away from the use of objective criteria in purchasing, regardless of favorable changes in the economy. New competitive strategies are needed.

COMPETITIVE FACTORS IN EVOLUTION: AN ANALYSIS

The way the firm competes successfully has been slowly altered by the sequence of developments discussed above as automotive technology has been perfected and competing products have become similar in more respects. Recent government regulations have also limited the firms' freedom to change product features. Through these trends, the essential features of firms' competitive strategies seem to have been altered. Market volatility decreased after World War II, the introduction of major new models has tended to have less effect on market share, price competition seems to have changed in importance, and consumer service has become a more important aspect of dealership policy. Evidence of such change is particularly apparent in Ford's and General Motors' product-line pricing policies in the transitional decades of 1920 and 1930. Ford was initially able to gain a dominant position by following what today would be called an "experience curve" pricing strategy. Prices were aggressively reduced as volume increased and manufacturing costs were reduced. This worked well while primary demand expanded rapidly. As the industry developed, further product-line price reductions proved unsuccessful in competition with General Motors. This is but one example of several changes that together constitute a pervasive change in the basis of competition. Table 2.5 summarizes the changes in four competitive variables that arise from the history of the industry. The systematic nature of these changes can be explored more thoroughly through a statistical analysis of the competitive variables that actually influenced Ford's market share for over seventy years.

Competitive Variables

Three types of independent variables can be used in the analysis to represent the three top cells in Table 2.5: (1) the price differential between Ford's product line and that of its nearest competitor (Chevrolet in recent years); (2) a function representing the introduction of major new models by Ford; and (3) an index of Ford's product-line prices in respect to per capita disposable income. Statistical regressions can be used to determine how changes in these three variables are associated with changes in Ford's market share over time.

Price Differential. The price differential is the difference between the median price of cars in the Ford product line and the median price for the nearest competitor, for example, Chevrolet. The nearest competitor is considered to be a competing car line with the largest market share of passenger cars in the United States market (other than Ford). Data on car prices from 1905 to 1973 were obtained from the trade literature.

Major Model Introduction. The introduction of a major new model is represented by the number of years since the prior new model introduction (model age), as illustrated in Figure 2.3.

The assumption is that at the time of a successful major model change (the zero age of a new model in Figure 2.3), the firm will begin to add additional market share to its existing level. As knowledge of the new

TABLE 2.5. The Changing Mix of Competitive Factors

Competitive Factor	Stage of Development	
	Early: (1905–48)	*Late: (1949–73)*
Competitive Pricing (Competitive Differential)	*Secondary Competitive Factor* Variations in product performance among competitive products makes price comparisons difficult. Initial purchasers are also more likely to be affluent and to value performance over price.	*Primary Competitive Factor* As the technology is perfected, the degree of standardization among competing products increases and most offer minimum acceptable performance. Under these circumstances, price becomes a highly important factor in competition.
Model Change (Major Innovative Change)	*Primary Competitive Factor* The potential for product improvement is great, and technological progress is rapid. The market reacts in a volatile manner to new model introduction.	*Secondary Competitive Factor* The technology is refined, and most of the purchasers' needs are satisfied by earlier product models. The market reaction will be more uncertain and influenced by subjective or style consideration.
Relative Product-Line Pricing (In Respect to Consumer Disposable Income)	*Primary Competitive Factor* "Experience curve" product-line pricing is accompanied by reduction in "real" prices and increases in market share as new purchasers are drawn into the market. Stated alternatively, trading the product line down in price is expected to attract a larger market as primary demand is increased.	*Secondary Competitive Factor* Once the market is fully developed and the product is accepted by purchasers, the new entry, price-sensitive market segment, is not expected to be as large as in early stages of development.
Channels of Distribution (Dealerships)	*Primary Competitive Factor* The dealer's personal contact with customer and his own reputation is expected to be important for a new high-priced product.	*Primary Competitive Factor* Mass dealership channels, cost, and quality of service are expected to be most important with a more mature product.

model diffuses to consumers throughout the market, further gains will be realized. At some time, however, the success will be noted by competitive firms, and they will respond to counteract their loss of sales. As competitors take retaliatory action, perhaps through the introduction of their own new model, the growth will slowly decrease and eventually reverse. Com-

FIGURE 2.3. Market-Share Response from New Model Introduction: Fitted by Parabola

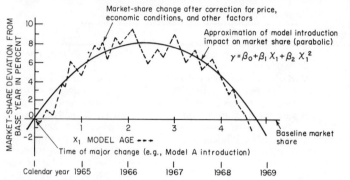

petitors will soon regain their original position, and market shares will be back to their original position.

This change in the initiating producer's market share can be represented as a parabola of a variable, model age, whose shape can be determined through regression. If x_1 is model age, it would take the form of the equation shown in Figure 2.3. Thus, through the use of data on the timing of new model introduction,* two terms of a multiple regression equation can be used to approximate the effect of model change on market share.

Product-Line Price Index. The ratio of Ford's product-line price to per capital consumer disposable income is used as an index of product-line prices relative to consumer purchasing power. Change in this index is expected to reflect overall product-line pricing strategy, as explained in Table 2.5. A steadily decreasing trend in this index would correspond to an experience curve pricing policy. It does not concern competitive pricing behavior, however, since competitive price differentials are reflected only in the earlier term.

Results of the Analysis

The entire period from 1905 to 1973 (except the World War II years) is included in the analysis. To show the difference in competitive factors as the industry developed, these seven decades have been partitioned roughly in half. The break point chosen was 1948 since the pre-World War II models were continued in production through this year. The differences between the two periods reflect systematic changes in the competitive environment. Variables are considered significant only when they have a 95 percent or higher confidence level.

The results are presented in Table 2.6, and the regression coefficients

* The models or years in which major changes were introduced include the following. For the years up to 1932, the introduction of models N, T, and A represented major changes. The new chassis introduction for the V-8 engine in 1933 is another. For later periods the model years 1941, 1949, 1952, 1957, 1960, 1965, and 1971 are considered major change years.

TABLE 2.6. Statistical Analysis of Competitive Factors: Determinants of Ford's Share in the U.S. Passenger Car Market (dependent variable)

	Stage of Development	
Competitive Factor	Early	Late
Price differential	Not Significant − 4.1* (70%)	Significant − 13.5 (99%)
Major model change Terms of parabola Model age Model age squared	Significant 3.5 (99%) − 0.1 (95%)	Not Significant − 0.3 (70%) 0.1 (90%)
Product-line price index (Relative to per capita consumer disposable income)	Not Significant − 4.1 (90%)	Not Significant .9 (60%)
Dealership	Increase in number of Ford dealerships is associated with increasing market share.	Increase in the average size of Ford dealerships is associated with improved market share.
Other statistics of regression Constant R square	 2.3 .532	 35.8 .50

NOTE: Variables offering confidence levels of 95 percent and above are considered significant.
  * The partial coefficient of regression is with the confidence level in parentheses.

and their confidence levels are given for each period. The coefficients show how great a change in market share accompanies a change in the indicated variable. These data strongly suggest that the competitive environment has completely changed as the industry has developed. Major model changes were a predominant competitive factor initially, but their role greatly diminished after World War II. This may be seen in Table 2.6 by comparing the magnitude and confidence levels of the parabolic terms. To simplify comparisons, the difference in magnitude of the parabola for the early and late periods (from a related regression analysis that also includes dealerships) is illustrated in Figure 2.4. These parabolas can be interpreted as an "average effect" of model change, for the top curve represents the average for five major model introductions in prewar years and the bottom one represents six for the postwar period. Not only is the magnitude greater in the earlier period, but the certainty of a favorable competitive consequence is better. In other words, Ford could be more sure of gaining a competitive advantage by introducing a major new model in the earlier period.

The importance of competitive pricing changes between the two periods. As expected, a decreasing price differential is associated with market-share gains in both periods, but the magnitude of effect is three times stronger in the postwar period and the uncertainty about effects is lower (99 percent confidence level versus 70 percent). In fact, price is the most important competitive variable in the postwar period. It is important to note, however, that these results do not pertain to conditions since 1973. Much different results might be expected in this more volatile market environment.

Changes in the coefficients of the price index confirm earlier observations about pricing strategy. Experience-curve product-line pricing proved more important during the initial phases of industry development and unimportant later. It would seem that such a strategy should be used with caution in the later stages of development.

The model for so simple a formulation is surprisingly powerful in representing the competitive environment. The fraction of total variance in market share explained by the variables is about 50 percent (R^2), and the results nicely support the prior conceptual model that preceded the statistical analysis.

Although not reported here, other more speculative but complex forms of the model have also been analyzed with similar results and an

FIGURE 2.4. Contribution of Model Changes to Ford Market Share (Versus Base Unit)

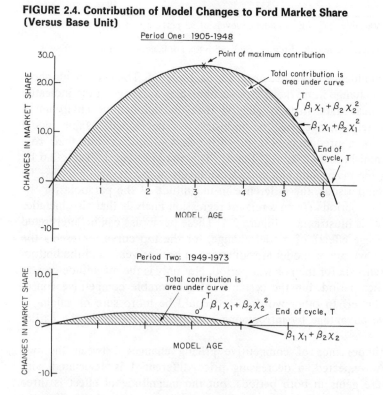

improved fraction of explained variance. When variables that pertain to channels of distribution are included, the results suggest that they are competitively very important in both periods. An increase in the *number* of dealerships seems to be associated with improved market share in the prewar period (99 percent confidence level). For the postwar period the *size* of dealerships seems most important to Ford. These trends lend support to the concept that appropriate channels of distribution shift as the industry develops.

Further analysis concerning which variables might stimulate change, or be "causal" as it were, have not produced fruitful results. The timing of relative changes in numbers of dealerships was systematically shifted relative to other variables to see whether a successful model change preceded an increase in dealerships or vice versa. This analysis showed no evidence of such a "leading" or "lagging" relationship. In a preliminary way, this suggests that a successful competitive strategy may require close timing and coordination among its various components. These later analyses provide the basis for the parabolas in Figure 2.4.

Economics of Major Model Change

Huge profits are at stake in the changes that have come about in the industry. The parabolas shown in Figure 2.4 provide a way of approximating the economic returns that accrue from a major model change. The area under each parabola represents the additional units that were sold because the change was made. Although the units used in the figure are percentages of the U.S. automobile market, they can be used to roughly approximate dollar-equivalent value if the contribution over variable costs per car is known.

For the average 6.14-year period that a major model change influenced the market in the pre–World War II period, additional unit sales were captured equivalent to 100 percent of annual U.S. automobile sales in an average year.* The gain in market share was only 25 percent in a peak year, but over six years the cumulative addition, as determined by the area under the parabola, was 100 percent. The comparable market-share gain for the postwar period is less than 5 percent, a decrease of 20 to 1. Table 2.7 extends these market-share figures to make a rough approximation for the value of a major model change in the prewar and postwar periods.

The differences between the two periods are quite sizable, ranging from about $1.5 billion for the earlier period to $.25 billion after World War II. Since the value of a model change rose from nearly zero when the industry was formed at the turn of the century, these numbers can be used

---

* As indicated in Figure 2.4, the area is the integral of $\beta_1 x_1 + \beta_2 x_1^2$ over the limit of 0 to T where T is the period of effect, is 100 percent of any one year's market share.

TABLE 2.7. Approximating the Value of a Major Model Change

	Prewar	*Postwar*
1. Annual U.S. car sales (cars in average year)	4,500,000	8,500,000
2. Additional market share captured by major model change (in units of percent annual market share)	100%	5%
3. Additional unit sales captured by major model change (item 1 × item 2)	4,500,000	425,000
4. Average price per car (in 1958 dollars)	$1,300	$2,100
5. Contribution per car to fixed cost, model change costs, and profit (assuming 25% contribution)	$ 325	$ 525
6. Value of new model introduction (item 3 × item 5)	$1,462,500,000	$275,625,000

to outline changes over time. This trend is illustrated by the upper curve in Figure 2.5.

The Net Value of Model Changes

The full significance of the decline is not shown by the value of major model change alone. The net value of a model change, or the difference between the value and the cost of a model change, is more informative. This is suggested by the gap between the two curves in Figure 2.5. The curve for the cost of model changes is based on industry estimates of actual model change costs during the postwar period for both Ford and General Motors (adjusted to 1958 price levels). The costs of particular model changes apparently are similar for both companies.

The implications of the curves are clear. The net value of an average model change fell nearly to zero in the postwar period. This explains the reduced rate of model change observed below (see Chapters 4 and 5). It may also explain why incremental change is relatively more attractive. The convergence of the two curves is also consistent with the shift in competitive emphasis to price and dealerships. These relationships clearly illustrate the magnitude of changes that have accompanied industry developments. If the two curves were to cross so that the net value of a major model change were negative, as suggested for the period since 1973 in the figure, then the automobile would be virtually a commodity.

Most of the data on which the model-change analysis rests pertain to the pre-1970 period. There is ample evidence that the market does value new models in the post-1970 period. Lightweight cars with more fuel efficiency and interior space have apparently gained in market share—the market now seems to be demanding this type of automobile. In fact, the market seems dynamic, sensitive to differences, and able to express its preferences. This is a far cry from a commodity market. The cost of model change does not seem to be as volatile as the value of model change,

FIGURE 2.5. Value and Cost of a Major Model Change

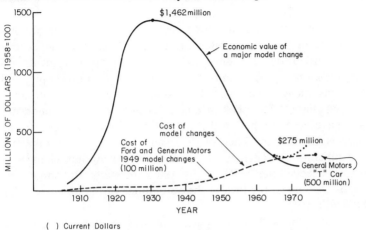

( ) Current Dollars

NOTE: Amounts in parentheses indicate 1958 dollars.

however, and these costs continue to rise. In the face of a continuing shift in consumer preferences and a rising cost of change, the industry's market power may concentrate even further among producers.

This analysis focuses attention on forces that induce technological change in the product and process and on the cost of making these changes. Previous studies have often concluded that static economies of scale in production were the major barriers to entry into the industry. These data suggest that the cost of change and the market's demand for change may be competitively much more important.

CHOOSING A UNIT OF ANALYSIS

As we have seen, the automobile industry has been fundamentally changed by progress in improving productivity and serving mass markets. Product innovation has been replaced as a major competitive factor by customer service and product-line policy. The development of highly efficient technologies for mass production has increased costs and raised design constraints to the point of slowing product change. Technological progress is no longer introduced by radical product innovation, but comes about as the cumulative result of incremental change. Forces outside the industry, like government regulations, political action, and fuel prices, now provide the primary stimulant for change rather than entrepreneurial competition within the industry.

These changes in innovative capability have come about slowly and cannot be attributed to any one factor. Rather, they seem to be generally associated with the competitive strategy choices of major firms and the technological trends that accompany the extensive development of mass production.

A sense of consistency and direction has pervaded the course of long-term development in the automobile industry. For decades, the central tendency in design led toward a universal car for all market segments. As new features made the car perform better, more reliably, more simply, and with greater convenience, the basic distinctions between high- and low-priced cars disappeared. The peak of convergence toward a common design seems to have been reached in the early 1960s; from that point to the present, there is growing evidence of divergence in design. To take full advantage of inherent consistencies in production and product changes, a unit of analysis is needed that will support systematic study. But should the unit of analysis encompass the firm or the automobile or the manufacturing process or the industry?

Salient features in the historical pattern of product and process development provide a framework of technological change that seems to apply outside the automobile industry as well as within. The technological histories of mass production in incandescent light bulbs, electronic calculators, and television share intriguing similarities with the history of the automobile. Progress in defining a unit of analysis must be made, however, before we can develop a common framework for comparison.

Such a unit of analysis properly includes the characteristics of the product, the constraints of the production process, and certain aspects of the particular firm's competitive strategy. During the early stages of development, the product alone might seem to be a useful unit of analysis. In more advanced stages of development, however, the production process takes on increased importance and, in the extreme, the process principally determines the characteristics of the product. (As an illustration, both the Oldsmobile and Ford's Model T were initially well-defined and unique entities. Today, however, little is communicated about a car by saying it is an Oldsmobile. To say that it was produced in a General Motors assembly plant for midsized Buicks, Oldsmobiles, and Pontiacs [a "BOP" plant] is much more informative.)

A special unit of analysis is therefore needed to encompass both the product and the characteristics of the manufacturing unit that produced it. A "productive unit," as I have defined it in prior studies, meets these requirements for a unit of analysis.[41] A productive unit is defined as an integral production process that is located in one place under a common management to produce a particular product line. The unit's characteristics are determined by a variety of factors—whether mass production is involved, how the production process is organized, and the cost and type of equipment and work-force skills. In a specific case, such a unit might be an automobile assembly plant for a given type of car or an automobile engine plant for a particular type of engine or a stamping plant and the intended body type. In other industries, the equivalent unit might be a plant for pocket calculators or a cold rolling mill. The important feature of this definition is that both product and process characteristics are considered jointly. Together they best represent constraints and opportunities for change.

By using the productive unit as the basis for study, an important reality about the technological development of the automobile can be addressed. The automobile is not well represented by just one productive unit; rather, several are important, and they may all be at different stages of development.

The stage of development in the productive units of the major components of the automobile must be evaluated to determine the development of the automobile as a whole. For example, as discussed above, the technology for mass producing automobile engines at Ford had undergone ten to fifteen years of development by the time Ford undertook the mass production of closed steel bodies. Although the mass-production technology for bodies ultimately became highly developed, in 1925 it was still a rudimentary process that required much hand fitting and stationary assembly work. Similarly, the automatic transmission at the time of its introduction in the early 1940s had the characteristics of an innovative product and demanded process innovation.

The maturity of an industry is often equated to many different factors like the rate of innovation, profit margins, and standardization of product as well as the industry's age. If the maturity of the automobile as a whole depends upon the development of the major productive units, however, then the chronological age of the car as a product, per se, is not as important in determining its vitality as is the development of major productive units. Innovation in major productive units up through the 1950s kept the car as a whole from reaching an advanced stage of maturity (see Chapter 6). It remains to be seen whether impending innovations in electronics, fuel engines, and frame and body designs can counterbalance the tendencies toward maturity.

Recent trends offer encouragement that such change is possible and may now be under way. If this is the case, then much of the responsibility must rest with forces external to the industry that have encouraged change. Even though the major automobile firms may have resisted change initially, forces have stimulated a new direction of development that in the long run will be in the vital interest of the industry and the firms themselves.

The concept of the productive unit and the way it normally evolves and is shaped by innovation are central issues in this book. The way a productive unit develops and changes or resists change, and its relationship to the structure of the automobile industry and to the automobile as a final market product, all require more study. These ideas are developed and refined in subsequent chapters.

3 TWENTY AUTOMOTIVE INNOVATIONS

Technological innovations are a leading edge in industrial progress; they create the capability for new products and production processes. If the very nature of innovation systematically changes with the maturity of a product and its manufacturing process, as suggested in Chapter 2, then to learn how changes come about, it makes good sense to examine the sequence of innovations in a given area for an extended period. Such a "longitudinal" study offers an opportunity to analyze the way that innovation may quicken, reverse, or otherwise alter developments. In addition, both product and process innovations require analysis because there are important interactions between them. Thus, in practice, we will use the productive unit as the focus for analysis.

In this chapter, twenty technological innovations are analyzed in order to clarify the way they have shaped the course of development of major automotive components and attendant production processes. I have not chosen innovation randomly for analysis, as would be appropriate for studying the general characteristics of the industry. Instead, I have selected samples of product and process innovations according to a few definite principles. First, the innovations occur in only two areas of automotive production—engine plants and assembly plants. Second, within these areas, balanced attention is given to both product and process changes over five decades. Third, the innovations have been selected becauuse of their commercial importance rather than their technological interest.

The engine plant and the assembly plant are selected for study because they seem to represent different states of development in the industry, and they cast new light on the conditions and actions that influence the development of a productive unit.

The picture of innovation that unfolds from this method of study differs considerably from the conventional view. Innovation is not a fortuitous, independent act by one party that furthers some independent goal. To the contrary, most of the innovations are highly interdependent, and they were the product of directed research and development efforts by many organizations over a long period. Technological innovation is seen to be more cumulative and consistent with a pattern of long-term development than has been suggested by previous studies.

THE TWENTY IMPORTANT INNOVATIONS

The objective was to select for study one of the most important product innovations and one of the most important process innovations in each decade from the 1920s to the present, for both engine plants and assembly plants. All told, one innovation was selected in each decade for each cell of the matrix below—twenty all told, as listed in Table 3.1.

SELECTION MATRIX

	Process	*Product*
Engine	Engine and related accessories	Engine plant and engine foundry
Automobile	Body and other major (nonengine) components	Assembly plant and body manufacturing

TABLE 3.1. Twenty Automotive Innovations

Decade	Automobile Design	Automobile Assembly	Engine Design	Engine Manufacturing
1920–29	Closed steel body	Use of seam welding in body and chassis assemblies	Aluminum-alloy piston	Cemented carbide cutting tools
1930–39	Independent suspension	Unit body construction	Automatic choke and downdraft carburetor	Cast crankshaft and camshaft
1946–55	Improved automatic transmission	Electronic-assisted scheduling for assembly	High-compression V-8 engine	Extensive automation of engine plants using transfer-line concept
1956–65	Disc brakes	Body corrosion protection	Aluminum engine	Thin-wall, gray cast-iron engine
1966–74	Energy-absorbing steering assemblies	Automatic chassis and body assembly	Electronic ignition	Programmable control

As the first step in selecting the twenty innovations, four to six candidates for each cell in each decade were identified from journal literature published at the time of the innovations. Knowledgeable individuals associated with each of the major U.S. automobile producers reviewed these candidates, suggested other candidates, and offered judgment about which were most important.* The innovation candidates that were judged as most important by at least one of these experts are listed in Tables 3.2 and 3.3, one list for engines and one for assembly.†

* Individuals with experience in research and development, operating divisions, and corporate staffs participated in the selection process. From eight to sixteen ratings were obtained for each cell, depending upon the period and whether product or process innovations were involved. A surprising degree of consensus was apparent, irrespective of individuals' corporate affiliation, except for the current decade. A majority identified the selected innovation as most important in almost every case.

† The exception to the procedure is found in the period prior to 1920. Candidates were not suggested for the early period, and there were several write-in innovations. These are listed for the earlier period to complete the tables.

TABLE 3.2. Thirty-three Technological Innovations in Mass-Produced Engines

Decade	Product Innovation	Process Innovation
1900–1909	Simple and reliable engine[a] (Model T)	Multiple simultaneous machining
1910–19	V-8 engine design	Continuous pouring of molten iron
1920–29	[b]Aluminum-alloy piston Crankcase ventilation Special exhaust-valve materials	[b]Cemented carbide cutting tools Dynamic crankshaft balancing
1930–39	[b]Down-draft carburetor [b]Automatic choke Low-cost V-8 engine	[b]Cast crankshaft and camshaft Precision boring Surface tunnel broaching
1945–54	[b]Short-stroke, high-compression V-8 New combustion-chamber design —OHV engine 12-volt electrical system	[b]Integration of engine plants with transfer lines Dynamic engine balancing Automatic air gauges in machining
1955–64	[b]Aluminum engines [b]Thin-wall, gray cast-iron cylinder-block engine Multibarrel carburetor	[b]High-tolerance iron-casting methods Automatic crankshaft grinding with measurement Segmented transfer lines for block and head Ceramic boring
1965–74	[b]Advances in electronic ignition Overhead cam engine on mass-produced cars Stratified-charge engine[c]	[b]Programmable controller for machining systems Electronic sensors and automated testing in engine line

SOURCE: Industry experts.
[a] Added by author.
[b] Subject of case analysis; see Appendix 1.
[c] Potentially important.

TABLE 3.3. Thirty-five Major Technological Innovations in Mass-Produced Cars and Assembly Plants

Decade	Product Innovation	Process Innovation
1900–1909	Lightweight durable chassis[a] (Model T)	Interchangeable parts and progressive manufacturing in automobiles (Cadillac) Overhead conveyor for parts
1910–19	Electric starter Electric lights[a]	Moving final assembly line
1920–29	[b]Closed steel body Hydraulic and four-wheel brakes Lacquer finishes (DUCO-pyroxylin)	[b]Welding in body and chassis assembly Growing use of light, powered hand tools
1930–39	[b]Independent suspension Power brakes All-steel body, turret top, and streamlining[a]	[b]Unit body construction High-frequency portable power tools Multihydromatic welding
1946–54	[b]Automatic transmission Power steering Air conditioning	Multiple nut runners Automatic spray painting Electrostatic painting [b]Electronic-assisted scheduling Higher-speed and automated stamping[c]
1955–64	[b]Disc brakes Improved suspension systems Alternator	[b]Body-corrosion protection Expanded use of special-purpose fasteners Mixing of body styles on assembly lines
1965–74	[b]Energy-absorbing steering wheel and column Energy-absorbing bumpers and front ends Electronic sensors of car mechanisms	[b]Automated chassis and body assembly Powder coatings (paint for body)

SOURCE: Industry experts.
[a] Added by author.
[b] Subject of case analysis; see Appendix 1.
[c] Not in assembly plant.

The twenty innovations selected for study, from these lists (Table 3.1), were those most frequently identified as important by individuals from two or more firms.

Data Limitations

Because this study looks backward in time, with sure knowledge about what has succeeded commercially, the data and conclusions have a very special interpretation and some limitations. They represent a stream of innovations regarded as commercially successful from the viewpoint of the major U.S. automobile companies today, but not all innovations that might have seemed important at the time. Although some precautions were taken to incorporate the viewpoint and optimism of the era by drawing on past industry literature, this does not circumvent the inherent limitations of the data. Therefore, it must be recognized that the lessons from these cases cannot reflect the uncertainties of the time, technical successes that failed for other reasons, or for what might have been. The lists show only what did succeed. Still, there is much to be learned from the successes if these limitations are recognized.

Defining Innovation

In a study of innovation, a definitional problem arises because the same set of general technical solutions or design approaches to a basic engineering problem present themselves year after year. A distinction must be made between the act of improvement and the general design approach that is improved. To solve this problem, I define each innovation as a major improvement or series of improvements in what I refer to as a "design approach."

The basic design approaches are long-lived. If a basic design approach is strong to begin with, its life may be greatly extended by a rapid rate of innovation. For example, V-8 engines and cast crankshafts are design approaches used respectively in engine design and in crankshaft manufacturing. The innovation in these design approaches consisted in improvements that made them more suitable for mass production. To take these examples further, Cadillac's superior V-8 design in 1915 constituted an innovation in the V-8 engine, and so did Ford's low-cost V-8 engine design in 1932. Ford made metallurgical and casting innovations in cast crankshafts that advanced this design approach at two different times, one in 1934 and one in 1951.

A single innovation has also often acted to advance several different design approaches applicable to different components of the car. For example, advances in the quality and maximum widths of rolled steel made the closed steel body more economically feasible, which in turn made baked finishes possible. These trends were reinforced by the development of pyroxylin paints, electrical welding, and other changes.

Types of Process Innovation: Evolution in Function

Functions served by process innovations change and evolve over time as a given productive unit matures. This pattern of evolution can be inferred from the full set of important process innovations listed for both productive units in Tables 3.2 and 3.3. These process innovations can be generally grouped according to four functions: introducing new process capabilities, organizing the process, integrating an existing process, and improving the overall process as a system.

For both the assembly plant and the engine plant the early process innovations served two functions—they organized the production process, and they put major new individual process capabilities into place. Subsequently, major innovations could integrate or weld the process into a more tightly organized unit. Then the individual process capabilities and the overall process configurations could be refined through innovations that made better use of information—innovations in the nervous as opposed to the muscular system of the process, as it were.

Referring back to actual innovations, the process-organizing character of the early ones in both productive units is evident in at least five cases: the continuous pouring of molten iron, multiple simultaneous machining, the use of overhead conveyors, interchangeable parts, and the moving assembly line. These were all innovations essentially in process organization.

The cluster of innovations that introduced process capabilities was interleafed and delayed somewhat in respect to the first one. In assembly the second cluster included welding, powered hand tools, and the lacquer-painting process. In engines such innovations included cemented carbide cutting tools, precision boring, surface tunnel broaching, and the metallurgical and foundry advances that enabled crankshafts and camshafts to be cast rather than forged.

The pattern in engine plants visibly diverged from that in assembly plants at the point when engine plants were extensively integrated with transfer lines, beginning with Ford's Cleveland engine plant innovation in 1951. Subsequently, in engines, innovations have functioned to refine and control existing processes and further to integrate the overall process configuration. The last advances have been achieved through innovations in information and control systems like dynamic crankshaft balancing, programmable controllers, the application of electronic sensors, and automatic testing. These have helped to link and integrate the manufacturing process into a common system that is tightly balanced and commonly controlled. There are obvious exceptions to the general pattern, such as the recent introduction of ceramic boring in engine plants, but in general terms the overall pattern is quite consistent.

In assembly, the early features of this general innovative pattern are quite evident, as just noted, but the later features have yet to occur. An innovation in integrating the assembly process that would be a critical turning point, as was the use of transfer lines in engine plants, has yet to be reached. A rapid build-up of mechanical integration is now taking place, however, as noted in Chapter 6 and in the case on automated body assembly (Appendix 1). Individual process capabilities, such as corrosion protection, special fasteners, and painting advances, are still being added.

The current mix of innovation functions in assembly is similar to the earlier, midrange mix of innovation in engines. This is consistent with expected differences in the development of these two productive units.

Another way of describing these changes in the type of process innovation is to examine what the innovation embodies. The innovations that embody independent new process capabilities are those that most frequently originated outside the industry, for example, ceramic boring, cemented carbide cutting tools, surface tunnel broaching, electronic sensors, or programmable controllers. The innovations in process organization more frequently embody practices that were developed within the industry, and hence these innovations originated within the industry. For example, the moving assembly line embodied a concept of process organization that Ford originated first in 1908. Ford's first transfer machine, in 1932, embodied basic process-organization concepts that Ford helped originate two decades earlier. Technological innovations of this type have several implications. They make the production process more capital-intensive and expensive; but they actually reduce barriers to entry into the industry. By embodying management skills in innovative equipment rather than organizational know-how, the critical knowledge for entry can be purchased as equipment.

LESSONS FROM CASE ANALYSIS

The twenty innovations can be placed into one of two groups based on the extent of their adoption throughout the industry. All but four or five of the twenty major innovations were broadly adopted shortly after they were introduced, and thus were nearly completely diffused. The other innovations were adopted by only a few firms and were subject to fluctuating degrees of adoption throughout the industry.

The first category includes the closed steel body,* the electric starter, hydraulic brakes, energy-absorbing steering assemblies, independent front suspension, 12-volt electrical systems, cemented carbide cutting tools, the moving assembly line, the automatic choke, the down-draft carburetor, and the extensive automation of engine plants. Each of these innovations led to a "dominant design," as I used the term earlier to characterize the choice of the internal-combustion gasoline engine, the Model T chassis, and the V-8 engine design. The dominant design met the needs of most market segments for most producers.

The second category, where diffusion was not complete, includes unit body construction, aluminum engines, automatic body assembly, cast

* The reader may wish to refer to the case abstracts in Appendix 1, but for the remainder of this chapter, these cases will be discussed without making explicit reference to the appendix.

crankshafts and camshafts, disc brakes, and the high-compression V-8 engine. The lower rate of adoption of these means the innovation did not achieve superiority in satisfying design requirements in all major market segments. Technological competition is most intense in these cases, for partial diffusion usually indicates the presence of highly competitive design approaches. Innovation, in the case of partial diffusion, is one more round in a continuing competitive sequence among alternative approaches.

Intense competition among design approaches as they advance through evolutionary development is evident in several pairs of cases: aluminum versus thin-wall cast-iron engines, cast versus forged crankshafts and camshafts, disc versus drum brakes, automatic chassis assembly versus manual assembly, and unit construction versus separate body and frame construction.

A dominant design is not typically the product of radical innovation. To the contrary, a design approach becomes dominant, as did the integration of engine plants with transfer lines and the closed steel body, when the weight of many innovations tilts the economic balance in favor of one design approach. Typically, the relevant design approach has already been in existence. It may appear radical in a particular application because the newly favored design approach replaces a much different alternative, but the competing approaches were very likely the product of evolutionary improvement.

Origins of Design Approaches

Many design approaches in current use have very early origins. They may have been used and then abandoned many times, depending on changes in market preferences and on innovations. The rich nature of exchanges that have come about is suggested by two examples.

The aluminum engine appeared in the Corvair as a major change in General Motors' car lines during the 1960s, but it had been used previously in the German Porsche. As the case study of the aluminum engine indicates, an innovation in aluminum castings by Kaiser Aluminum and General Motors, among other advances, contributed the necessary technology to advance this approach to a state suitable for higher-volume, low-cost production. The push for a lightweight, economical car like General Motors' Corvair and Ford's Falcon provided the impetus for the innovation. In a sense, the import penetration of the Volkswagen into American markets provided stimulus for what might appear to be a technology transfer from Porsche, a sister car in Europe. But was the prior West German application the major originating application in the development of this approach? The evidence suggests not. Aluminum engines were used in the United States before World War II, by the Franklin car among others. Before this, the aluminum air-cooled engine was developed in France, but the first known automotive application was even earlier—in the United States in 1895.

The aluminum engine is a design approach that has been steadily advanced and refined here and in Europe through successive applications in the automobile industry and in other industries—such as the Wright brothers' airplane and U.S. military trucks in World War I. Contributions have come at different times from different industries in different countries.

The unit construction body provides another example. To Ford and General Motors in 1960, the introduction of small cars with new unit construction bodies, like the Ford Falcon and the Corvair, represented a major departure from their existing product lines.† This design approach promised material, weight, and labor savings. Although American Motors and Chrysler had used unit construction earlier, the more commercially popular applications of this design since World War II had been made in Europe. The Renault, Peugeot, Fiat, and the Ford Taunus, among others, were of unit construction. This seems to be a clear-cut case of international technology transfer, but it really is not. Ford had adopted unit construction in 1936, for example, when the Lincoln Zephyr was introduced, and automobile historians have traced the direct impact of this car on the early body styling of the Volkswagen Beetle before World War II.[1] The second-generation 1961 Volkswagen Beetle grew out of engineering work done by the U.S.-based Budd Company, which also supplied the tooling. Should this be counted as a transfer of technology? Actually, the origins of the unit construction approach date back even further, at least to 1903, when the English Vauxhall Iron Works produced such a body.

These two cases illustrate several characteristics of technological change that are also typical of other cases. A given design approach may have an early origin, but this does not necessarily mean the rate of progress is slow. Changes in market preferences, like the switch to small cars, may call earlier design approaches back into use. Such changes are sometimes thought to indicate progress, when in fact they indicate only change. Progress depends on the contributions of innovations, not vacillation among design approaches.

Interdependence in Innovation

The degree of interdependence among innovations is very high. For example, a number of other innovations have either given impetus to or impeded the two design approaches discussed above. Of the cases considered here, advances in welding, lighter engines, automated body assembly, as well as market trends toward smaller cars, have acted in support of one another. Not all change is mutually reinforcing, however. Innovations that

---

† Ford's product line in the 1950s relied exclusively on separate frame and body construction. The 1958 Lincoln began a broad switch to unit construction in large cars.

provide a capability for variety and change, such as electronic-assisted scheduling, have not favored the small-car trend. The use of unit construction leads to a car design that is inherently more expensive to change than when separate body and frame construction is used. Similarly, the thin-wall cast-iron engine grew out of an innovation by Ford that was competitive with General Motors' aluminum engine. Sufficient improvement was introduced in the traditional cast-iron technology to suppress the aluminum engine as a major approach—at least to the present.

The aluminum engine and unit construction bodies are just two among several examples of competition in the twenty cases. There are close parallels in the history of disc brakes, the V-8 engine, and cast crankshafts and camshafts.

Individual innovations have solved specific problems or added new features, but they have seldom been independently decisive in causing one approach to dominate its competitors. Often a shift in market preference coupled with an innovation causes one approach to gain in preference over another, as with the shift toward small cars and unit construction bodies. Because improvements are cumulative, the chance decreases with time that a single innovation will change a favored approach.

Incremental versus Radical Innovation

Incremental innovations give impetus to and further shape the direction of existing design approaches, functioning as steps in an underlying long-term trend. Radical innovations introduce entirely new approaches like Mazda's rotary engine.

The evidence suggests that it is misleading to judge the significance of an innovation by its apparent novelty. Incremental innovation has been very important because it is cumulative and because it builds on existing approaches. For example, the rubber engine mount, a seemingly trivial change, had a cumulatively significant impact. As revealed through the case study of high-compression engines, the rubber engine mount contributed to the smooth performance of 6- and 8-cylinder engines. Consequently, there was no need to use high-cylinder-count engines, like the V-12s, to achieve the same result mechanically. In this way, the engine mount reduced the mechanical variation in the engine line.

A focused sample of innovation in a particular productive unit, as presently analyzed, thus shows that advances are highly interrelated. A series of coherent innovations may so improve a given underlying design approach that subsequent innovation is much less likely to cause a competing approach to become preferred. The incidence of apparently novel product change is not necessarily a sign of cumulative long-run progress. In many instances it may be more an indication of changing market preferences or a weak and unsuccessful design approach.

International Technology Transfer

Several writers have recently asserted that transfers of automotive technology from Europe to the United States have been greater in recent times than transfers in the reverse direction. My data were not collected to address this issue specifically, but the present evidence does bear on the question.

In respect to design approaches that have long histories, such as disc brakes, aluminum engines, and others discussed above, there sometimes seems to be simple evidence of significant transfers when little was in fact transferred. Ongoing improvements in underlying design approaches continue to be derived from the contributions of many firms and countries within and without the automobile industry. The market shift to smaller cars has caused the return to many design approaches that were developed by U.S. firms in even earlier periods. Many of these were improved by European firms that had a head start in small cars. In this limited sense, there seems to have been an increase in technology transfers.

The data suggest the need for care in analyzing technology transfers, however. By selecting the right base year for comparison, one can demonstrate almost anything through simple counts.

In respect to more recently originated design approaches the picture is clearer. In these cases, which are heavily based on electronics, the United States still apparently has a strong leadership position.

One European versus American comparison that appears to be valid is the relative development of process eqiupment in the engine and assembly plants. As discussed in the case on automated assembly (see Appendix 1), assembly plants for small cars in Europe and Japan appear to have become more automated and advanced, while those in the United States have continued to emphasize flexibility for product change. For the engine plant, the United States has maintained the lead in automation for many years.[2]

Innovation by Major Automobile Firms

A number of studies have found that for established industries, major innovations have usually originated outside the industry.[3] As a corollary, major U.S. automobile manufacturers have been criticized for relying heavily on both suppliers and firms in other industries as sources of innovation.[4]

An increased reliance on outside sources to originate process-equipment innovation is expected as a productive unit advances in development (see Chapter 4). Such a shift seems to have come about in the engine plant, where all major automobile firms have come to rely heavily on machine tool firms for their process-equipment advances. Case data indicate that the major firms are much more involved in originating specific process innovations for assembly plants than for engine plants. One explanation for this is that the engine plant became so highly organized that there is little opportunity for process-organization innovations. The traditional expertise of the major firms was no longer needed, at least until the current energy problem arose. Beyond this shift in engine plants, there is no indication that the major firms have increased their reliance on outside sources of process innovation.

Reliance on outside firms has not increased appreciably, but it remains very high. There has been a strong reliance on outside sources from the beginning of the industry. There was much interindustry contribution even before the automobile industry could be considered "established," and this has continued to the present. As many as five or six of the twelve early innovations in Tables 3.2 and 3.3 involve transfers from originating industries: aluminum-alloy pistons (aircraft); hydraulic brakes (aircraft); multiple machining (existed at least prior to 1902); continuous pouring of molten iron (Westinghouse-to-Ford transfer); cemented carbide cutting tools (German); interchangeable parts (Singer and others).

Suppliers and other firms originated other innovations that have been studied: high-speed grinding and ceramic boring (machine tool), carburetors (supplier), lacquer finishes (Du Pont), and sensors for automatic testing (electronics). Of course, the automobile industry made reciprocal contributions in advances like welding, transfer machines, painting methods, and so on. If anything, for the car as a whole, there seems to be less reliance today on out-of-industry firms than there was earlier. On balance, however, the issue of the originating innovative source does not seem to pertain globally to an analysis of changing industry characteristics, but does pertain to the development of particular productive units, as discussed above.

One pattern is evident in the innovative activities of the major manufacturers. Each of the major companies seems to have more frequently made contributions in a particular area. The list below indicates areas of innovation by General Motors and Ford where a major and identifiable contribution was found.

Ford has been predominantly innovative in process technology in general and in metallurgical and foundry innovations in particular. General Motors has been more active in developing major components that add performance features to the car. This tendency has continued for decades, and it extends up to recent years.

Diffusion of Process Innovations: A Consequence

The major innovations in engine and assembly plants have diffused rapidly. A dominant design implies almost complete diffusion, and many of

Ford	*General Motors*
Mechanized moving assembly	Electric starter
Welding in body and chassis assembly	V-8 engine design
Cast crankshafts and camshafts (1934 and 1952)	Cemented carbide cutting tools
	Independent front suspensions
Transfer machine (1932)	Automatic transmission advances
Economical V-8 engine production	Electronic ignition systems
Integration of engine plants with transfer lines	Energy-absorbing steering assemblies
High-speed automated stamping	Aluminum engines
Thin-wall gray cast-iron engine	
Electrocoating (corrosion protection for bodies—1968)	

the innovations led to dominant designs. The process-organizing types of production-process innovations have also diffused rapidly. As a generalization, it seems that, among the major firms, engine plants and assembly plants have developed in a common mold. The rapid adoption of major innovations by many firms in the industry implies that their engine and assembly plants were at equivalent stages of development. To explain this argument more fully, let us consider the type of innovations that were adopted. As listed in Tables 3.2 and 3.3, they are: the moving assembly line, multiple machining, continuous pouring of iron, the closed steel body, automatic chassis and body assembly, the integration of engine plants with transfer lines, programmable control, electronic-assisted scheduling, and the mixing of styles on the assembly line. Each of these carries a technological mandate for product volume, standardization of design, and labor-task characteristics, and, of course, equipment characteristics themselves. The rapid diffusion of these innovations among the major companies means that development milestones have been achieved at about the same time in different firms.

The diffusion pattern for major innovations has important competitive implications, but for different reasons than are usually recognized. Since the Model T, no one firm has achieved a major production-process advantage over others, for they have all evolved in a very similar way. In practice this means that no firm sustains a competitive advantage through product innovation. When all firms have the same process capabilities, then any one firm can replicate the product innovations of any other. Under these circumstances, the incentive for significant product innovation is weakened.

Factors Stimulating Innovation

The findings of Jacob Schmookler's[5] classic study suggest that innovation is stimulated largely by demand growth. His analysis of patent data shows that technological development lags behind rather than leads market growth. Another related hypothesis is that process innovations that lower prices stimulate other technological innovations through their effect on primary demand.

The present data on innovation fail to confirm the idea that major technological innovation lags behind demand growth. The converse may be more nearly correct. Some of the most important innovations in the industry were made under weak demand conditions and made apparently to stimulate demand. This is evident in Ford's initial innovations, which supported its entry into the industry, and by both General Motors' and Ford's response to the Great Depression of the 1930s. Ford responded to the depression by investing heavily in the most advanced process equipment,[6] and some of its more important innovations appeared during this period. It was then that Ford developed the first transfer machine, the cast camshaft and crankshaft, and—probably of more importance—the first mass-produced V-8 engine. General Motors innovated in independent suspension and began work on automatic transmission and power brakes. Most of these had the effect of adding major new features to the car rather than reducing costs. This was consistent with the economic conditions of the time, however, because the middle- and lower-price market segments had little purchasing power. It would seem, as William T. Hogan observes,[7] that the major companies tried to stimulate demand by introducing new technology during sales downturns. There is no indication that major advances were delayed by slow market growth.

After a minimum scale of operation is reached, further increases appear unimportant in stimulating innovations that improve productivity. Current engine plants at Ford operate at much lower capacities than the Highland Park and Rouge plants of the 1920s (see Chapter 5). The sequence of developments that led up to the modern engine plant began during the late years of the depression and had the effect of *reducing* the capacity utilization in individual engine plants. Yet, significant improvements in productivity have certainly been realized during this period. The weight of evidence suggests that increases in the scale of operations in individual plants have not been a factor in stimulating innovation or productivity.

Other sources of innovative stimulation could be reviewed, but a statistical explanation does not seem appropriate here. In the automobile industry, the most important explanatory factor in innovative activity seems to be the competitive strategies of the major firms (see Chapter 2). The very purposeful nature of innovative activity stands out conspicuously in the twenty case studies. Most of the innovations met needs that were envisioned from the beginning of the industry, and they developed from purposeful effort and directed research and development (R&D) programs. When a few firms control most of the market, their competitive strategies are of overriding importance in determining the course of technological progress. This, rather than statistical factors, should be given primary attention.

Competition and Product Innovation

The major product innovations listed in Tables 3.2 and 3.3 reveal the automotive features that were competitively important in their introductory years. The first innovation was a reliable automobile at a reasonable price —the Model T. Then came electric starters, then closed steel bodies, then streamlined bodies, and so forth. Each innovation first rose in competitive importance; it then diffused widely, and then came to be expected by the customer. Each of these innovations represents a feature that at first was available only in expensive cars, then in many cars, and ultimately became a standard aspect of all cars. With wide adoption, each wave of new features became "packed down" in the product technology or taken for granted by customers, and fresh innovations were again needed for competition.

These lists profile the nature of technological competition in the industry. We can see two types of product innovations: those that enhance the recreational value of the car and those that enhance the car's transportation efficiency. From the early period through the 1960s, virtually every major innovation identified in Tables 3.2 and 3.3 improved the car's recreational performance, rather than its efficiency. Each innovation added new features to make the car perform better, to make it easier to drive, more attractive, safer, more comfortable. In this way, the market broadened so that the group of owners and drivers became very large. Since 1960, however, this has changed (as discussed further in Chapter 7).

The connection between the concept of productive unit and these major competitive innovations is direct. The innovations mark the introduction of new productive units in the overall manufacturing process or major changes in existing ones. For example, the introduction of the closed steel body and the automatic transmission mark the beginning of new manufacturing processes as well as new components. The product innovations introduce both new components in the car itself and new changes in assembly plant operations. Further upstream in the manufacturing process, however, these components are the products of different productive units, and the innovations are milestones of their economic creation, change, and destruction. As automatic transmissions were introduced, for example, the existing manual transmission plants were rendered almost obsolete.* The manual transmission plant, as a productive unit, was replaced by a new one. Major product innovations destroy old paths of backward vertical integration and create opportunities for new ones. Product innovations thus generally reduce the degree of backward integration (as shown directly in Chapters 5 and 6).

---

* Ford reportedly sold its manual transmission line at the peak of automatic transmission adoption. When small cars were introduced, new facilities were acquired.

FIGURE 3.1. Diffusion of Selected Competitive Features

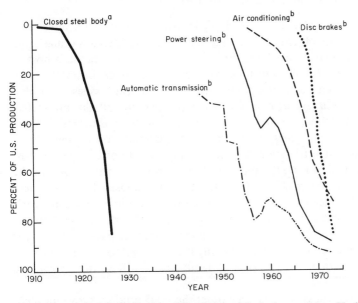

SOURCES: Ralph C. Epstein, *The Automobile Industry* (New York: A. W. Shaw Co., 1928), p. 112; and *Ward's Automotive Year Book, 1974*, p. 124.
[a] Percent of car lines with closed steel bodies.
[b] Percent of cars with indicated feature.

Figure 3.1 superimposes diffusion data for a few new product features on a common inverted scale to signify the way that innovations are introduced, broadly adopted, and ultimately packed down as routine features. Curves in the figure show how the closed steel body, automatic transmission, power steering, air conditioning, and disc brakes were first introduced, then rapidly adopted in most U.S. cars, and finally accepted as almost standard. Each of these curves can be conceived as a profile of the development of a productive unit. These five innovations mark the birth or change of major productive units and the destruction of the predecessor units the innovation replaced. Each major innovation has increased the complexity and size of the car. The declining number of man-hours per thousand pounds of Ford cars (Figure 2.2) shows, however, that these innovations have not proportionally increased the real economic costs of the car overall. The smaller cars in the line are not presently much heavier than mainline cars in the 1920s, which indicates that the labor requirements of new features have been offset by other efficiencies. Costs and labor hours per car have been held down, even though new features are added, because there are productivity improvements with increased volume according to a learning-curve relationship once the new component has been standardized and introduced into mass production.

INNOVATION AND THE MANAGEMENT OF CHANGE

Taken collectively, these trends in innovation present an interesting conceptual picture of the issues that must be considered in managing technology at the corporate level. From the corporate viewpoint, a host of different productive units must be managed to produce a single, high-valued product that has many components, like the car. Issues somewhat like a portfolio management problem are present, for all the productive units change over time. Innovation to create new features is essential, but if too much innovation occurs at once, costs may exceed an acceptable limit. There is an incentive for the producer to limit the rate of change, for cost must be controlled to keep the total price of the product within reach of the consumer. The problem differs from those in the industrial sector, where increased performance means higher value in applications that can justify higher product prices. Once the innovative feature is perfected, costs begin to decline along the learning curve, the technology is packed down, the diffusion becomes complete, and all competitive advantage is lost. Another innovation is needed, or the basis of competition will shift to cost, and profit margins will fall.

As this process continues over time, the final product grows in complexity. As more productive units are integrated into the overall manufacturing process, the cost of product change also increases. The higher cost of change means that it is more expensive to introduce new automotive features even though to do so is no less important from a competitive viewpoint.

By the 1960s the car had reached a highly developed state insofar as the existing American market was concerned. The innovative potential of the automobile industry had run down, so to speak, as regards major innovations with recreational application. At least this seems to be the case according to the innovation lists in Tables 3.2 and 3.3. Innovations that had yet to diffuse no longer offered conspicuous new features that added to the recreational quality of the vehicle. To be sure, there were opportunities for safety and pollution advances, but these were not likely to add much excitement to the consumer's automotive purchase decision in the 1960s.

Under such conditions, the purchase decisions would be expected to hinge more on transportation utility than on recreation. In short, the car was becoming a commodity. This interpretation is consistent with the prior statistical analysis of competitive performance during the postwar period and the recent penetration of low-cost imports in the American market (Chapter 2).

The important performance-improving innovations, like automatic transmission and power steering that have advanced over the years, were all envisioned from the beginning of the industry. They were, in fact, the targets of innovative effort from the beginning. Once these improvements were realized, it was as if the mainspring of a giant clock had unwound.

Now, in the mid-1970s, the conditions seem to have changed more completely than at any time since World War II. Encroaching petroleum supply restrictions, rising gasoline prices, fuel economy regulations, and the erosion of consumer purchasing power have completely changed the environment for innovation. Tangible objectives for innovation that relate to new consumer needs are apparent, and new technologies on which such innovations might be based, such as electronics and new propulsion systems that will consume less or new forms of energy, are in the wings, so to speak.

Some innovations have been introduced into mass production in the time period since the data on innovation were obtained from industry experts. The catalytic converter is a particular case, having proved much more successful than the respondents were willing to predict at that time. This uncertainty is in itself perhaps the strongest evidence of greatly accelerated innovation. Some recent or impending innovations include: catalytic converter; stratified-charge engine; mass-produced advanced lead acid batteries; dual displacement engine; computer engine control (analogue and digital); transverse engine power train configuration; lightweight body and components parts (plastic, aluminum, etc.); and lightweight body design.

Both the major producers and suppliers seem to be responding to the market's demand for change. Opportunities for technological innovation can once again be important to the competitive behavior of the major producers. The type of innovation that results will very likely require a reversion to an earlier stage of development. This is explored further in the two following chapters on engines and assembly plants. The success of these emerging trends will depend upon the major firms' leadership through their programs for innovation and research and development.

4 A GENERAL MODEL: INNOVATION AND PROCESS CHANGE IN A PRODUCTIVE UNIT

Intriguing regularities in the course of technological progress appear throughout the history of the automobile industry. A definite pattern is evident in the sequence of events that accompanied developments like the closed steel body or the automatic transmission, from their initial introduction through design improvements and the beginning of mass production to standardization and, finally, their wide adoption throughout the industry. From the common elements of product and process development in this pattern we can construct a general model of technological change that may be applicable to the automobile industry and perhaps to other similar industries as well.[1] Such a general model helps to explain the underlying forces that stimulate and shape technological progress.

DIFFERENT INNOVATION PATTERNS

The unit of analysis for this model is particularly important, for it captures both product and process characteristics in one entity—the productive unit. The productive unit consists of both a manufacturing unit and the product line produced. The types and sources of material inputs, the scale of operation, production-process equipment, necessary work-force skills, methods of organization and supervision, all help to characterize important production-process traits. The degree of product standardization or the rates of change, product-line diversity, and product design complexity provide useful product-line descriptors. A productive unit would typically be an operating unit of a firm that is located in one geographic area under the management of one senior executive. An engine plant and the

I wish to gratefully acknowledge James M. Utterback's contribution as coauthor of this chapter and some related points in Chapter 7. His contributions have been particularly important in regard to the aspects of competitive strategy, organizational consideration, sources of stimulation for innovation, and the considerable work done in relating the model to prior research.

line of engines it produces is one productive unit. An assembly plant and the particular car it produces is another.

Current knowledge about technological change is fragmented because there are few, if any, paradigms whereby insights about one product or industry can be applied in another. For example, much may be known about the management of technological change in rocket engines, but the application of this knowledge in another setting, such as the scientific instruments industry, is conjectural. This chapter presents a model of innovation and change that may be broadly applied and that interprets disassociated findings as parts of a common pattern.

One Pattern of Innovation

One pattern of technological innovation can be seen in the important changes that occur in established high-volume product lines, such as incandescent light bulbs, rolled steel, refined gasoline, and auto engines. Such products constitute the mainstream of current economic activity in industrialized nations. The kind of innovation that takes place in these industries is of particular interest because its impact is large and immediate.

The markets for such goods are well defined, the product characteristics are specific and often standardized, and competition is primarily on the basis of *price*. Per-unit profit margins are typically low. The production technology is efficient, equipment-intensive, and specialized to a particular product. In many respects, the product is defined by the process rather than the process by the product. The nature of technological change is greatly influenced by the characteristics of the process technology, as the development of Ford's small car, the 92A, illustrated. Change is costly because in such an integrated system product and process innovations become linked so that an alteration in any single feature has ramifications in many others.

In this environment, innovation is typically inncremental in nature and has a cumulative effect on cost and productivity. For example, Samuel Hollander has shown that more than half of Du Pont's reduction in the cost of producing rayon was the result of process improvements that could not be identified as formal changes.[2] John L. Enos's data show that less-striking developments in petroleum-cracking processes resulted in productivity gains that were often more significant in toto than the gain from the original process choice.[3] Kenneth E. Knight shows that new computer systems or major systems changes have contributed greater individual gains than minor product or systems improvements, but these minor changes accounted for more than half of the ultimate gain because they were so numerous.[4] Incremental innovations, such as the use of larger railroad cars and unit trains, have resulted in drastically reduced costs in moving large quantities of materials by rail, as reported by William Hogan.[5] While cost reduction seems to be the major focus of innovation in this pattern, both

Knight's study of computers and Rodrick W. Clarke's study of rocket engines[6] note that major advances in performance result from the sum of numerous small engineering and production innovations.

Typically, this pattern results in a situation where economies of scale in production and the development of mass markets become extremely important. Such productive units are usually divisions of large firms and are located to reduce factor costs of materials, labor, or transportation.[7] The firm is vulnerable to changed demand, technical obsolescence, and the need to maintain production volume to cover fixed costs.

A Second Pattern of Innovation

While minor product variations can be accommodated within the first pattern as described above, major changes in the firm constitute a distinct second pattern. Richard Normann contends that product variations may easily originate within the large, highly structured firm, but that new products that require reorientation tend to originate outside this type of firm.[8] If they originate within, they tend to be rejected. Radical product change involves identification of an emerging need or a new way to meet an existing need.[9] Here innovation is an entrepreneurial act, involving the introduction of a new product and often the formation of a new firm established to exploit the innovation. This case is like the automobile industry in its early years.

A variety of studies suggest that many new products in different industries share common traits. Innovations occur in disproportionate numbers in geographic regions characterized by proximity to affluent markets, strong science-based universities (or other research and development institutions), and entrepreneurially oriented financial institutions.[10] Innovative products typically compete with predecessor products on the basis of their own superior functional *performance* rather than lower initial cost, that is, they are performance-maximizing rather than cost-minimizing innovations, and they command correspondingly higher profit margins.[11]

When a major product innovation first appears, performance criteria are typically vague and poorly understood. Users may play a major role in suggesting the ultimate form of the innovation as well as the need for it, perhaps because they have a more intimate understanding of performance requirements. For example, Knight states that 76 percent of the computer models that emerged in the period 1944–50 were developed by users and were usually produced as one or two of a kind.[12] The corresponding figures for 1951–53 are 44 percent, followed by 20 percent in 1954–56, 16 percent in 1957–59, and dropping to 5 percent for 1960–62. A more recent study by Eric von Hippel of four scientific instruments shows that the prototype for the basic instrument was developed first by a user in each case.[13] As development continued, manufacturers took a greater part in initiating variations, including eight of forty-three major improvements and fourteen of forty-six minor improvements.

In this second pattern of innovation, the diversity and uncertainty of performance dimensions for major new products might be expected to require a more flexible organization and technical approach and a greater degree of external communication than in the first pattern. Robert A. Schlaifer and S. D. Heron have argued that a diverse and responsive group of firms struggling against established companies to enter the industry contributed greatly to the early advances in jet aircraft engines.[14] The first jet engine represented a relatively small performance advance over the piston engine, but once initial operating experience was gained, a series of advances led to rapid improvement. New enterprises also led the advances in application of semiconductor technology, according to John E. Tilton, often transferring into practice information from other firms and laboratories.[15] Tilton argues that economies of scale have not been of prime importance because the rate of product change makes production technology designed for a particular product rapidly obsolete.

Connecting the Two Patterns

In the first case, the product is standardized, change is incremental, production systems are rigid (*specific*) but efficient, information about needed product features is relatively visible, and the economic impact of any improvement is large and immediate. In the second case, product design is subject to radical change, product characteristics are in flux, the emphasis of product innovation is on improved functional performance rather than cost reduction, production systems are flexible (*fluid*) but inefficient, and even major innovation has little immediate economic impact. These patterns are not independent of one another, however. It is apparent in the automobile industry and several other industries that products currently represented by the *specific* pattern were much more like the *fluid* one at the time of their origin. This is represented in the lower part of Figure 4.1, where characteristics of the *fluid* (*F*) state are given in the left column, those of the *specific* (*S*) state to the right, and the path of *transition* (*T*) by the arrow.

As will be evident in the examples of transition considered below, several different productive units appear to have followed the same path of change. The predominant mode of innovation shifts from radical product innovation to incremental innovation, and process innovation increases in relative importance to product innovation. This is represented at the top of Figure 4.1. Sources of innovation, types of stimuli for innovation, production-process characteristics, productivity rates, product-performance characteristics, and organizational content all change as the productive unit

FIGURE 4.1. Transition, Boundary Conditions, and Innovation

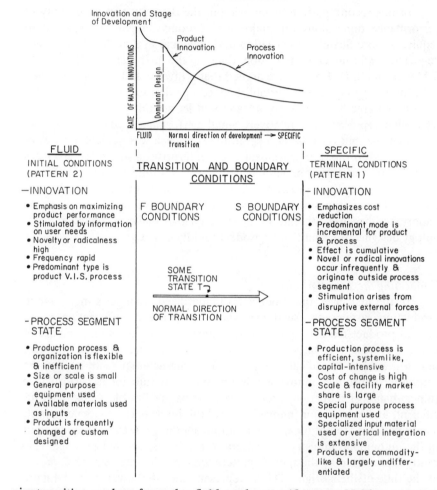

in *transition* evolves from the *fluid* to the *specific* state. Neither extreme pattern by itself represents an attractive stable state for a firm.

LESSONS AND EXAMPLES OF TRANSITION

Tilton's study of technological and economic developments in the semiconductor industry from 1950 through 1968 indicates both that the rate of major innovation has decreased and that the type of innovation has shifted with the development of the industry. Eight of the thirteen product innovations he classed as most important occurred within the first seven years, before 5 percent of the industry's total sales for the period had occurred.[16] Established firms, those that entered the industry early from a prior vested position in vacuum tube markets, met subsequent competition from new entrants like Fairchild, IBM, and Texas Instruments by emphasizing production considerations and process innovations. The newcomers sought entry through product innovation. As a consequence, these three very successful new firms were responsible for 46 percent of the major product innovations and only 11 percent of the process innovations that Tilton considered up to 1968. Conversely, three comparably established firms, General Electric, Philco, and RCA, made only 25 percent of the product innovations but 33 percent of process innovations in the same time period.[17] Such an emphasis on process innovation did not prove to be an effective competitive stance so early in the development of the industry, for by 1966 the three "established" receiving-tube firms held only 18 percent of the market collectively, while the three new firms held 42 percent. This changing mode of competition has had a pronounced effect on the development of the industry. As costs and productivity have become more important, the rate of major product innovation has decreased, and process innovation has increased in competitive importance. This pattern is similar to that of the automobile industry.

In the aircraft industry the development of the DC-3 stands out as a major turning point both in the type of product innovation that took place and in the market structure of the aircraft and airlines industries. Almarin Phillips's study of aircraft technology and economics points out that the DC-3 was a cumulation of prior innovations.[18] It was not the largest or the fastest or the least expensive airplane to operate, but it was the most economical large, fast plane. The features that made this design so competitively successful were introduced and proved in prior aircraft, such as the Ford Trimotor, the Boeing 241, the Douglas DC-1, the DC-2, and the Lockheed L-10.

Reacting to requests from the airlines about needed operating improvements, Douglas designed the DC-3 and flew it first in 1936.[19] Around eleven thousand were subsequently produced, and of these some thousand were still in use in 1966. Phillips observes that the DC-3 was so successful that, aside from the turbine-powered transports in Britain, no major innovations were introduced into commercial aircraft design until the new jetliners appeared in the 1950s. Instead, many refinements were made, such as stretching the design, adding appointments, and so forth, with the result that the airline operating costs per passenger dropped 50 percent.[20] However, production methods in airframe manufacturing were not correspondingly advanced as in the capital-intensive industrial sectors, even though the product was standardized. Without this constraint, product designs returned to a more fluid state after World War II and have remained fluid ever since.

The electric light bulb in its present form also came about through a long series of evolutionary improvements, starting with a few major innovations and ending in a highly standardized, commoditylike product. From 1909 to 1955, after the initial tungsten-filament and vacuum-bulb innovations, a series of incremental changes were made, including better metal alloys for the filament, the use of "getters" to assist in exhausting the bulb, and the coiling of filaments. In association with these changes, the price of a 60-watt bulb decreased (with no inflation adjustment) from $1.60 to $.20 per unit, the lumens output increased by 175 percent, and the amount of direct labor content was reduced more than a factor of 10, from 3 to 0.18 minutes per bulb. Over the same period, the production process evolved from a flexible job-shop configuration,* involving more than eleven separate operations and a heavy reliance on the skills of manual labor, to a process that was virtually embodied in a single machine.[21]

One common thread in these examples is the shift from a pattern of radical product innovation to one of evolutionary product innovation. This shift is related to the development of a dominant product design and is accompanied by heightened price competition and an increase in process innovation. Tilton's work on semiconductors, as discussed earlier, suggests that this shift may have come about because of competitive action and reaction in the industry. Newly entering firms emphasized product innovations as a basis for gaining initial market positions, and existing firms reacted to retain their market positions through cost-reducing process innovations. Process considerations cannot long be ignored by new firms, however, in an industry where prices have been reduced continually for more than a decade. For example, by 1973, Texas Instruments, originally a major new firm in the semiconductor industry, had shifted much attention to process innovation and planned to develop a single machine that would produce 4 percent of world market requirements for integrated circuits.[22] It had contributed to none of the major process innovations in Tilton's sample prior to 1968.

In yet another case, Robert D. Buzzell and Robert E. Nourse trace innovations in processed foods.[23] Their data show that new food technologies such as soluble coffees, frozen vegetables, dry pet foods, cold breakfast cereals, canned foods, and precooked rice came very early and from individuals and small organizations that were experimental practitioners or otherwise relied heavily upon information from users. As the industry has developed, the firms have increased in size, and marketing, production, and distribution methods have been greatly improved, but on

---

* The term "job shop" refers to a particular type of production process. General-purpose equipment is used, and it is usually organized so that common types of equipment that require similar worker skills are grouped together. A wide variety of different products can be produced by routing the work pieces back and forth among different equipment groups. Such a system is flexible, but has high inventory levels and slack resources.

the basis of new products that extended rather than replaced the earlier basic technologies. The predominant source of ideas for this type of new product innovation is no longer the experimental practitioner. As Buzzell and Nourse show, some 60 percent of the ideas for new products now come from the larger firms' own research and development organizations and almost none from users. The transformation has been very significant, affecting type of innovation, source of information, size, method of operation, and the use of formal research and development. Not all firms in this industry are large, however. There is evidence that new firms still find modes of entry for innovative products through market niches generated by consumer enthusiasm for health foods or for natural or convenience food products. Frozen orange juice concentrate provides one such example,[24] and packaged yoghurt another.[25]

ASPECTS OF REGULARITY IN TRANSITION

Each aspect of change is significant and important in its own right. When viewed collectively, however, the individual aspects become part of a larger and regular pattern of transition. These regularities encompass the role of a dominant product design, the characteristics of the product line, the changing nature of innovation, improvement in direct labor productivity, changes in the production process, performance criteria, the stimulus for innovation, and the organization's means of coordination and control.

A Dominant Design

The superior designs of products like the DC-3 and the Model T Ford[26] seem to mark turning points in the development of their respective productive units. These designs were synthesized from individual technological innovations that had been introduced independently in prior products. The important economic effects of a dominant design afford a degree of enforced product standardization, so that production economies can be sought, and provide a bench mark for functional performance competition, so that effective competition can take place on the basis of cost as well as product performance. Product design milestones are also apparent in other product lines where evidence is available on patterns of development over time. Sealed refrigeration units for home refrigerators and freezers, the development of an effective can-sealing technology in the food-canning industry,[27] and, in the locomotive industry and railroads, Charles Kettering's[28] standardized diesel locomotive can be considered dominant product designs.

Product-Line Diversity

Changes in product-line diversity also accompany transition. Initially, the product tends to be made to customer order or to exact specifications, and in this sense the product line is diverse. Frequent model change is forced by major innovations that rapidly make existing products obsolete. As was the case in the early years of the automobile and aircraft industries and later in the computer industry, there were initially many radically different product versions. The impact of a dominant design decreases the diversity in product line, and the subsequent advances in production processes cause even further decreases.

The Type of Innovation

Before a dominant design is achieved, product innovation is manifest in the introduction of radically different products. Subsequently, however, innovations act to improve an existing design and are necessarily more incremental but also more cumulative in effect. As a product becomes standardized, production volume rises, and cost becomes an increasingly important basis of competition. These concurrent changes stimulate process innovation through reduction in product variation, increased competitive pressures, and rising demand for greater output. As shown at the top of Figure 4.1, the predominant type of innovation will shift from major to incremental and will result in an overall decrease in major innovation. The rate and importance of process innovation will also increase relative to product innovation. These trends are illustrated by the changing mix of innovation in the semiconductor industry (as discussed above), and in the competitive interaction between Ford and General Motors in the early years of the automobile industry.[29] An analysis of the relative mix of product and process innovations among 330 innovations from 77 firms in the railroad equipment, computer, and housing supply industries also supports these hypotheses.[30]

Productivity Improvements

As mentioned earlier, unit costs of incandescent light bulbs have fallen more than 80 percent since their introduction; airline operating costs were decreased by half through the development and improvement of the DC-3; semiconductor prices have been falling by 20 to 30 percent with each doubling of cumulative production. Transition in the auto industry began with the introduction of the Model T Ford, which resulted in a price reduction from $8,000 to less than $1,000 (in 1958 dollars). Similar dramatic reductions have been observed in the unit costs of computer core memory and television picture tubes.[31] A linear percentage cost reduction with doubling of cumulative production of a product has been commonly represented as a learning or experience curve.[32] Although the causes of this phenomenon are not well understood, there is evidence that the occurrence of the learning curve is related to the transition of a productive unit, in that it depends on a standardized product design, a reduction in market uncertainty, predictability in organization and work-force incentives, and advances in production-process technology.[33]

Production-Process Changes

In the early fluid state, the production process is inchoate, the duration of labor tasks is long, there is reliance on skilled labor often organized along trade-craft lines. Flows of work in process are erratic, inventories are high, and general-purpose equipment is utilized. In general, the organization of the production process is like a job shop: there is slack, and capabilities are flexible even though they are not "efficient" in the same sense as mass-production facilities. With transition, the division of labor is increased, the work force is deskilled, and its tasks increasingly become those of the operative.

In the midrange between the fluid and specific states, some specialized process equipment begins to be purchased or is originally developed through mechanical analogy to manual tasks as process innovation and "islands of automation" begin to form in the process flow. In the extreme specific state, the process is mechanically integrated to form a near-continuous flow, is designed and purchased as a system that has well-defined capacity limits, is highly automated, and is designed so that product and process change become synonymous. In important instances these advances have so altered capabilities that product change has become very costly[34] and has decreased the productive unit's ability to respond to external forces for change.[35]

Changes in Product-Design Criteria

The performance criteria for product and process design (the bases of competition) change from ill-defined and uncertain targets for innovation to well-articulated design objectives. In the fluid state there is a proliferation of product-design criteria or performance dimensions.[36] These frequently cannot be stated quantitatively, and the relative importance or ranking of the various dimensions may be quite unstable.[37] Clarke has shown that manufacturers are likely to produce an innovation where the performance requirements are clearly specified, but that users are likely to introduce the innovation where performance requirements are ambiguous.[38] The facts that performance requirements are uncertain in the fluid state and that users are the likely sources of innovation under these conditions fit nicely with Knight's and von Hippel's findings, as discussed earlier, that users are the source of major product innovations. One way of viewing regulatory constraints such as those governing auto emissions or safety is that they add new performance dimensions to the set faced by the engineer and may lead to designs that give better performance on a larger number of dimensions.[39] The criteria for design are clearer for productive units approaching the specific state, but the highly developed structure in this state may reduce the productive unit's capability to exploit new opportunities for change.

Shifting Roles of R&D and Market Needs

The predominant stimulus for innovation varies as the productive unit evolves from the fluid toward the specific state. Innovations are first stimulated by market needs, but later by technological opportunities. The studies of innovation in computers, foods, scientific instruments, and rocket-engine technology show that initially the user is highly involved in originating major innovations. Then, as the productive unit develops, formal (R&D) organizations contribute increasingly to innovation. For example, Buzzell and Nourse observe that in recent times the main source of stimuli for food companies' new products has been the firms' own R&D programs.[40] The automobile firms did not establish formal R&D organizations until mass markets were developed, even though at an earlier time bicycle firms had research laboratories. While true that this change in the relevance of formal R&D to product innovation might be explained by an economywide shift toward a greater reliance on R&D as a source of innovation, other results show that more complex factors are at play. Peter R. Richardson's recent study of innovation and R&D activities in the Canadian mining industry explores the relationships among the development of the firm, sources of innovation, and R&D expenditures directly.[41] Using cross-sectional data on contemporary firms, he found that firms with larger total sales volume, or market share in mining operations, also placed greater reliance on formal R&D activities as a source of innovation. He observes that the extent of the firm's reliance on R&D changes because the nature and extent of uncertainty change.

The present model helps to explain how transition would increase the prominence of R&D as a stimulus for innovation. In the initial fluid stage, market needs are ill-defined and can be stated only with broad uncertainty. So there is uncertainty about the relevance of the outcomes that might be achieved through R&D (the targets of R&D activity), even if investments of R&D resources were made to bring about such outcomes. This has been called "target uncertainty,"[42] and its influence on decision making in R&D projects is very different from that of technical uncertainty. The expected value from any R&D investment is reduced by the combined effects of target uncertainty and technical uncertainty. The decision maker has little incentive to invest in risky R&D efforts as long as target uncertainty is high.

As the productive unit develops, however, uncertainty about markets and appropriate targets for R&D is reduced. Therefore, R&D projects bearing the same level of technical risk are made increasingly more attractive, and larger R&D investments are justified. At some point before the mounting consequences of transition make the cost of implementing technological innovation prohibitively high, and before increasing cost competition erodes margins below levels that can support large indirect-expense categories, it would be anticipated that the benefits of large R&D efforts would reach a maximum. Although R&D expenditure data are not readily available on a productive-unit basis, the apparent characteristics of the main business lines of corporations with high R&D rates provide support for this explanation. These corporations tend to sustain main business lines that fall neither near the fluid nor the specific boundary conditions, but are represented by the technologically active middle range. Jesse W. Markham observes that corporations with high R&D spending rates tend to be large, to be integrated, and to have a large relative market share.[43]

Organization and Control

Coordination and control over the productive unit also vary with the changes in product and production process within the firm. Jay Galbraith amply illustrates the impact of an abrupt innovative change on a large, established air-frame manufacturer.[44] It changed the ability of the organization to coordinate its activities successfully through the usual means of goal setting, hierarchy, and rules. In a situation that may be interpreted as a reversal in the normal direction of transition, he shows that as task uncertainty increases, the organization must increase its capacity to process information through increased investment in vertical information systems, creation of lateral relations, liaison and project groups, and so on. James M. Utterback and Elmer H. Burack have hypothesized that changing coordination requirements extend to the creation of formal technology forecasting and planning groups, which would be organizational manifestations of normal directions of movement from a fluid to a transitional state.[45] Burack adopted a unit of analysis very similar to the present productive unit in a study of highly automated production systems.[46] His analysis shows that as these production systems evolve toward the specific state, the controls that are necessary for both the regulation of process functions and management also change. Job procedures, job descriptions, and systems analyses are extended to become more pervasive features of the production network.

These results suggest ways in which the firm would modify its organization as well as its means of coordination and control as the productive units it manages develop. As products become more stable and standardized, altered only by incremental change, one would expect firms to deal with complexity by reducing the need for information processing through the use of buffers, slack resources, and the creation of self-contained and homogeneous units and tasks.[47] A reduction in the rate at which technological change takes place increases the available time for principal organization groups to anticipate and adjust to the changes.[48] Each of these considerations helps to explain the firm's impetus to divide into homogeneous productive units as its product and process technology evolve.

The changes in control and coordination that are hypothesized to accompany the unit's transition imply that the structure of the organization will also change, becoming more formal, having a greater number of levels of authority, and a greater division into units that are internally homogeneous. Several studies of firms have shown that organization structure varies with changing process technology, and also that this variation is accompanied by a specialization in subordinate units and different rates of product change and innovation as anticipated in the present hypotheses.[49] For firms that are very large[50] or rapidly growing,[51] the relationships between the characteristics of the productive unit and the total firm appear to be less important. This factor would be consistent with an observation that larger firms tend to support multiple productive units in different stages of development. To summarize, the available evidence confirms that as firms move toward more rigid process technology, standard products, and higher levels of efficiency,[52] corresponding changes in means of control and coordination and organization structure can be expected.[53]

A SYNTHESIS

The model of development in a productive unit is shown in Table 4.1. Each aspect of change has been identified independently in the preceding section, and now they are related as joint variables that change together. Table 4.1 presents the major regularities, the joint relationships, and the normal direction of transition in summary form. The fluid and specific boundaries appear at the top and bottom of the table respectively. Within the table are listed the milestone events that represent common stages of transition, as manifested in innovation, product-line characteristics, production process, organizational control, and kind of capacity. The structure of the table embodies some principal ideas found in our model: that there is a normal rate and direction in technological progress, that progress in one aspect is dependent on that in others, and that a certain degree of evenness in progression among many different elements is essential to the advance of any one. The hypothesized relationships among many variables are at once consistent with the general and detailed findings of many previous studies of innovation. They conflict with some others, but they are helpful in explaining many of the dilemmas raised in earlier studies.

The Shift in Origin of Process Innovation

The distinction made between product and process innovation and the relationships between the two are also central to the present argument. A productive unit in the fluid state uses general-purpose process equipment, which is by definition purchased. In the transitional state the firm is expected to originate some process-equipment innovations for its own use. In the specific state, entire processes are designed as technologically integrated systems that are specific to particular products and developed and produced by specialized equipment-supplier firms. Therefore, in the specific state, major process innovations are expected to originate outside the firm. However, most process-equipment innovations are expected to come from supplier companies in all stages. Viewed from the perspective of a given firm, most innovations are therefore product innovations. In the aggregate, many of these new products are process equipment for use by other firms.

This is consistent with George J. Stigler's work on *The Organization of Industry*.[54] He points to the generality of the notion of phases in industrial development: from young to maturing to declining. From this perspective, he considers how subsidiary firms that supply production-process equipment will develop with evolving phases. This would lead to a shift in the originating source of process innovations from the user segment in early stages of development to the supplier firms in later stages. Firms in various phases of development are also seen to differ in the market structure they face, in the division of labor and equipment specialization of production processes, and in the responsibilities the firm must accept in innovating to satisfy its own needs for process technology and material inputs.[55] Although Stigler's work does not focus on characteristics of innovation, the nature of evolutionary change that he identifies is much the same as the characteristics of transition discussed above, even though derived from very different data sources.

Connections with Prior Research

J. R. Bright examines the conditions that enable application of process automation in several different processes involving complex manufacturing and assembly tasks. He suggests the importance of a parallel progression among several factors, as shown in Table 4.1: predictability in product and input material characteristics, regular process flows in production, well-specified and routine labor tasks, and a sequence of cumulative incremental product and process innovations. All of these joint enabling conditions were present in several different industries in which an evolutionary sequence of development toward a high level of automation was observed.[56]

Edward Harvey applied a framework, compatible with the present

TABLE 4.1. Summary of Hypothesized Relationships between Innovation and the Evolving Structure of the Productive Segment

Innovation	Product Line	Production Process	Organizational Control	Kind of Capacity
		Fluid Boundary		
Frequent and novel product innovation market stimulated.	High product-line diversity produced to customer order.	Flexible, but inefficient. Uses general-purpose equipment and skilled labor.	Loosely organized. Entrepreneurially based.	Small scale, located near technology source or user. Low level of backward vertical integration.
Cumulative product innovations usually incorporated in periodic changes to model line. and Increase in process innovations—internally generated. and Technology-stimulated innovation.	At least one model sold as produced in substantial volumes. Dominant design achieved.	Increasingly rationalized process configuration with line-flow orientation, relying on short-duration tasks and operative skills of the work force. "Islands" of specialized and automated equipment introduced in some parts of process.	Control achieved through creation of vertical information systems, lateral relations, liaison and project groups. Control achieved by means of goal setting, hierarchy, and rules as the frequency of change decreases.	Centralized, general-purpose capacity where scale increases are achieved by breaking bottlenecks. Facilities located to achieve low factor-input costs, to minimize disruption, and facilitate distribution.
Cost-stimulated incremental innovation predominates. Novel changes involve simultaneous product and process adaptations and are infrequently introduced.	Highly standardized product with few major options. Commoditylike product specified by technical parameters.	Integrated production process designed as a "system." Labor tasks predominantly those of systems monitoring.	Bureaucratic, vertically integrated, and hierarchically organized with functional emphasis.	Large-scale facilities specialized to particular technologies, capacity increases achieved only by designing new facilities.
		Specific Boundary		

Normal Direction of Transition →

one, for forty-three essentially single-product firms in the food, chemical, and plastics industries, as well as in the machinery and electronic equipment industries.[57] His results show a progression among four characteristics of each firm: bureaucratization of organization, rate of product change, product-line diversity, and the "specificity" of the process technology, a measure indicating the degree to which the production process exhibits strong line-flow qualities. In a related line of inquiry, D. J. Hickson examined joint relationships among size, organizational structure, the extent of the production-process line-flow quality, and the input of technology for an even larger and more diverse group of British firms, including service organizations.[58] Here again, results show strong consistency among these characteristics, even though the industries are very different. Focusing on health care delivery, Charles Perrow explains the necessary conditions for transition in terms of concomitant and parallel progress in process technology. Standardization of product (service task), scale, and organizational structure are similar to this model.[59]

Taken collectively, this evidence suggests that the present concepts of boundary conditions and transition apply to a variety of productive units. A good description of a common path of development is promised for products in the industrial sector that involve complex manufacture and assembly, but there is also the suggestion that the model need not be so limited.

WHERE THE MODEL APPLIES

Where does this model of the development of productive units apply? Where does it not apply? What would be contrributed if it were known to be valid? How much is really known about the hypothesized characteristic? And, of these unknowns, which questions would it be most useful to answer first?

Applicable Products and Processes

The model applies most directly to a productive unit in which multiple inputs are combined and transformed through a complex production process that yields a highly valued product whose characteristics may be varied. The key phrases here are "productive unit," "complex production process," and "product whose characteristics may be varied."

Some confusion about application may exist because the terms "firm" and "productive unit" have sometimes been used interchangeably. Also, results from the present model are sometimes coincidental with findings that have been obtained from other units of analysis, such as firms, industries, or innovations. It is important, however, to recognize that my model pertains uniquely to the productive unit and not to the other classes of definition.

The model provides the most useful insights for complex production processes in instances where the features of the product can be varied. In cases where the product of a productive unit is definitionally standardized (for example, sulphuric acid, nylon, or copper), the prospect of radical product innovation is definitionally limited, if not practically impossible. Without the prospects of interaction between product innovation and process development, the evolution toward mass production can be much more rapid, and it will be constrained by other factors. While some important aspects of the model would still seem to apply in such instances,[60] they are special cases that are not addressed directly. The more interesting applications are to situations where product innovation is competitively important, difficult to manage, and needs to be viewed in the context of the full range of other implications that are identified through application of the model.

There is some evidence, as noted in the previous section, that applicability need not be limited to industrial products per se, but may extend to services where there is a complex process for producing or delivering a highly valued, standardized service. This seems to be the case with the evolution of communication services like the telephone system, and the initial stages of development might apply to certain health care services. In the latter case some intriguing parallels are apparent where well-defined procedures and delivery technologies are evident, as with some acute surgery units and in primary care with multiphasic screening.[61]

Exceptions in Application

The notion of evolutionary transition is a characteristic of the model that may be particularly troublesome. In some cases transition may not have occurred or may have occurred very rapidly, either because the productive unit initially began at a high state of development, or because development has simply failed to come about.

The pattern of very rapid progress appears to occur with some chemical products and other continuous-flow processes where advanced, elaborate, and large-scale process equipment is used to make a new product virtually from the initial product introduction. This exception extends beyond the pure continuous-process industries to certain products with low unit values, like cigarettes, and simple plastic and metal products, where the available process technology defines the mode of operation and may have made the product feasible in the first place.

APPLICATIONS AND EXTENSIONS IN THE AUTOMOBILE INDUSTRY

There are important questions about the model that need to be answered. All of the evidence considered shows that the normal direction of transition is toward a more rigid process structure, more homoegeneous products, increased substitution of equipment for labor, and so on. Is change evolutionary, or does it come in steps and stages? What are the forces that constrain abrupt change and cause progress to come about through a steady and cumulative progression? Is it possible that a lateral move offering both flexibility and efficiency may be realized through advances in process-equipment technology, or is transition always in one direction? That reversals do occur is indicated by studies of firms' workflow structure and organization both before and after major changes, in the design and production of new commercial aircraft[62] and in the early major model changes in the automobile industry.[63] More needs to be known about these questions and the conditions that lead to these observed outcomes.

The automobile industry offers visible evidence of a large increase in product-line variety and diversity since the mid-1950s, accompanied by continued process automation. The emphasis on frequent style change has continued throughout the period, in apparent contradiction to the model. Our first question, then, is whether the present model has any practical significance in this situation, where there is visible evidence of contrary trends. To find the answer, we will analyze the development of the engine and engine plant at Ford as a unique productive unit. The separate aspects of product-line change, process-equipment development, the characteristics of task and direct labor, and patterns of vertical integration will be considered over an extended period of time to clarify the forces that pace technological change. We will look at whether the anticipated evenness and direction of development in each aspect are present as anticipated, and whether the concept of a productive unit has operational relevance and can be measured and defined in units that have practical significance. In Chapter 6, we will use the same approach to analyze the development of Ford assembly plants, as a contrasting case in which development has not advanced as far.

5 THE AUTOMOBILE ENGINE PLANT: EVOLUTION TOWARD AN EXTREME

Today, four-cylinder gasoline engines for Ford's small cars pour out from the glistening, highly automated engine plant in Lima, Ohio. Seven decades ago, in 1906, Ford first began production of another four-cylinder engine for its Model N, using the rudimentary capabilities of the Bellevue Avenue plant near Detroit.

According to conventional wisdom, the production method should have been the malleable servant of product design and market. Yet, in this case, after years of six-cylinder V-8 and V-12 engine production, it is the engine design—the product—that has come full circle, back to a design seemingly akin to the early ones, while the production process has been irreversibly altered through cumulative progress. The progressive development of the engine plant over this period has set off subtle but powerful forces that have shaped innovation in many ways.

THE ENGINE PLANT AS A PRODUCTIVE UNIT

A modern automobile engine plant like Ford's Lima plant offers a degree of automation unparalleled in any other manufacturing process turning out a product of comparable complexity. Principal engine components are machined, inspected, and delivered by integrated transfer lines, approximately every three-quarters of a minute, from a sequence of machining operations that are performed without direct operator intervention. These transfer lines, such as shown in Plate 4 move major parts through automated operations that would otherwise have to be performed on more than 150 different stand-alone machine tools.[1] Although the number of distinct machining operations on a four-cylinder engine has increased many times, the number of direct man-hours per engine has been reduced one hundredfold from that required in very early plants.[2] Many models of varying designs were produced in the early plant; today each engine has its own devoted facility, and even a seemingly minor design change can cause a shutdown of many months or the replacement of all tooling. The differences between the modern process and its 1906 counterpart are almost total.

PLATE 4. *a*, Crankshaft Machining Department—Ford's Highland Park Plant, 1915; *b*, Automatic transfer line for cylinder block—Engine Plant around 1970. (Photographs courtesy of the Ford Motor Company.)

FIGURE 5.1. Current Engine Plant Operations (Productive Unit)

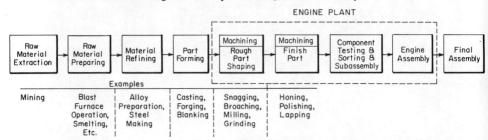

The modern plant is not the simple result of rational choices by Ford, as many picture it. Rather, it is the outcome of a complex evolutionary progression that has gone on for more than seven decades. The losses in flexibility and the highly standardized product lines have come along with impressive gains in productivity and, as it turns out, a better working environment. These all make up a complex package of changes in effective labor tasks, equipment design, material inputs, and production-process organization. To understand and manage technological change in a productive unit as a whole, these independent aspects must be studied.

Currently at Ford an engine plant is a separate organizational entity—a cost center with its own management structure, building, and support staff, reporting functionally to the Engine Division. The current engine plant and the line of engines it produces are the same as a productive unit, and therefore the two terms will be used interchangeably. This unit includes the operations within the broken lines indicated in Figure 5.1. The generalized chain of vertically related process operations that lead up to the delivery of a complete engine is shown in this figure, with examples of types of operations that would be included. In reverse order, the plant typically includes: testing, engine assembly, component testing and subassembly (of machined parts), finish machining, and rough machining.

The definition of an engine plant is clear today. But the operations now bounded by geography, management, and operational control systems were not always circumscribed in this way. To maintain consistency in historical comparisons, the engine plant, as a productive unit, will be taken to include the final engine assembly and testing operations and other process operations closely tied with them: that come under the same level of management supervision, that are linked together with major process flows, and that are located in the same plant complex. This definition represents the set of operations currently included in an engine plant.

THE PROFILE OF CHANGE AT THE CORPORATE LEVEL

The very early characteristics of engine manufacture at Ford (1903–4) were essentially those of an assembly operation. Energies were focused on design and the final assembly.[3] "The motors and most of the parts that went into these models were assembled in their [Dodge Brothers] machine shed and then loaded for delivery to the Ford plant on Mack Avenue."[4] The Ford Company, however, quickly developed the capability to produce the engine and many other components. By 1906, because of high demand for the Model N, Ford faced the problem of insufficient capacity to produce enough engines to meet orders.[5]

Initial Manufacturing Characteristics
The available evidence about the engine-manufacturing process at Ford in this beginning period, 1905 through 1909, suggests that it was at first characterized by low division of labor; reliance on skilled mechanics; a job-shop arrangement with erratic flows of work in process; the use of very general-purpose, nonspecialized capital equipment; hand-to-mouth purchasing procedures; crude production-control systems; and rapid, rather fluid, changes in engine design. Progress in rationalizing the process was extremely swift, however, so even though numerous descriptions exist, it is difficult to pin down the exact characteristics of the process in any one year. Some idea about initial characteristics in this era can be drawn, however, from four accounts of manufacturing at Ford: that of Charles Sorensen, who was Ford's overall production manager from the Model T era up through World War II and a Ford employee since 1905; the extensive accounts of two nationally known engineers of the era, H. L. Arnold and F. L. Faurote, who studied Ford facilities and manufacturing methods; the work of academic historians who studied Ford, Allan Nevins of Columbia University, his colleague Frank E. Hill; and the most critical historian Keith Sward, who has challenged many legends about Ford. These books describe the characteristics of labor tasks, process organization, process equipment, purchasing, and product design, providing in addition a notion about how these began to evolve toward a higher degree of development.

Major production tasks were initially ill structured, relied on a low division of labor, and depended on the skills of the craftsman mechanic. "At Ford's and all other shops in Detroit the process . . . still revolved around the versatile mechanic. . . . Ford's assemblers were still [by 1908] all-around men. To be sure time had added some refinements. In 1908 it was no longer necessary . . . to leave his place of work for trips to the tool crib or the parts bin. Stock runners had been set aside to perform this function. Nor was the Ford mechanic in 1908 quite the man he had been in 1903 . . . the job had been split up ever so little."[6]

The initial process organization was erratic and more like a job shop, organized functionally rather than as a line flow. "In the [shop] previous to the time when any attempts at Ford shops systematizing were made and chaos reigned supreme . . . the Ford . . . four-cylinder casting travelled no less than 4,000 feet in course of finishing, a distance now [in 1913] reduced to 334 feet."[7]

"Ford and his engineers made their first notable strides in production merely by organizing again and again the various departments of their new plant that were given over to the making of parts. . . . Had the company laid out this vast array of equipment [added after 1906 to expand production] along old fashioned lines, it would have grouped each class of machinery in a department by itself . . . the lathes here, power drills there and so on."[8]

The capital equipment initially employed was general-purpose, "off the shelf," and employed at relatively low intensity. "Until then [the move to the new Highland Park Plant in 1910], our production had been carried on with standard equipment; we had little experience with special machines such as, for instance, a drill capable of boring more than 40 holes at one time on four sides of a cylinder block. After moving into Highland Park we began developing special type machines, multiple-spindled drills, milling machines with multiple heads at different angles."[9]

"The Ford foundry as first started had no distinctive features whatever. . . . The shovel and wheelbarrow regined supreme, everything done by hand, nothing by machinery when, May 10, 1910, the first Ford Model T cylinders were made from wood patterns."[10]

Purchasing was initially hand-to-mouth and dominated by the suppliers. "Until then [1907] the large requirements like tires would be handled as an individual job by Mr. Ford and other large items by Couzens. Buying was on a hand-to-mouth basis, generally in quantities no larger than were actually needed for short periods. Flanders stabilized some of this helter skelter buying by setting production schedules of fixed monthly output [aggregate planning]. As volume increased with rising production . . . Diehl [Ford's new Purchasing manager] required large suppliers to submit prices covering six and twelve month periods. . . . His buyers were instructed to look for at least two sources of supply and be sure of competitive bidding. Next he required each bidder to submit prices based on material, labor and other overhead and even the amount of profit. Under such a system there was no question about costs being kept down and the savings were tremendous."[11]

Product design was fluid and changed frequently and radically. Referring primarily to his work on the design of the power train for the Model T, Sorensen notes: "Actually it took four years and more to develop the Model T. Previous models [2-cylinder, 4-cylinder, and 6-cylinder since 1903] were the guinea pigs, one might say, for experimentation and development."[12]

"During the first five years of its existence the Ford Company experimented with eight different models. . . . Diverse in design these . . . were equally dissimilar in price. Then in 1908 it introduced the Model T engine, which was to be standardized for almost two decades."[13]

The underlying course of these initial fluid conditions and the subsequent evolutionary but rapid development of engine manufacturing is perhaps best summarized in Sorensen's words, from his perspective of having developed through this period with Ford: "Henry Ford had no ideas on mass production. He wanted to build a lot of autos. He was determined, but like everyone else at that time, he didn't know how. In later years he was glorified as the originator of the mass production idea. Far from it; he just grew into it, like the rest of us. The essential tools and the final assembly line with its many integrated feeders resulted from an organization that was continually experimenting and improvising to get better production."[14]

At the end of this period, in 1908, the Model T was introduced. From a production base of 10,202 engines in this year, production approximately doubled every two years for the next fifteen years, reaching two million in 1923, initiating a sequence of evolutionary change that was to continue at varying rates for decades later.

Corporate Product Line: Passenger Car Engines

The composite history of Ford's U.S. passenger-car engine line for all plants is summarized graphically in Figure 5.2. Beyond providing the obvious data about frequency of model change, this figure enables us to draw subtle but significant insights from patterns of new-engine introduction. Systematic change in at least three aspects of the product line can be observed: the standardization of the engine model itself vis-à-vis other engines and the line of passenger-car models, the trends of mechanical variety in the engine line, and the diversity of the entire engine line.

Each engine in the figure is represented by a straight line that indicates both the years it was in production and its cubic-inch displacement (CID). The CID is the volume of space that the pistons sweep out in one complete stroke of operations; it is a function of the engine's mechanical size that is exactly determined by the engine's bore and stroke. For several reasons, CID provides a particularly useful single dimension for describing an engine: it is a fundamental measurement that determines an engine's basic capability for developing horsepower; it can be altered only through changes that affect both design and manufacturing; and it reflects the overall physical size of the engine.

Localization of Model Change. The impact of model change or production of the engine and other major components has been localized as standardized component lines, or families, have been adopted. In the initial period (1903–8), the engine was standardized by car model: when the car

FIGURE 5.2. Ford Engine History

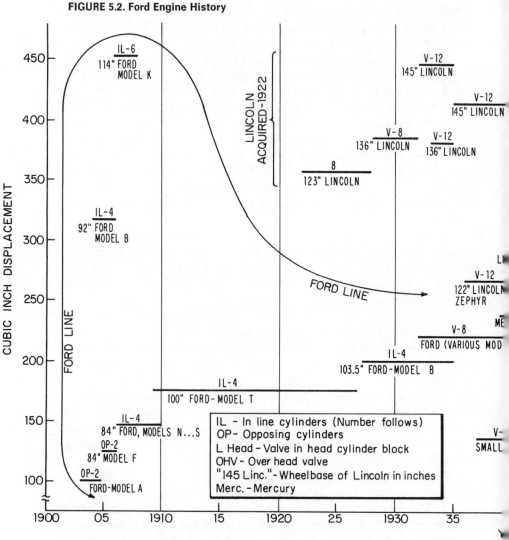

SOURCE: Appendix 2.
NOTE: The match between engine and passenger car is illustrated by listing some of the major passenger car lines on which the engine was either standard or optional.

model was changed there were simultaneous design changes in engines. This is no longer the case. Change in the engine line is now managed independently, so that model changes in the car that might introduce a higher-powered engine need not involve redesign.

The transition between these two states can be traced in Figure 5.2, where the car model is listed below the line for each engine, and, for the early years, the car's wheelbase length in inches is given just before the

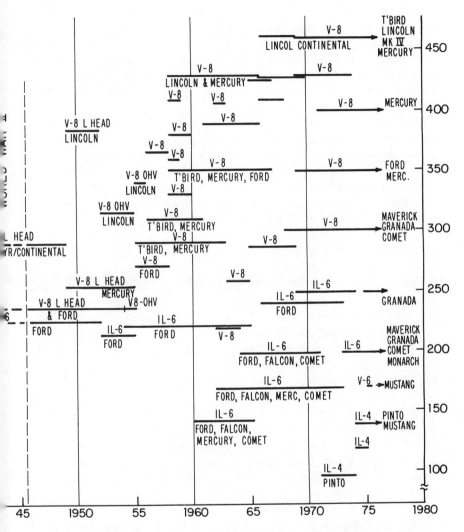

Only the major passenger car line is noted, and special appointment series within the major car lines, such as LTD, Parklane, Marquis, etc., are not identified separately. See Appendix 2 for more detail.

model name. From this data it may be noted that engines and cars were initially designed as a unit, for car model, wheelbase, and engine all changed together. Engines were uniquely associated with a particular car model in this way, through several model changes in the Ford and Lincoln line, until 1931.

The engine began to be standardized by car line rather than car model with the introduction of the 221-CID V-8 engine. This was the automobile industry's first low-priced, mass-produced V-8 engine, and it turned out to be a dominant design. From 1932 through 1942, while the 221-CID V-8 was employed as the principal engine for the Ford car line, the wheelbase was lengthened from 106 inches to 112 inches and then to 114 inches, the steel turret top was introduced, the body was streamlined, the running boards were absorbed into the body, and headlights were integrated into fenders. Mercury initially had its own engine, the 239-CID V-8, and the Lincoln had a set of V-12 engines.

In this mode of technological change, incremental improvements and innovations were managed by car line. Major improvements, however, such as the overhead-valve engines, were introduced (around 1952) across more than one engine in the line. This across-the-line pattern of engine changes in 1932, 1948, 1952, and 1955 is evident from Figure 5.2.

Finally, in recent years, an entirely different pattern emerges, as is apparent in Figure 5.2. The engine line is now systematized or "rationalized" so that engines regularly differ from one another by exactly 50 CID. The engine line is now also standardized, and the introduction of new designs is staggered. The engine line is managed separately to serve all car models in their class. Changes in car models need not be tied to engine changes, and vice versa. These altered relationships have localized the impact of model changes both in engines and the car as a whole.

Growing Engine-Line Diversity. The absolute diversity of the engine line has increased, as indicated by the number of engines in the line, while mechanical novelty has decreased. Figure 5.2 shows the build-up, from one engine in the early Model T era to the present seven or eight engines. During some years around 1960, there were as many as nine. But the number of plants has also increased, thereby offsetting product-line diversity increases for individual engine plants.

Decreasing Structural Novelty. A third aspect of product-line change is the tendency for engine designs to become similar and for major changes to occur less frequently. Table 5.1 illustrates this point by listing innovative engines, major structural changes in engine design or in manufacturing method that incorporate "Ford Firsts," and organizational and production changes that concern the engine segment. The entries are events which Ford or others have emphasized as particularly important. The engines so designated are but a few of those shown in Figure 5.2, but they have propelled about one-third of all the motor vehicles Ford has produced in the United States.

When the entire product line is considered, we see more diversity and more incremental changes. Highly visible radical innovation has declined overall through the early 1970s. This cannot be taken, however, as evidence that change has become less significant or that innovation has stopped. Rather, important changes have become evolutionary in nature and less individually identifiable. The changes are not less significant in a

TABLE 5.1. Major Design, Process, and Organizational Changes or Innovations in Ford Engines

Year	Application	Change or Innovation
*1903	8-hp 2-cyl. (opposing engine)	Adjustable spark advance
*1904	3/8-CID 15-hp IL-4 (in-line 4-cylinder engine)	Horizontally mounted engine with torque-tube drive as opposed to side-chain drive
*1906	149-CID IL-4 and 453-CID IL-6 engines	Unitary engine and transmission
*1907	149-CID IL-4 engine	Cylinder head made as separate, removable part
*1908	New 177-CID Model T engine	First truly mass-produced, lightweight, reliable engine. Vanadium steel used on critical components (crankshaft and rods), single casting "en block" block
1922	358-CID V-8 Lincoln engine	Lincoln company purchased
*1924	Engine manufacturing	Constant temperature inspection
*1927	New 200-CID Model A engine	Aluminum pistons, mushroomed-type valve stems; offered improved cooling and lubrication
*1928	Engine manufacturing	Dynamic crankshaft balancing in production
*1932	New 221-CID V-8 engine	First low-cost, mass-produced V-8 engine to achieve single-piece complex casting for block in continuous production
†1932	Engine manufacturing	First in-line transfer device
1932	New 448-CID V-12 engine for Lincoln	
1941	New 226-CID IL-6 engine	Added to product line as low-cost engine. The first IL-6 since 1907
1945	Lincoln-Mercury Division established	Beginning of product division organization
1952	New 215-CID overhead valve (OHV), short-stroke 6-cylinder engine	First conversion to new higher-performance, short-stroke, higher-compression engines. All engines changed over to OHV by end of 1954—start of "horsepower race"
*1952	Cleveland engine plant	First engine plant fully integrated by automated transfer lines. Beginning of decentralization of engine manufacturing
*1959	Thin-wall, gray cast-iron engines introduced	Improved casting technology and metallurgy permits weight and cost reduction and higher precision in manufacture
1960	The merger of previously separate Lincoln-Mercury and Ford engine lines into a common line is begun	Consolidation of divisional engine lines into one corporatewide line begun
1970	New CID 4-cylinder metric-based engine introduced	Detroit-designed engine introduced for new Pinto from Ford Germany

SOURCES: *Ford Firsts* and *Ford Facts and Figures,* various years.
   * Engines or changes that introduced widely recognized "Ford Firsts" or innovations.
   † Added by author.

total sense. The methodology and conclusion of many past studies assume that innovation must be structurally novel to be significant. A careful consideration of advances in engine design helps to explain why the need for novel change has decreased. The last few years are different, however, in terms of novelty. Despite the smooth consistency with which radical change has decreased over this long period, there are subtle signs of an upsurge in novelty following 1970. The V-8 engine, which nearly reigned supreme at one point, has developed a growing list of challengers. The introduction of the small in-line four-cylinder overhead cam engine and of the V-6 are two examples. The recently announced introduction of an engine with adjustable displacement is another. These changes foreshadow a strong reversal in the historical transition toward the specific state of development. If these changes are borne out in mass-produced engines, they will show that reverse transition can be realized in a mature productive unit.

Self-Limiting Technological Innovation

Technological advances made radical change less necessary, at least least until the pollution and energy problems added new constraints on design. Radical structural changes by themselves contributed only nominally to advances in technological capability. Some causes of this self-limiting effect are illustrated by the following simple analysis, which considers how horsepower and CID advances have influenced the car manufacturer's efforts to differentiate his product line of cars. To develop the analysis, we will use data on actual Ford engines, beginning with the very early period, 1903–8.

Early engines did not produce much power. If a large car or truck was to be designed, then a large engine was needed. Large engines were mechanically complex and much more expensive than small ones. Therefore, if a line of cars was to be produced for both high- and low-price segments of the market, a line of engines was needed that varied substantially in size. From 1903 to 1908, Ford experimented with different models that were to serve different market segments.[15] The engine designed for the large and high-priced Model K was 453 CID, larger by 353 CID than the low-priced Model A engine. Even with this much mechanical variation, only a 32-horsepower advantage was achieved. The state of the art in this era offered a horsepower-to-CID trade-off ratio of only 32/353, or 0.09. What this meant was that performance improvement necessitated a great deal of mechanical novelty in order to achieve larger engine sizes. The Model T was superior as a car in its era because it innovated in the use of a vanadium-steel alloy to achieve a high strength-to-weight ratio and could be powered by a moderate-sized, 177-CID engine.

Over time, steady progress was made in advancing engine performance. Improvements were made in precision machining to give higher RPM engines, higher compression ratios, better balance, and reliability. Better metals were developed, as were improved fuels, and new knowledge about engine design was gained. These improvements were reflected not just in higher horsepower engines, but also in a more flexible capacity for producing engines that offered a wide range of power with less mechanical variation. By the mid-1950s only a relatively small amount of mechanical variation among different engines in the line was needed in order to achieve large performance differences. A difference of only 207 CID in 6- and 8-cylinder engines supported horsepower differences of 245 brake horsepower (bhp) vis-à-vis a range of 353 CID for only 32 bhp in the earlier period.* This meant that the capabilities of the more recent period supported a horsepower-to-CID ratio of 245/207 or 1.18, compared to a ratio of 0.09 in the earlier period. Of course, some of the improvement is illusory, since a less conservative basis for rating horsepower was used in later periods. In large part, however, the gain was real and had important implications beyond the obvious improvement it afforded in the car's performance. It meant that much less variation in design and in manufacturing was needed to achieve a given level of change in performance. Thus it supported the automation of manufacturing processes, made novel innovation less necessary, and, of course, made possible the horsepower race of the late 1950s.

As the capability to produce high-performance engines has increased, there was less *need* to introduce novel mechanical designs—the need for conspicuous structural change diminished. Rather, large changes in product performance could be realized through incremental mechanical changes or trade-offs. It became easier than before to support a wide diversity in the performance of vehicles in the product line, since only relatively small differences in manufacturing process are needed to produce engines that perform differently. Under these circumstances it is not surprising to find the historical trends in product change and diversity that we have observed. It is also interesting to note that the major, or innovative, engines contributed in only a minor way to the important trend in increased horsepower-to-CID capability.†

Recent regulation and fuel efficiency goals have created a need for major innovations to adapt the product to the changed environment.

* Brake horsepower (bhp) is the engine rating that has traditionally been used for U.S. automobiles in specifying engine power. The rated bhp varies with the speed at which the engine is rated and overstates the "delivered" horsepower the engine actually provides to propel the automobile. Th present analysis is based on "advertised" brake horsepower.

† The brake horsepower (bhp) to CID ratio has advanced from 0.10 in 1903 to 0.70 for the 122-CID 4-cylinder Pinto engine in the 1970s. The eight engines designated as most innovative since 1927 have contributed only 0.125 of this improvement, based on rated horsepower data for the referenced engines and their predecessors.

CHANGE WITHIN THE PRODUCTIVE UNIT

While product-line diversity and the rate of product change have risen companywide, an exactly opposite trend is apparent at the level of the individual plant.

Product-Line Changes

The addition of more engine plants has offset companywide increases in the number of different engines. Initially there was one plant, and aside from the Lincoln facility, which produced its own engines from 1922 until World War II, there was but one engine plant until September 1951, when the Cleveland engine plant began to operate. By February 1955 a second Cleveland plant was in operation.‡ The U.S.–Canadian Auto Pact in 1965 enabled duty-free shipment of engines made in Canada. By 1970, operations in Canada were expanded so that there were two Ford engine plants in Windsor, Ontario. The impact of these additions on diversity is shown in Table 5.2, which, for selected years, compares the number of different engines in the total line to the number of engine plants in operation.

Decreasing Product-Line Diversity. The data in Table 5.2 suggest that the diversity accommodated by any given engine plant has been decreasing

‡ The Highland Park plant was the main Ford facility from 1910 until the late 1920s. Operations were steadily expanded at the giant Rouge River facility, which was known at one time as the largest single industrial facility in the world. The Lincoln plant was devoted exclusively to Lincolns, with a peak production of 30,000 units per year (1937), compared with the maximum of more than 2,000,000 car and truck engines produced per year in the single Highland Park facility in 1923.

TABLE 5.2. Product Diversity per Segment

Year	Number of Different Engines	Number of Plants	Ratio of Engines to Plants	Total U.S. Motor-Vehicle Unit Production Volume*
1905	2	1	2	1,599
1915	1	1	1	501,462
1923	2	2	1	2,019,000
1939	4	2	2	826,341
1947	3	1	3	1,091,229
1952	4	2	2	1,323,578
1959	8	4	2	2,124,390
1968†	8	6	1.3	3,200,748
1973†	9‡	6	1.5	3,811,927

SOURCES: Appendix 2 and Ford press releases and news announcements.
* Includes two Windsor plants after 1965.
† Total motor-vehicle production is given, since most trucks use the reported engines.
‡ One of the small 4-cylinder engines is produced abroad.

since the 1950s. Effective diversity was probably the highest in 1906, when the 6-cylinder engine was added to the line, but it is difficult to pin down the actual number of different engines produced. Diversity was certainly at its very lowest during the periods of product standardization in the Model T and the Model A. Another peak is apparent in the period of the post–World War II start-up, when capacity was being expanded. Since this time, management has apparently found that effectiveness was improved by specializing the engine plants.

Declining Model-Change Rates. The rate of engine-model change has also decreased over time on a per-plant basis. The maximum rate of change occurred in the pre–Model T period. A second peak occurred from 1954 to 1960. In the later period, Ford implemented the concept of separate product divisions, so that there were competing lines of engines for Lincoln and Mercury. During the same period, the so-called horsepower race began. Nevertheless, the *rate* of model change was higher in the earlier period, when there was effectively only one plant. During the initial period, six new engines were introduced in five years. In a comparable five-year period from 1954 through 1959, during the horsepower race, there were from three to four engine plants and eleven engine changes. The rate of change per plant was, therefore, less than half the earlier rate.

After the horsepower race, and up to 1973, the rate of change stabilized a great deal more. A ranking of all engines by the number of years they were in production shows that only twenty-six, or 45 percent, out of fifty-nine engines in toto were produced for five years or more. Seventeen, or 63 percent, of these twenty-six engines were produced after 1959. The rate of change now seems to be increasing again but this cannot be definitely confirmed.

Equipment and Process Change

The explosive growth in volume that followed the introduction of the Model T led to a new approach in mass production. The approach shaped labor tasks and process configuration, and, perhaps most important, it set a pattern of process-equipment innovation in engine plants that was to hold throughout the industry.

Ford's approach, as described in the literature of the time, merely involved the repeated application of the following steps, as demand doubled and redoubled:

> (1) Redesign the flow of work so that parts move in a more nearly linear or progressive flow, and progressive operations are physically adjacent or linked with gravity feed conveyors or mechanical transfer devices.
>
> (2) Use a separate, wholly devoted machine tool for each operation in the work-flow sequence, rather than reroute the work back to a common machine (drill press, milling machine, etc.).

(3) Obtain the most appropriate machine tool for the operation to which it is to be applied without regard for its shared application or alternative future use.

(4) Group common operations and perform them simultaneously at one machine or station (for example, drill twenty-four holes at once in the cylinder block).

(5) Modify available machine tools with special power heads, jigs, and fixtures to increase capacity and reduce direct labor requirements.

(6) Encourage machine-tool companies to offer new, special machine tools that meet unique process-flow requirements and reduce direct labor.

(7) Develop special machine tools that cannot otherwise be obtained.

"The policy [in the 1910s] was to scrap old machines ruthlessly in favor of better types—even if 'old meant only a month's use.' "[16] At the same time, Ford established a machine-tool development group, relying heavily on German-born machine-tool designers and makers. "Now aware that Ford was scrapping old and installing high-production equipment, machine tool builders flocked around Emde [the German-born chief of Tool Development] with their latest development."[17]

The way that equipment characteristics developed under the force of this policy is shown by three indices that relate to steps 1, 4, and 6 above. An estimate of the degree of automation (as this term has been defined by James R. Bright in his book *Automation and Management*[18]) is used as a surrogate for step 6 above—the degree to which special machine tools are used. The various levels that Bright suggests are given in Table 5.3. The three indices are:

Transfer Span: A measure of the extreme state in mechanically linking adjacent operations—the number of stations that are connected so no operator is needed. Stated alternatively, this is the number of different machine-tool operations that are linked and whose operation is controlled by an automated transfer-machine mechanism.*

Grouped Operations: The maximum number of different operations performed simultaneously (not necessarily automatically) by a machine at one station.

Automation Level: An estimate of the highest level of automation achieved in any machine tool based on Bright's automaticity scale.

Articles written before World War II frequently emphasized process-flow descriptions and the particulars of equipment, especially new innovative equipment. The maximum number of grouped operations and the maximum transfer span have been identified from this literature, assuming

---

* A transfer machine is a mechanical device that automatically moves a part that is being machined, inspected, etc., from one work station to an adjacent one. Normally it is automatically activated and interlocked with the affected machines so that they all work as a unit.

TABLE 5.3. Mechanization Index

Initiating Control Source	Type of Machine Response	Power Source	Level Number	Level of Mechanization
From a variable in the environment	Responds with action Modifies own action over a wide range of variation	Mechanical (Non-manual)	17	Anticipates action required and adjusts to provide it.
			16	Corrects performance while operating.
			15	Corrects performance after operating.
	Selects from a limited range of possible prefixed actions		14	Identifies and selects appropriate set of actions.
			13	Segregates or rejects according to measurement.
			12	Changes speed, position, direction according to measurement signal.
	Responds with signal		11	Records performance.
			10	Signals preselected values of measurement (includes error detection).
			9	Measures characteristic of work.
From a control mechanism that directs a predetermined pattern of action	Fixed within the machine		8	Actuated by introduction of work piece or material.
			7	Power tool system, remote controlled.
			6	Power tool, program control (sequence of fixed functions).
			5	Power tool, fixed cycle (single function).
From man	Variable		4	Power tool, hand control.
			3	Powered hand tool.
		Manual	2	Hand tool.
			1	Hand.

SOURCE: James Bright, *Automation and Management.*

that the most advanced developments were described. The automation level was determined in the same way, with the intent of determining the most automated aspect of the engine-manufacturing equipment as reported for the year in question. The estimate of automation refers to a particular machine as it ranks on Bright's scale, "Seventeen Levels of Mechanization." The values for all three indices are tabulated in Table 5.4.

The data in Table 5.4 show that equipment development has been steady and coherent over very long periods. Cumulatively the changes have

TABLE 5.4. Selected Equipment Characteristics of Newest Plant in Period

Periods	1910–12	1913–14	1924–26	1927–28	1932	1935–36	1947–48	1952–53	1970–72
Transfer span (number of linked stations)	1	1	1	1	2	3	8	150	150+
Number of grouped operations	24	45	48	34	83	83	32	12	20
Automation level	5	6	6	6	6	6 or 7	6 or 7	10	16

SOURCE: See Appendix 3.
* Introduction of the Cleveland Engine plant, September 1951.

completely altered the characteristics of engine manufacturing. The contrast that is apparent in early and modern engine manufacturing processes, as shown in Plate 4, suggest the significant change that has taken place. They have led to: (1) a manufacturing process that is specialized to a particular engine design; (2) a completely altered set of work-force skills; (3) a change from labor-saving to capital-saving process innovations; and (4) a large increase in the cost of product change.

Process Specialization. The early growth in the number of grouped operations is in fact a trend toward greater specialization and mechanization in individual machines. The mode of equipment development up to the sharp break point in 1952 sought direct labor reductions by making machine tools that grouped as many operations as possible. The trend was representative of more than just the peak occurrence that Table 5.4 reports. In each period within the plant there were many grouped operations that approached the reported peak number.

Each cluster of grouped operations can be visualized as an "island of mechanization" that grew in the process flow. As it grew, it became increasingly specialized to a single process function. The growth of mechanized islands was paralleled by the use of relatively flexible mechanical conveyors to couple machine groups into a system. For example, conveyors were first introduced at Ford in its radiator line around 1912.[19] But by 1936 Ford reported that it had the largest completely mechanized installation of handling equipment ever set up in any industrial enterprise. In that year Ford reported: "Over 700,000 feet of monorail and belt conveyor equipment alone are used at Rouge River."[20]

Standardization of the engine was a necessary condition for growth in grouped operations. There is evidence that the trend in grouped operations reversed with the introduction of new engines. A reversal may be noted in the 1927–28 period following the introduction of the Model A, and a dip also occurred with the introduction of the V-8 engine in 1932, although this is not evident in Table 5.4.

By the late 1930s, applications of the transfer-machine concept ushered in a new form of specialization, and the transfer span began to build up rapidly. This trend led toward higher levels of integration in the process work flow. Ford's Cleveland engine plant was a culmination of efforts to integrate the process mechanically rather than to seek advances in individual machines by grouping operations. In the Cleveland plant, the principal machining operations for each major engine component, such as cylinder blocks and heads, became one giant grouped operation that functioned as a common machine. Automation began to increase rapidly after transfer lines were extensively adopted in this plant.

Automation. Advances in process equipment, that is, sophistication achieved through the use of feedback and other features of automation, apparently lagged behind rather than led other advances. Gains in grouped operations were achieved early, largely by combining existing functions in a single machine. Progress was late in functions normally associated with higher levels of automation, such as feedback and machine self-correction, represented by levels 10 and above on Bright's scale of mechanization. These levels were reached only after extensive process integration was brought about through application of the transfer-machine concept—not before it. The transfer-machine concept itself was introduced first in 1932 on the innovative new 221-CID V-8 engine. This engine proved to be a dominant design.

These trends suggest that the roles of a dominant design and of management in making the process flow consistent and regular are critically important in making equipment advances possible. This fits with the idea that equipment advances are achieved through mechanical or electronic analogies to manual or simple mechanical processes. Before the analogy can be made, however, the prior processes must exist as a consistent and regular model of operation. These observations point to the important interrelationship among product design, regular process flow, and equipment innovation.

Labor Skills. The role and skills of the work force were completely changed when the engine plant was integrated through the use of transfer lines. Direct labor in the manufacturing process was almost eliminated. One estimate placed the decrease in direct labor associated with machining operations at 90 percent.[21] This figure is probably accurate, but it does not reflect total labor-cost reduction because of a corresponding increase in the skills and numbers of indirect work-force employees. Nevins placed this total engine plant work-force reduction at 20 percent.[22] The impact on the nature of labor tasks will be considered in the following section.

Shift in Mode of Innovation. The 1952 change was a turning point in the objectives of future equipment advances. The Cleveland plant seems to have made the first major innovative change that relegated direct labor costs below indirect and capital investment costs. The synchronous transfer line, with its short, entirely machine-paced cycle, promised to move engine parts through machining operations at almost twice the rate previously achieved and thereby to achieve an offset in the traditional trend of capital-labor substitution ratios. It offered twice the capacity of a comparable semiautomatic line, by one estimate.[23] Since then, the important changes in engine manufacturing have emphasized overhead and capital savings as much as or more than direct labor savings. This is indicated by some of the engine-plant equipment advances made after 1952 that were reported as important by industry experts (Table 5.5; see also Chapter 3).

These improvements since 1952 have, among other things, continued past trends by increasing the extent of the process that is linked by au-

TABLE 5.5. Recent Advances in Engine Lines

Description	Factor Improvement	Use
Programmable controllers	Ease changeover cost and time. Reduce maintenance manpower and downtime; increase utilization of plant.	Contributes to equipment flexibility and automated location of equipment failure.
Ceramic boring	Quality improvement in machining and increased tool life; decreased downtime.	Higher-speed cutting and better-machined surfaces, reducing number of machine tools by as much as one-third.
Nonsynchronous transfer lines*	Improved utilization, eased maintenance, and increased flexibility in the process.	Loss of one in-line machine does not shut down entire line or plant.
Automated engine assembly	Reduction of labor content in assembly and improved consistency.	An extension of mechanical pacing, and an increase in machine-performed insertion, fastening, and testing in engine assembly.
High-speed grinding	Increase equipment utilization; decease in number of different operations.	Increases throughput and allows substitution of grinding for other operations.

* A nonsynchronous line is one where successive operations are actuated by the entry of the part. In such a line, machines or portions of the line can be run independently if necessary, small buffer inventories created, etc.

tomated transfer,* particularly in engine assembly. The primary emphasis has changed, however, in an important qualitative sense. Improvements like nonsynchronous transfer lines and programmable controllers are more systemslike innovations than independent changes to particular operations and equipment. They resemble system-improvement innovations in bulk processes like refineries or chemical plants more than they do the independent innovations of the early 1910s or 1920s in particular machines (for example, camshaft-shaping machine, unitary casting, crankshaft-balancing machine). These changes altered the nature of process innovation in the engine plant.

Flexibility and the Cost of Change. Equipment used in the period before 1910 could flexibly accommodate product change, but the high degree of equipment specialization introduced in the 1910s and 1920s greatly reduced this flexibility. The five engines introduced from 1903 through 1908 did not require significant machine-tool replacement or equipment writeoff.† In contrast, the changeover from Model A to Model T involved almost one year's shutdown, the purchase of 4,500 new machine

* The extent of process operations integrated by transfer lines has continued to increase because more assembly operations have been incorporated, transfer lines for smaller parts have been added, and links in the line have been closed. It is difficult to show this by counting stations, however, for many of the stations are not equivalent to previous machining operations.

† Both balance-sheet data and documentary evidence support this view.

tools, and the rebuilding of 53,000, estimated at well over half of the engine-plant process equipment.[24] Similarly, five years later the change-over from Model A to the V-8 engine involved a shutdown of several months and the replacement of half the machine tools in the engine plant.[25]

After this early period it is difficult to assess this type of flexibility on a comparable basis, for the structural changes to the engine were planned with longer lead times; in most of the cases there were several engine plants so change could be staggered; and engine design changes were not often of the same magnitude as the 1932 V-8. The overhead-valve engine introduced in the 1951 Ford involved changes of moderate magnitude.[26] Although shutdown cannot be used as a measure, it is clear that after World War II the plants have not been flexible. In general, a changeover to a new engine requires an entirely reengineered line with new equipment. If nothing else, the difficulties with pollution-control changes demonstrate a characteristic inflexibility in equipment.‡

Changing Task Characteristics

The work environment and critical skills that the work force contributes have turned inside out over the seven decades we are examining. In their predominant mode, the tasks in engine manufacturing first called for the skilled craftsman. Then mass production initially demanded the short-cycle, repetitive tasks of machine operation—an operative stage. Finally, tasks changed back to the broader ones of process-systems monitoring, more craftsmanlike in nature. The stages are shown in Table 5.6. For the engine assembler, the same cycle may be noted, except that the last stage has not been reached.

The very early period, from 1903 to about 1908, is marked as the era

‡ In an interview in 1972, one manager of an engine plant comparable in complexity to Ford's cited a six-month shutdown caused by changes made in an engine to introduce pollution-control modifications.

TABLE 5.6. Changing Labor-Task Characteristics

1903–7 High Skill	1908–12 Semiskilled	1913–51 Operative	1952–present Systems Operation
Tasks demanding trade-craft skills	Experience and some skills required	Manual dexterity	Knowledge of process equipment
Long-duration tasks that include unpredictable operations	Long-duration tasks that are repetitive	Short duration; repetitive, predictable tasks	Monitoring patrol and intervention
Trade-craft union	No union	Growth of industry union	Industry union

of the jack-of-all-trades, the craftsman, and the trade union.[27] Individual workers were responsible for the satisfactory completion of a large component or identifiable part of the engine. Tasks were typically of long duration. For example, initially one man had the responsibility for the total final assembly of an engine. This took a little over nine hours.[28]

During the transition to mass production, tasks were better defined and structured so that high skills were not required, but task durations were still relatively long.[29] The influence of trade craft unions in the automobile industry reportedly ended for all practical purposes by 1910.[30]

In the third period, from around 1913 to 1951, only the skills of the operative were required. The division of labor was high, and each worker was responsible for the repetitive execution of one operation. Motor assembly provides an example. The rate for the moving-assembly-team method, which Ford reportedly adopted in 1913 after considerable experimentation, involved an average cycle time of twenty-four seconds per operation in the case of the flywheel magneto and fifty-nine seconds for the motor. The duration of the tasks performed by individual operators ranged widely, however, from six seconds to six minutes; most tasks required between ten seconds and one minute.[31] The distribution of times was not much different in 1932.[32]

At present, the nature of the work in the engine plant is essentially a systems operation. This change accompanied the introduction of transfer-line integration in 1951. For example, Bright's data on the Mercury cylinder-block line shortly after it was placed in operation in 1954 indicate that 78 percent of the workers assigned to it had responsibilities described as either "setup" or "patrol." He notes that only 19 percent of the operators actually "operate" their machines. He comments on the overall nature of work in an engine plant as follows:

> The worker is becoming more of an observer. His activity covers a wider geographical portion of the production line. This almost invariably requires familiarity with more kinds of machinery. His job is losing its need for repetition. It is one of random activity, to some extent dictated by chance and to some extent by choice.
>
> While considerable labor is still required in assembly, the core tasks have changed dramatically from earlier periods. They concern the operation and maintenance of a system that carries out work, not the performance of work itself.[33]

In the later period of automated engine plants, the short-duration task is still present as noted for the Pinto engine, but primarily in assembly.[34] Even here, progress is being made in performing these short-duration tasks with machines.

Job Enlargement—A Folly? The progression of labor-task characteristics through these stages raises an intriguing question about the best way to improve the quality of the job environment for the worker. Many writers have recommended that more challenging jobs be given to workers by arbitrarily changing the division of labor to provide longer-duration tasks that are less repetitive. If such a policy had been implemented at Ford in the 1920s or 1930s, would the work environment in engine plants be as challenging as it is today? One may argue that it would not!

Task characteristics clearly have evolved through the less-than-challenging operative period to one that offers a less routine, more challenging work context. There is reason to believe that advances in equipment development may have depended in an important way on the conditions of the prior stage. Many equipment developments have been made through mechanical analogy to short repetitive tasks. that ultimately made those undesirable tasks unnecessary. In this sense, the less desirable operative stage of task characteristics may be an important stage in an overall pattern of development. But can development proceed other than through such an evolutionary process? Are the difficult work conditions of the operative phase essential in achieving a more desirable state? If they are, then ill-conceived premature efforts to enlarge job content by increasing task durations and making tasks less routine may thwart long-run advances that eliminate unpleasant tasks entirely.

The Changing Nature of Capacity

The reliance on vertical integration as a source of input materials and components, the types of process operations that are included in the engine plant itself rather than other supporting plants like foundries, and the way these are organized, all represent important characteristics of development. In the absence of comprehensive data that would exactly define these properties, a useful perspective can be obtained by analyzing a sample of engine components, their sources, and associated manufacturing processes.* By examining the way that selected components have been handled over time, a great deal can be learned about the engine plant as a productive unit and how it changes over time. The analysis of these data (see Table 5.7) indicates the development of backward vertical integration and some aspects of organization.

The engine components selected for study are: cylinder block, crankshaft, pistons, piston rings, crankcase, carburetor, distributor, radiator core, and starter. The origin and process steps for each component were identified for eight time periods from 1910–11 to 1970–73. The

* A wealth of data is available on fragmented specifics of engine manufacturing. The problem is to comprehend aggregate characteristics from this data. Because engine manufacturing was physically integrated with other operations until the Cleveland plant was introduced in 1951, special approaches must be taken to determine these characteristics.

TABLE 5.7. Aggregate Segment Changes for Eleven Engine Parts

	1910–11	1914	1924–26	1927–28	1932–34	1945–47	1952–53	1970–73
Purchases	All steel stock Steel alloy stock Iron ingots Carburetor Radiator (No starter, 10 parts total in sample)	All steel stock Steel alloy and forging stock Iron ingots Carburetor (No starter, 10 parts in sample)	Rolled steel and most forged steel stock Starter Piston rings (11 parts in sample)	Rolled steel stock Aluminum pistons Piston rings Starter Some alloys	Distributor Some aluminum pistons Some alloys Piston rings	Carburetor Aluminum pistons Piston rings Some alloys	1/2 carburetors Aluminum pistons Piston rings Some alloys	Piston rings Some steel and alloy metals
Number Previous Ford operations		37	39	50	46	50	55	59
Discontinuations Process and part changes and process deletions		None	Stopped producing piston rings	Introduced purchased aluminum pistons	Deleted distributor production	Deleted carburetor production Dropped cast steel pistons		
Resulting operations deletions			3	4	5	8		
Additions Backward-integration thrusts		Radiator production	Coal and iron ore mining Iron production Some steel alloy preparation (from scrap in electric furnaces) Carburetor production	Increased production of special alloys	Steel production: furnaces, blooming and rolling mills Production of cast steel crank and camshafts and some pistons Starter production	Distributor production	Carburetor production	Aluminum casting plant for pistons and small parts
Resulting additions to operations		2	14	0	19	4	4	2
All Ford operations, net	37	39	50	46	50	55	59	61
All Ford backward-integration steps	3.4	3.5	4.5	4.2	4.5	5.0	5.4	5.5
Segment concentration Backward-integration steps	3.4	3.5	4.2	3.6	3.9	3.3	2.2	2.1
Specialization number of feeder plants separately managed	0	0	1	2	3	4	6	11+

SOURCE: See Appendix 3.

108

same standard set of nine operations was used to define process steps in each period and for each part. The definitions of these operations or process steps are the same as those used in Figure 5.1 to describe the scope of current engine-plant operations. The locations of operations and the flows between them help to describe the degree of centralization and the extent of backward integration at each time period. An examination of the changes that occurred in these flows between different periods yields some idea of dynamic relationships.

First, changes in the average number of steps provide a profile of vertical integration for the corporation as a whole. This is indicated by the degree to which all process operations for the sample of parts are performed within the engine plant itself or within Ford. In 1927, for example, six of the nine standard operations (or seven, counting assembly) were performed within Ford on cylinder blocks. A high degree of backward integration is evident for this part because Ford mined its own ore, transported it, produced iron ore in its blast furnaces, and so forth, up to assembly. The crankshaft and connecting rod at this time were forged at Rouge River from purchased rolled steel and do not exhibit the same degree of backward integration.[35] For the entire sample of parts in this period, the average number of integration steps back from assembly was 4.2. The range for individual parts was from 1 to 6 steps. This is considered a vertical integration index, and it is 4.2 for the sample in 1927.

Second, data on the sample are used to indicate the degree of concentration among operations within the engine plant itself. This is suggested by the number of steps that are included within the organizational limits earlier defined for a productive unit. Before World War II, the iron-making, foundry, and machining operations were all linked by extensive conveyors and other mechanical transfer devices, so that the productive unit effectively extended backward along the chain of vertical integration much further than it does today.[36]

Finally, an *index of specialization* is created from the same basic data. The degree of specialization among different productive units within the corporation as a whole is indicated by the number of decentralized plants that feed parts or components into the engine plant. At one time almost all functions were integrated into the giant Rouge River plant. Slowly, over time, separate specialized plants were organized to produce carburetors, for example, or radiators. These changes represent specialization of facilities.

The three indices—vertical integration, concentration, and specialization—for eight periods are summarized in Table 5.7. The table also attempts to clarify changes that occurred from period to period by noting whether specific parts were made or purchased, the processes that were discontinued since the prior period, and new manufacturing processes undertaken (backward integration moves) since the prior period. An accounting format is used, showing deletions and additions since the prior period.

Data in this table provide a focus for considering three relationships over the long period under consideration: (1) the relationship between backward integration and product change, (2) the waxing and waning of centralization over time, and (3) the tendency of productive units to be formed out of a centralized industrial complex as the industry matures.

The term "focus for consideration" is emphasized. While it is true that these data reflect changes in only eleven parts, a reading of the far more extensive but fragmented accounts of changes at Ford and at other major firms strongly suggests that these trends are more pervasive than is indicated by the small number of parts considered.

Vertical Integration versus Product Innovation. The strong backward-integration thrusts of the early periods and the continuing backward-integration moves in following periods present the most conspicuous pattern in Table 5.7. Notice the build-up in the index of backward integration. Starting from a vertical integration index of 1.0 in 1903 and 1904, when all engine parts were purchased, Ford integrated backward very rapidly, adding machining capability in the 1906 to 1909 period, extensive foundry operations in the early 1910s, and iron making in the 1920s. By 1924, hot molten-iron charges were being directly transferred in foundry operations without recourse to the intermediate production of solid iron "pigs" and the resulting energy loss, inventory costs, and lost motion.[37] The level of vertical integration achieved during this 1924–26 period, identified with an index of 4.5, was to be a peak for several years. But why was there a reduction in the overall level of vertical integration after the late Model T era?

The answer lies not in a policy change but in the relationship between product innovation and vertical integration. Each major product change has destroyed the chain of backward integration built up to that point. Even with the Model T in the 1920s, the addition of the electric starter reduced the percent of value added by Ford, since the starter and generator were purchased components. Then, on the Model A, aluminum pistons were introduced along with the use of cold rolled-steel forged parts. Whereas Ford had previously made its own pistons, an outside source was now used. Ford reintegrated into pistons through its own innovation in cast-steel pistons in the 1930s,[38] but these were again replaced by improved supplier-produced aluminum pistons in the late 1940s. It was not until the early 1950s that Ford integrated backward in a major way into aluminum-casting facilities that could supply piston requirements. A similar picture is evident with carburetors and distributors, as indicated in Table 5.7.

The view of vertical integration traced out here is dynamic. The degree of vertical integration is not static as long as major product changes are taking place. It is rather the equilibrium condition of a continuous effort to extend integration backward in the face of the constant erosion caused by product change. As the technology of product design advances, so that novel change is made less necessary, vertical integration can be maintained without such continuous effort. For most of the postwar period, when the product technology can be characterized as more mature, the level of backward integration seems to have been extended even further and with less turmoil. This is true, at least, for the sample of parts considered here.

Now, with the introduction of computers, including new sensors and microprocessors, the degree of backward integration will be decreased again. As sources for the most advanced electronics are sought out and until the costs for such components are reduced, these new forms of control will represent a significant increase in cost versus the components made by the automobile companies. The old cycle wherein product innovation reduces vertical integration is repeating.

Focusing the Factory. Changes in the concentration of a productive unit seem to be linked to its phases of growth and maturity. The engine plant was brought into existence as an integral element of the manufacturing process for making cars, and, as such, it included many heterogeneous process technologies at first, like distributor production, foundry operation, and so on. Over time, similar technologies have been grouped and separated into separate plants under separate management. The last major change noted here came about in the late 1960s, when engine foundries were organizationally separated from engine plants with the explanation that the management problems were much different.

Concentration (see the second index, from the bottom of Table 5.7) first increased with the horizontal and vertical integration achieved in the early years. Then separate productive units began to be created, drawing heterogeneous technologies out of engine units. After World War II, the trend toward more specialized units began to reduce the concentration of the engine plant. By the era of the Cleveland engine plant, only homogeneous technologies were included in an engine plant; hence a concentration index of only 2.2, versus the earlier 1924 peak of 4.2.

These changes produced a long-run cycle: growth, then a decrease in the concentration of the productive unit, coupled with an increase in specialization of related units.

The trends in vertical integration and organization are clearly tied to a global pattern that encompasses equipment trends, product-line standardization, and the entire range of changes that have been observed in the engine plant. The rapid initial extension in vertical integration, the struggle to retain a high degree of vertical integration, and the subsequent leveling off are related to patterns of product change, standardization and advances in equipment technology, and work-force characteristics. The trend toward specialization in different productive units seems to offer greater efficiency, since homogeneous technologies can probably be managed more effectively. At the same time, specialization does not support rapid change, so it also increases rigidity. These trends and the other evidence considered above seem to support the central idea of the present model, that a productive unit evolves through parallel changes in a cluster of variables. The engine plant, as a productive unit, has advanced over time through complementary changes in a number of factors that are mutually reinforcing and difficult to reverse.

CONCLUSIONS

The course of development in the engine plant has been distinctly evolutionary in nature, but cumulatively the total extent of process change has been great. Parallel changes have come about in many different aspects, and these are highly interrelated and dependent on one another. For the period up to 1973 the findings are as follows:

(1) There has been an overall reduction in the mechanical novelty of the product line. Although the absolute number of product options has increased, the real variety has decreased.

(2) There is an apparent increase in the diversity of the product line, but for individual plants, or productive units, the diversity has decreased over time in both an absolute and a qualitative sense.

(3) The overall rate of change has decreased at the level of the productive unit, and the impact of product change has been localized through the introduction of a modular product line.

(4) The mode of change has shifted from radical fluid change to incremental change, but incremental change is apparently important to cumulative technical progress.

(5) Major innovations have been self-limiting, since they have reduced the need for further novel change.

(6) The characteristics of process equipment have changed from general-purpose tools to specialized equipment systems, but this development has seemed to lag behind the overall development of the productive unit.

(7) Equipment development is very cumulative in effect and seems to have a pervasive impact on many other aspects of the productive unit.

(8) Labor tasks and required skills have changed with equipment development in three phases: from craft skills to operative skills to systems-monitoring skills.

(9) The concentration of operations within the engine plant has first increased and then decreased. With the decrease in concentration the segment has become more specialized, organizationally decentralized, and the technology more homogeneous.

(10) Vertical integration has increased overall, but the degree of vertical

integration is not stable. Product innovations erode the chains of vertical integration so that continued backward-integration moves are needed.

Despite the consistent and pervasive nature of these trends, there are now good reasons to conclude that a new period has begun. Innovation and change in the recent 1970s support the idea that the direction of normal development can be reversed through severe changes in the market environment. Regulatory actions by the government and the threatened gasoline shortage (as discussed in Chapter 2) have had their effect on the course of development in this productive unit. The pattern of evolution laid out in Chapter 4 represents a central tendency in technological progress but not an inevitable one.

6 THE AUTOMOTIVE ASSEMBLY PLANT: OPTIONS FOR FLEXIBILITY

The assembly plant, as the final stage in the production of the automobile, is the locus of product change. It must accommodate the full range of changes in automotive designs, in components, and in production-output rates that the market demands; and so, more than any other productive unit in the automobile industry, the assembly plant should mirror systematic changes in product or market maturity, if there are any.

Going by outward signs, the assembly plant and its car line have developed exactly contrary to the productive unit's typical pattern of development, as proposed in Chapter 4. Consider, for example, two peak years at Ford, as shown in Table 6.1.

Product-line diversity and product change seem to have increased at both the corporate level and the individual plant level over this fifty-year span. Yet, as the historical analysis in this chapter will show, these outward signs are deceptive, and in terms of trends at the assembly-plant level, product diversity and change have actually diminished.

THE ASSEMBLY PLANT AS THE UNIT OF ANALYSIS

Development of the assembly plant has differed from that of the engine plant because the two are dissimilar in product complexity, process technology, and the degree of change and uncertainty in their product lines. As will be seen, however, the assembly plant's actual course of develop-

TABLE 6.1. Two Peak Years of Production at Ford

	1923	1973
Unit production	1,825,766	2,706,161
Number of passenger car plants	30	14
Number of passenger car models	Model T, Lincoln	Ford: Torino, T'Bird, Pinto, Maverick, Mustang; Mercury: Montego, Cougar, Lincoln MK IV, Continental, Comet.

114

ment corresponds closely to the proposed model of development in Chapter 4. If we contrast the engine plant and assembly plant, as two different productive units, common aspects of development are clarified and distinguished from features that depend upon a particular technology.

Assembly Plant Definitions

The principal process operations of the assembly plant include body building, protective coating and painting, cushions and trim operations, chassis build-up, and final assembly.* The important functions of body building, coating, and painting are more nearly manufacturing than assembly operations.

In the traditional method of construction, the main body enclosure is manufactured, painted, and then set down over the assembled chassis in the final assembly line. Figure 6.1 illustrates the way that these components and functions mesh together in the assembly plant.† The top line in the figure is the body-building process. Chassis build-up starts with the frame line, shown down the left-hand side of Figure 6.1, and becomes the final assembly line, as shown across the bottom. Other components are added as shown. The two pictures in Plate 5 show the operations where the automobile body merges into the final assembly line for two different eras: 1914 and in the 1970s.

The moving assembly lines for chassis build-up and final assembly have not changed much since their origin at Ford in early 1914.[1] But other functions, particularly the body-building and painting operations, have changed substantially.

In the following sections, the terms assembly plant and productive unit will be used interchangeably as the unit of analysis for most of the period in question. First, we will look at the initial, companywide characteristics of Ford's product (car) line. Subsequently, we will analyze trends at the individual plant level: product-line characteristics, equipment developments, labor-task characteristics, vertical integration, and organization.

* The terms body, chassis, and frame are defined as follows: the car frame is the rigid steel structure on which the wheels, engine, and entire power train are mounted. The chassis is the entire lower part of the assembled car, including frame, power train, wheels, brakes, etc., excluding the body. The body is the passenger enclosure and outer shell, presently manufactured in the body-building section of the assembly plant from several thousand stamped metal parts.

† This process illustration is for cars that have separate frames and bodies. Currently, as shown in Appendix 2, this includes the top end of the Ford, Lincoln, and Mercury line. For lighter cars, the Granada and Monarch down, unit construction is used. This refers to a design in which there is no separate frame. Frame and body are designed as one unit. This has implications for final assembly, for there is no separate chassis, and flow is more nearly in a single-line operation.

FIGURE 6.1. How an Automobile Is Assembled

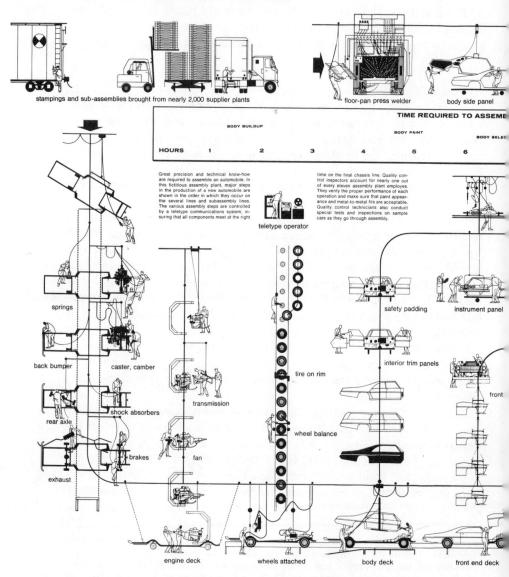

stampings and sub-assemblies brought from nearly 2,000 supplier plants

floor-pan press welder

body side panel

TIME REQUIRED TO ASSEMBLE

BODY BUILDUP

BODY PAINT

BODY SELEC

HOURS	1	2	3	4	5	6

Great precision and technical know-how are required to assemble an automobile. In this fictitious assembly plant, major steps in the production of a new automobile are shown in the order in which they occur on the several lines and subassembly lines. The various assembly steps are controlled by a teletype communications system, insuring that all components meet at the right

time on the final chassis line. Quality control inspectors account for nearly one out of every eleven assembly plant employes. They verify the proper performance of each operation and make sure that paint appearance and metal-to-metal fits are acceptable. Quality control technicians also conduct special tests and inspections on sample cars as they go through assembly.

teletype operator

springs

back bumper

caster, camber

shock absorbers

rear axle

brakes

exhaust

transmission

fan

tire on rim

wheel balance

safety padding

instrument panel

interior trim panels

front

engine deck

wheels attached

body deck

front end deck

THE PROFILE OF CHANGE IN FORD PASSENGER CARS AND ASSEMBLY PLANTS

The characteristics of assembly operations at Ford were initially influenced by the search for a successful corporate strategy and by the stream of technological innovations that changed the car and manufacturing methods. Both caused fluid change in product and process.

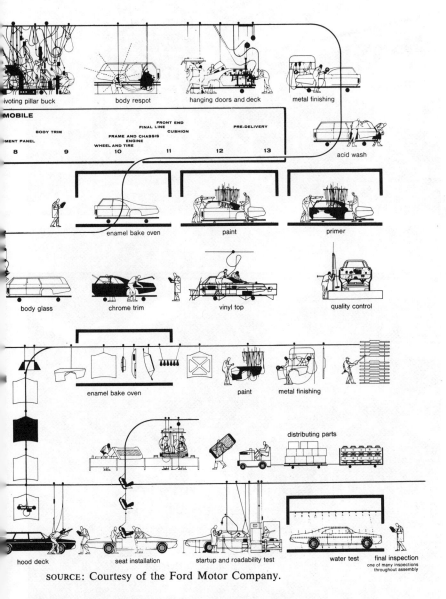

ivoting pillar buck body respot hanging doors and deck metal finishing

MOBILE

BODY TRIM FRONT END FINAL LINE CUSHION PRE-DELIVERY

FRAME AND CHASSIS
ENGINE

IMENT PANEL WHEEL AND TIRE

8 9 10 11 12 13

acid wash

enamel bake oven paint primer

body glass chrome trim vinyl top quality control

enamel bake oven paint metal finishing

distributing parts

hood deck seat installation startup and roadability test water test final inspection
one of many inspections
throughout assembly

SOURCE: Courtesy of the Ford Motor Company.

Formulation of a Corporate Strategy

The controversy within Ford between the years 1904 and 1906 has been described as the "battle for the cheap car." As different points of view prevailed, the company changed its product lines. A series of models first addressed the low-priced market, then the high-priced market (with the Model K), and then the low-priced one again.[2] The consequences were a

PLATE 5. *a*, Body drop onto chassis at Highland Park Plant—at time of introduction of moving assembly line, 1914; *b*, Body drop for final assembly, 1974. (Photographs courtesy of the Ford Motor Company.)

118

wide fluctuation in products and operating characteristics. By the end of 1906, however, the controversy was settled with the resignation of Alex Malcomson, the death of John Gray, the first president of the Ford Motor Company, and a publicly announced policy that asked, "How low can we sell it [our car] and still make a small margin on each one?"[3] The emphasis on cost reduction was vigorously pursued through cost competition, high-volume standardized production, infrequent model change, and extensive backward vertical integration. This policy was followed through the Model T and Model A era until around 1931. Only after a decade of unsuccessful competition against General Motors did the policy of annual model change and frequent product improvement become accepted at Ford. So the transition from fluid model change to standardized high-volume production and then to annual model change was in part a matter of competitive corporate strategy.[4] The transition was also influenced by technological change.

Major New Technologies Introduced

Technological innovations at first increased the variety and scope of production operations and kept the production process unsettled.

The impact of the early innovations on operations can be visualized from their descriptions. A few that Ford introduced are as follows: left-hand steering wheel on a production model, 1908; steel running boards, 1909; the moving assembly line, 1914; electric lights made standard, 1915; baked enamel finishes by dipping parts, 1917; starter available as option, 1920; pyroxylin paint in multicolors and closed steel bodies, 1925.[5]

The electric lights probably had the least immediate impact of items in this group, but they were an opening wedge. They represent the first major auxiliary application of the cars' electrical system in a long, important sequence that is still growing today. The ampere load is one measure of this trend. From a few amperes in 1915 the load grew to twelve amperes in 1930, thirty-five by 1940, and forty to fifty by 1948.[6]

The pyroxylin (DUCO) painting innovation and the closed steel body had a much more disruptive and immediate impact on operations. Body manufacturing and painting were not initially included in the scope of assembly activities at Ford. The initial car models, A, B, and so on, through the Model T, were standardized only in regard to the chassis. A variety of bodies were purchased,* and even as late as 1914, 90 percent of the painting was performed by suppliers.[7] Thus, the famous moving-

* The Briggs Body Company and Budd were to become Ford's major external supplier of bodies, from the 1920s even up to recent times, but in the very early years various sources were used. Sorensen describes how he and Henry Ford dealt with Fred Fisher (later of GM's Fisher Bodies) to purchase a body for the Model N, at a price of $72. Charles E. Sorensen, *My Forty Years with Ford* (New York: W. W. Norton and Co., 1956), p. 83.

assembly-line innovation in 1914 related almost exclusively to the final assembly operations.

Ford apparently achieved complete backward vertical integration into closed steel body production at the time when steel bodies were introduced to replace wooden ones, in 1925.[8]

Other characteristics of the assembly plant in the initial period reflected conditions that were compatible with unsettled technologies, market uncertainty, and strategy change. Ford's organization was relatively informal.[9] Skilled craftsmen who had the capability to adapt readily to change were employed,[10] and general-purpose equipment was used.[11]

Decentralization of Assembly Plants

Following the moving-assembly-line innovation, the period from 1914 to 1916 was marked by a more rapid rate of capacity decentralization than has occurred since that date, as shown in Table 6.2 below.[12] Like concentric waves after a stone is thrown into water, Ford's assembly plants sprang up throughout the United States and abroad.† Each plant was located in a major city such as New York, Boston, or San Francisco, at a freight break point. The plant served its region as its production source, as a regional sales office for dealership supervision, and in training local repairmen.

After 1925 each plant was equipped with the light hand tools needed to "frame"‡ the major steel body sections and with extensive painting lines. The introduction of these process capabilities and the decentralization of assembly capacity created the basic outline of today's assembly plant.

The Broadening Line of Cars

There has been extensive model proliferation in the Ford Motor Company's line of U.S.-produced cars that have been advertised and sold as separate passenger vehicles.** As shown previously, there was only one

---

† Although Table 6.2 describes only decentralization and expansion in the United States, overseas expansion was also extensive. The first Ford plant outside North America was an assembly plant established in 1911 in Manchester, England. The Model T was used extensively in Europe during World War I, and afterward Ford expanded assembly and other manufacturing operations throughout the world. The original plan called for six European divisions. In each a dealership was first established, then as volume warranted, an assembly plant would be built and ultimately other supporting manufacturing operations added. Each was modeled after the U.S. plants. By 1924 there were assembly plants in Manchester, England; Cork, Ireland; Bordeaux, France; Copenhagen, Denmark; Buenos Aires, Argentina; Sao Paulo, Brazil; Antwerp, Belgium; Trieste, Italy; Barcelona, Spain; and Rotterdam, Holland.

‡ Major body sections were shipped preassembled, and these were aligned and fastened together to form a body in an operation called "framing."

** A car is considered to be a separate product if it has a separate name, is marked by a separate product-line division (for example, Lincoln, Mercury, Ford), and has a different body and chassis configuration, generally as indicated by different wheelbases. For example, by this definition the Maverick and Cougar were differ-

TABLE 6.2. Decentralization of Final Assembly

	1911	1913	1914	1915	1916	1917	1918	1919	1920
Assembly plants[a]	1	9	13	24	29	28	27	26	25
Unit volume (hundreds)	32	203	308	501	735	622	435	820	420
% Cars produced centrally (Final chassis Assembly)	100	90[b]					7[c]		9[c]
% Dollar sales by branch sales office	67	79	80	86	88				

SOURCES: Branch Assembly Plant Records, Ford Archives, Henry Ford Museum, Greenfield Village, Dearborn, Michigan; and Nevins and Hill, *Ford: Man, Times, Company.*

[a] Many of the pre-1915 plants were for "knock-down" units and did not carry out full final assembly. Following 1918, however, the included plants had moving assembly lines.

[b] Arnold and Faurote, *Ford Methods and Ford Shops,* p. 12.

[c] Calculated from production records, Ford Archives, Henry Ford Museum, Greenfield Village, Dearborn, Michigan.

model from 1909 to 1922, the Model T, but by 1973, twelve different passenger cars were offered to the market.

The use of common body/frame families has made such large increases in product diversity possible without great efficiency losses, even though unit sales volume has not quite doubled. These body families are listed by both the year and car line in Appendix 2, and they are summarized graphically in Figure 6.2. Although car bodies and frames have developed in a distinctly evolutionary pattern, some thirty-six discrete body/frame families are identified in this figure. Each family is a major model in which designs are distinct from the prior and succeeding models. Each family generally has a unique wheelbase, weight class, design, and in early years an announced model number. A given body design in Figure 6.2 is referred to as a "family" because since World War II one body design is shared with several passenger cars that have only minor differences in body parts.†† A number preceding each bar gives the wheelbase in inches, and, where applicable, the model designator is inside the bar. Years that Ford considers major model change periods are indicated at the top.[13]

The important and changing competitive role of bodies can be traced in Figure 6.2. The body has changed over time, as engines did, from a purchased option to just another component of the car.

Successful early models, such as the Model T or A, were chassis models, and they used unique components that were optimized for a particular chassis. The body was added almost as a purchased consumer

---

ent cars in 1973 even though they shared essentially the same body. They had different appointments and were respectively Ford and Lincoln/Mercury cars.

†† Industry experts point out that the body can be stretched by adding extended parts in some locations to increase the wheelbase for different configurations, say station wagons or four-door cars, without great loss in the overall commonality of parts.

FIGURE 6.2. Major Ford Body Frame Families

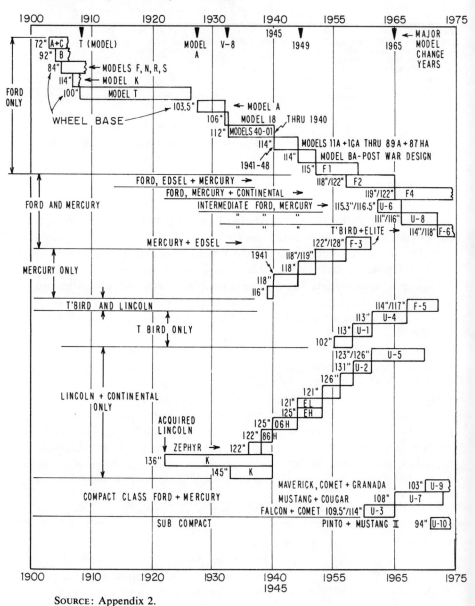

SOURCE: Appendix 2.

option. In this case the standardized product sent to market was the model, the entire chassis, and not a body style. Major components were manufactured in productive units that were tooled, organized jointly, scheduled, and even linked by conveyors to produce a particular model.[14] At Ford in the 1920s and 1930s, these major productive units were scheduled to form a single giant manufacturing process.* So in this instance the addition of a new model or a model change would have significant implications throughout the system.

The relationship among standardized components is different today, as may be seen in Figure 6.2. The primary product unit is now a marketing concept, a Mustang, Cougar, and so forth, and it is composed of particular choices from lines of standardized components like body/frames, engines, and transmissions. These are all shared with other cars in the line. Speaking in generalities, the car itself is now a styling rather than a technological concept, and by and large only its appointment features are unique to it. The technology is embedded in the component lines.

Product-Line Diversity. The line of cars is seen "downstream" by the market, but it is the line of common body/frame families that has implications for the product diversity of "upstream" productive units like stamping plants, frame lines, body-component fabrication facilities, and so on. As shown in Figure 6.3, the diversity of body/frame families has not grown as rapidly as the number of cars.

The two superimposed plots in the figure are: a simple count in each year of the different passenger cars in the product line and the number of different body/frame families, taken from Appendix 2. The upper, dashed curve represents market diversity, and the lower, solid line more nearly reflects the diversity impact on frame and stamping plants. The spread between the two curves suggests the use of common body components. The diversity imposed upstream has been only approximately doubled by a sixfold increase in the number of cars in the product line. Within limits, the major components, including bodies, can now be changed independently of one another. Because the plants that produce them have been technologically and managerially decentralized, the impact of change has been localized.

Mechanical Variety. It is difficult to quantify exactly mechanical or structural variety for bodies, but a measure of mechanical differences like size, capacity, or weight of the different models or cars in the line provides a general indication of variety. To the extent that cars are larger and weigh more, they are designed differently. Design does in fact change rather completely with weight and size in the current Ford product line, since "unit body construction," a form of body construction without separate frame, is used for small cars, while an entirely different design, embodying a separate frame, chassis, and body, is used for large cars.

* As an example of the tight integration, one Ford document written in 1924 documents the hourly movement of material through production of the engine and final assembly in just three days. Starting with iron ore delivery on the dock at 7 A.M. Monday morning, a cycle of blast-furnace operation, casting, machining, assembly, motor testing, shipment to an assembly plant, and final assembly has the car with engine delivered by Wednesday afternoon (*The Ford Industries*, 1924, pp. 15–17).

TABLE 6.3. Mechanical Variation by Market Segments: Ford Car Prices and Sizes

	Smallest Car				Largest Car				Range		Ratio
Year	Model	Wheel-base (inches)	Price ($)	Weight	Model	Wheel-base (inches)	Price ($)	Weight	Price range ($)	Weight range (lbs.)	Price ratio ($)
1906	Ford N	84	500	1,050	Ford K	114	2,500	2,000	2,000	950	2.1
1909	Ford T (Touring)	100	850	1,200	Ford T (Landaulet)	100	1,200	—	350	—	
1925	Ford T (Touring)	100	310	1,607	Lincoln K	136	4,600	4,750	4,290	3,080	1.4
1929	Ford A Touring	103.5	460	2,150	Lincoln K	136	4,400	4,500	3,940	2,350	1.7
1936	Ford 40 Sedan 4 d	112	580	2,850	Lincoln K	145	4,300	5,740	3,720	2,890	1.3
1939	Ford 922 A	112	665	2,525	Lincoln	145	5,000	5,900	4,335	3,375	1.3
1941	Ford 11 A	114	840	3,033	Lincoln Custom	138	2,950	4,380	2,110	1,347	1.6
1947	Ford 6 GA	114	1,234	3,213	Lincoln 66 H	125	2,337	4,015	1,103	802	1.4
1953	Ford	115	1,400	2,977	Lincoln Capri	123	3,699	4,310	2,299	1,333	1.7
1964	Ford Falcon	109.5	1,985	2,358	Lincoln	126	6,916	5,393	4,931	3,035	1.6
1974	Ford Pinto	94.2	2,292	2,443	Lincoln Continental	127.2	7,637	5,361	5,345	2,918	1.8
					Lincoln MK IV	120.4	9,198	5,337	6,906	2,894	2.4

SOURCE: *Automotive Industries*, statistical issue, various years.

124

FIGURE 6.3. Corporate Product Diversity: Ford Passenger Cars versus Body Families

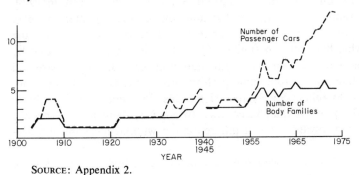

SOURCE: Appendix 2.

If weight and wheelbase are used as indicators of mechanical variety, then (as shown in Table 6.3) mechanical variety has remained rather constant over time. Table 6.3 also compares the largest and the smallest car product line for selected years from 1906 to 1974. Wheelbase, weight, and price are all listed, and the ranges of weights and prices are given for various years.

The year 1925 offered the largest weight and wheelbase range of the years shown, but there is really no significant trend in the ranges from the original to the current period. The difference between the largest and smallest car is about three thousand pounds. These measures suggest a rather constant mechanical variation between the highest- and lowest-priced market segments over the years.

The future may not change this spread in weight variation greatly. It all depends on the rate with which fuel economy regulations occur and the industry is able to stay ahead of the tightening standards through techno-logical innovations. One prognosis would be that the large and small ends of the line will both become smaller and lighter but that a range will be maintained. Some have forecast a reduction in mechanical variety among different car lines to near zero as regulatory standards tighten. Given each firm's incentive to differentiate its product, however, a more likely forecast is that seating capacity will be maintained through technological innova-tion.

In contrast, for engines, an advancing technological capability made it possible to achieve the full performance range and to differentiate the product line in the market with less and less mechanical variation. In other words, the high- and low-priced market segments came to be served in engines without novel structural changes among different engines in the product line.

The variation in bodies, when viewed in terms of prices and weights, is not much different from that in weight alone. The variation across the product line in 1974 was $1.80 per pound, as shown in Table 6.2. This is not significantly different from the ratio of $2.10 in 1906 or $1.70 in 1929. If the price ranges were adjusted for inflation, an even greater range in weight variation per dollar of car price would be observed, exactly the reverse of what happened in engines. Of course, it can be argued that by current industry practice, market segmentation depends directly on size and price rather than on the functional performance of the car. Although pricing formulas do relate closely to weight, this does not refute the basic argument. The point is that, in contrast to engines, there has not been a systematic trend toward product differentiation without mechanical variation.

Presently there has been some indication of a higher ratio of price differentiation for a given degree of mechanical variation. The 1974 Mark IV offered a higher, or more advanced, ratio than for any prior period. General Motors' 1975 Cadillac Seville was also decreased in weight versus price. Given recent fuel-economy regulation, this might be indicative of future body designs, as discussed above. It remains to be seen how comparable higher prices can be maintained over the long run, however, without the use of weight or size as a surrogate for an expensive car. The reduction in mechanical variation, as seen during the 1950s and 1960s, was a sign of maturity in the product and its market. As energy usage becomes more scarce or tightly regulated or as new energy sources are introduced, the trend toward maturity can be expected to reverse.

Rates of Product Change. Four distinct periods are apparent in the rate of major model change based on body/family lives shown in Figure 6.2. In the initial period, change was fluid, and the average body production life was 2.5 years (1903–7). Then, during the period of standardization, the average body life went up to 10.7 years (1908–32). From 1934 through 1960 lives were short, only 3.8 years; after 1960, they averaged 6.1 years.

The overall trend in the rate of change is as anticipated. The initial period had body/frame families with significantly shorter lives than any other period. Next in order is the period from 1933 to 1960. From 1960 to mid-1970, the rate of change declined further. Because of recent fuel-economy regulations the rate of model change can be expected to increase again as cars are "downsized" and plastic and aluminum are substituted for steel. Aside from the period of extreme standardization from 1908 to 1932, the overall trend is toward an even slower rate of change. The eighteen-year life span of the Model T is responsible for deviation from the trend during the second period. It is questionable whether the Model T is truly an exception to the declining rate of change that is otherwise apparent. This problem will be considered later.

Annual Model Change—An Incremental Mode. Annual model change has increased in importance with the trend toward a slower rate of major model change. Beginning around 1932, Ford started to shift its policy away from model standardization by giving much more attention to feedback from dealers. A policy was adopted regarding annual model change that was much more like that of General Motors.*

The change in physical appearance of Ford-line bodies during the late 1930s was dramatic, and much of the change was introduced through annual model change on the common 112-inch Ford frame.† This was the heyday of the *annual* model change in a car line.

Since 1960 the focus of change has been more at the component level. Common engines, transmissions, steering gear, as well as bodies, have come to be adopted across car lines.‡ The unsynchronized timing of new body/frame family introductions during the later period suggests that decisions are now made in respect to particular body/frame families for particular market segments rather than across the product line or in respect to a particular model. The Mustang and Pinto were exceptions at the time of their introduction, but even their bodies came to be shared with other cars.

Major Body Changes versus Annual Model Change. Table 6.4 shows how the weight of the car has changed over time. If it can be assumed that weight increases, at least in the early years, came from the addition of new features, than weight trends can be used in a limited way to make inferences about modes of product change. For this purpose, Table 6.4 breaks down weight change into two modes: (1) the discrete step changes in weight that were implemented by introducing major new body/family designs, and (2) the incremental year-to-year changes in weight that resulted from annual model changes. Particular body/frame families included in Table 6.4 have been chosen to present a connected history of the lightest-weight sedan for the smallest Ford car series since 1908. Although these data lack precision, because included car options and the standards for reporting weight and body types are not entirely comparable from year to year, they are helpful in identifying major trends.

These statistics show that the incremental mode of change predominated over major design changes in its effect on the car's weight. Since the 1960s, annual model change has had much more influence over model

---

* According to Nevins, Ford initially followed a policy whereby dealer comments and other market feedback had little weight in year-to-year modifications to standardized models. This was reportedly changed during the 1930s, but it was not until complete reorganization took place after World War II that design changes came to be highly responsive to market information. (Allan Nevins and Frank Hill, *Ford: Decline and Rebirth* [New York: Charles Scribners, 1962], pp. 109–21 and 317–45).

† During the ten-year period from 1931 through the 1941 model year, the following changes were introduced in the main Ford line. The first mass-produced V-8 engine was adopted, the body changed from box construction to a streamlined design, the all-steel turret top was introduced, headlights were integrated into fenders, four-wheel hydraulic brakes were introduced, the running board was integrated into the body, and a rationalized body series was adopted (see Appendix 2).

‡ Beginning around 1960, Ford's U.S. manufacturing facilities were consolidated under a functional management structure that served the respective car divisions.

TABLE 6.4. Weight Changes by Models for Smallest Ford: Discrete New Model Introduction and Weight Growth during Years of Production*

Model Designation†	Years	Average Percent Annual Weight Growth while in Production	Percent Weight Increase of New Model over Prior Model
Model T 100"	1908–26	1.9 (cumulative 34%)	—
Model A 103.5"	1927–31	1 (cumulative 4%)	+34
Model 40, etc. 112"	1933–40	2.3 (cumulative 18%)	+12
Model 11A, etc. 114"	1941–48	0.8 (cumulative 6%)	+25
Model BA, etc. 114"	1949–51	0.5	− 6.9
Ford 115" Ford F 1 family	1952–58	0.4	+ 4.3
Ford 115" Ford F 2 family	1957–65	0.6	+ 5.2
Falcon 109.5" UBC-3	1960–65	3.4	−33.7
Falcon 111" UBC-8	1966–69	3.0	− 4.1
Maverick 103" UBC-9	1970–74+	1.9	− 5.4
Pinto 94.2" UBC-10	1971–74+	4.8	−31.5
Cumulative	1908–74	183.6‡ (from annual weight growth)	−21.2 (from discrete changes

SOURCE: Computed from definitions of body/frame families in Appendix 2 and weights given in *Automotive Industries: Statistical Issue* (or corresponding section in early years), various years.

 * Body weight is shown for least expensive 4-door sedan, for the smallest car series in the product line, or the nearest equivalent of those reported in *Automotive Industries*. Body weights are not entirely comparable, however, due to option and definitional changes.

 † Model definitions are contained in Appendix; UBC refers to a particular unit body construction.

 ‡ Compound cumulative weight increase from 1908 to present using the annual growth rate for smallest model in production as indicated in list above. For example, the rate of 1.9 was used from 1970 to 1971 (Maverick) while 4.8% (Pinto) was used for remaining years.

weight than have major model changes. Even in the earliest years, however, this source of weight increase equaled that brought about by the major design changes. In later years this annual weight growth has acted to offset all weight reductions achieved by initial design decisions.

If it had not been otherwise offset by planned design decision, the cumulative compound effect of annual weight growth would have led to a 183 percent increase in car weight. Starting with a 1,200-pound Model T in 1908, the compound weight-growth rate from annual change would produce a 1974 car that weighed about 3,400 pounds. This weight, in fact, falls between the listed 1974 weights of the midsized Torino and Maverick. For the smaller car, of course, major design introductions have offset this increase. The Pinto is 1,000 pounds lighter.

The cumulative weight-growth rates help to confirm a suspicion that the early standardized models were not actually very standardized. Competitive pressures forced the addition of features to the Model T like the starter, a larger radiator, lower body, and closed steel body. These additions increased its weight by some 34 percent overall. They added about the same percentage weight to the Model T as did the planned design changes that were incorporated in the next-generation car, the Model A. It might also be noted that the features added during this period of apparent standardization were important functional improvements. The actual rate of change during the early period of standardization (1908–32) was higher than the calculated body-family lives indicate.

A Diversion on Model Change

It may be significant that the history of the major new design introductions at Ford presents a mix of both increases and decreases in weight. Of thirty-three long-lived bodies that were examined, the weights of twenty increased over the preceding models and of thirteen decreased. In contrast, the annual weight-growth rate from incremental change was consistently positive in thirty-four of the thirty-five body/frame families analyzed. These statistics imply that weight growth may sometimes occur unintentionally in small cars, as improvements are made and design difficulties are fixed. No doubt there have also been many intentional changes to trade up weight and capture a more affluent market segment. The rapid weight growth in small cars following 1960, as shown in Table 6.4, may well have resulted from such actions to increase the features offered on small cars. A general understanding of the weight growth of designs in other industries, such as the space program, however, gives reason to believe that it is in part unintended and hard to control. Periodic major model redesign is needed to capture all necessary improvements in a clean, simple design in order to control weight effectively.* To the extent that such weight increases are an important inherent phenomenon, and the present data raise this possibility, long-lived models may not contribute as much to lower prices as the learning-curve theory and the simple economics of change might imply.

Generally, throughout the Ford corporation, product-line diversity has increased, and, while the rate of change slowed during the 1950s and 1960s, it is still fluid by comparison with that of automobile engines. Annual, or incremental, model change became an important mode for

---

* The Volkswagen provides a good example of extensive weight growth in a supposed standardized model. At Ford in a number of instances major new designs took weight out without changing the market segment addressed. This is notably the case with the major design year, 1949, which Ford considers one of the company's four most important model change years. The 1949 Ford involved a weight reduction of some six hundred pounds.

PLATE 6. *a*, Assembly room—Ford's Piquette Avenue Plant around 1907; *b*, Welding robots in van body transfer line—Ford's Ohio Truck Plant, 1975. (Photographs courtesy of the Ford Motor Company.)

130

introducing new automotive features as the frequency of major body models decreased.

Period by period, the rate of major model changes was at a maximum during the initial period, 1903–7; it has been the slowest during the 1960s and early 1970s. There appears to have been a plateau of flexible change during the intervening period that recently gave way to a further slowing of change. Now it is likely that the rate of change will increase again, reversing the recent tendency toward the specific state.

Change has come to be managed on a component-line basis rather than by chassis model or passenger-car line. This shift in the impact of change has of itself influenced opportunities for major innovation, since any change in a line of components has ramifications for the cars in all market segments.

CHANGES AT THE ASSEMBLY PLANT LEVEL

Conditions in the individual assembly plant mirror some of the aggregate changes at the corporate level, but in other respects, such as product-line diversity, there are important differences. Perhaps the most important trait is the great consistency in conditions over time. To examine these conditions, let us look at different aspects of individual assembly-plant characteristics.

Product-Line Changes

A simple indicator tells a great deal about diversity in body construction at the assembly segment level. Figure 6.4 shows the average number of different vehicles that have been produced per plant in Ford passenger-car assembly plants. This graph shows that for an average plant, the number of different passenger cars and light trucks has not increased, despite large increases in the Ford product line as a whole.† Quite to the contrary, there has been a surprisingly constant level of diversity over many decades. The reduction since 1965, however, reflects a significant change in the trend. The decrease from an average of 2 to 1.5 cars per plant has come about because of the way cars are allocated to assembly plants.

The steep downward trend in recent years has occurred because an increasing fraction of assembly plants produce but one car, or two cars derived from the same common body. This is in marked contrast to the years before World War II, when all Ford products were produced in many of the thirty-two assembly plants.‡

This graph also shows that trends in the rate of change in the product have likewise followed a downward trend. In Figure 6.2 we saw that the

---

† Light trucks are included since cars and truck were traditionally assembled in most Ford assembly plants from the 1920s until the 1960s.

‡ Further data on allocation by assembly plants are given in Appendix 4.

FIGURE 6.4. Assembly Plant Product Diversity: The Average Number of Different Vehicles per Ford Plant (Based on Wheelbase Differences)

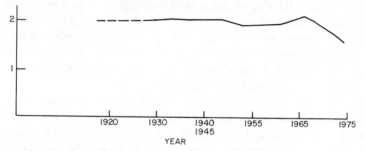

SOURCE: Appendix 4.

rate of product change in major body designs has slowed. Since there has been a decrease in the base number of vehicles per plant to which the average rate of change per model would apply, it follows that the rate of change has decreased even more at the assembly plant level. This indicates that both product diversity and change have followed a roughly similar pattern—there has been a decline from a high initial rate to a plateau maintained until the 1960s, and since then the rate has declined further.

Equipment and Process Change

According to popular impressions, the assembly plant is equipped only with portable powered hand tools, mechanized moving assembly lines, and painting booths. This view recognizes little substantive change in concepts of process organization since Ford's moving-assembly-line innovation in 1914 and little progress during intervening years in introducing equipment to improve labor efficiency. This image is valid only in certain process functions. While it seems reasonably accurate to characterize the final assembly process as stable, to do so ignores the important "body construction" functions that from the very beginning involved more cost than did final assembly. The pictures in Plate 6 illustrate this point by showing two pictures, one of car assembly in Ford's Piquette Avenue Plant around 1907 and the second of welding robots in the new Ohio Truck Plant.

The Introduction of New Process Technology. Technological innovations in body production came about rapidly at the centralized Rouge River facility following Ford's backward integration into bodies in 1925. Many of these innovations are listed and discussed in Chapter 3 and Appendix 1.

When Ford introduced the Model A in 1927, new body-fabrication processes were also introduced. Among these were welding presses and new techniques for seam and resistance welding. The techniques were applied to fabricate components from sheet steel for the simple, boxlike bodies. A rapid sequence of advances in die making, basic steel, and welding fixtures and techniques followed. The following description of the fabrication of a "stream-lined Ford body section," written in 1935 by a writer for *Mill and Factory*, illustrates the advances achieved in just ten years. Ten years earlier, in 1925, when Ford introduced steel bodies, the quality of steel was limited, and welding technology was still in a rudimentary state. "One of the most impressive sights . . . is the welding of the rear body assembly. Here the rear panel and two quarter panels are placed together in a huge balloon flash welding machine, a man pushes a button, the machine closes, there is a shower of sparks and the three sections are welded into one by means of 72″ seams in seven seconds.[15]

Assembly plants were not initially equipped with such mechanized welding capabilities. At Ford assembly plants, major body components were received already fabricated and only framed (joined to form a box-like, three-dimensional form) in fixed locations. They were then riveted and spot-welded together. Process equipment was limited to light, portable hand tools, presses for riveting, and portable welders.[16] By 1932, some specialized equipment came to be introduced in assembly, providing small islands of semiautomation among the otherwise general-purpose equipment.

Following World War II, assembly plants and engine plants at Ford were reorganized along major product lines (Ford and Lincoln Mercury). Now the company had separate operating divisions, and each had its own manufacturing capability. This encouraged specialization of assembly plants. At this point more advanced body-fabrication equipment began to be introduced into assembly plants. In the mid-1950s, more and more welding equipment was installed in the assembly plants, including some specialized welding presses, such as the Clearing press, which performed 144 welds at one station.[17]

Advances in process equipment within Ford assembly plants have proceeded along two major paths following this date. The first has been through the development and extension of "islands of mechanization" at different points in the overall assembly process. There are one or two examples of early "islands of mechanization" in the 1930s, where both the level of mechanization and the number of grouped operations were distinctly higher than other operations in the process.* These "islands" were greatly extended in the 1950s to include automatic tire-mounting and inflating equipment and automatic painting equipment. Some of the "new islands" introduced since 1950 are: a self-aligning door-hanging fixture; an

---

* The earliest example of a semiautomatic machine in assembly plants was noted in 1932. It was described as a merry-go-round for the semiautomatic inflation of tires. A machine group that serves the same set of functions is currently used, but it is now a truly automated multistage operation (Joseph Geschelin, "Scheduling in L-M Plants," *Automotive Industries*, November 15, 1953, p. 35; and Joseph Geschelin, "Ingenious Equipment Speeds up Export Plant," *Automotive Industries*, August 13, 1928, pp. 269–75).

TABLE 6.5. Ford Assembly Plant—Equipment Characteristics

	1914	1927	1930–36	1936–38	1953–55	1964	1970	1974	1975
Transfer span[a]	1	1	1	1	1	1	2	6	20[b]
Group Operations[c]	1	1	1	1	144	144	190	130	120
Mechanization level[d]	4	4	4	4	8	9	9	12	12

[a,c,d] These are keys to literature sources that described the equipment whose characteristics are tabulated above. Appendix 3 includes a brief description of the equipment and the complete reference.

[b] Estimate for new Econoline plant placed in operation in early 1975 (C.L. Knighton, "Manufacturing the Third Generation Econoline," Paper presented at the Society of Automotive Engineers Congress, Detroit, Michigan, February, 24–28, 1975).

automatic wheel aligner; multiple nut runners with controlled torque;[18] the electrocoat process for rust prevention; and automatic car-testing equipment.

The second and perhaps more important path of mechanization has been through the rationalization and integration of the body construction process. Automatic welding equipment combined with body alignment fixtures have been integrated into the flow of body construction,† and transfer lines have been introduced. The transfer lines, similar to those in engine plants, use transfer machines to automatically move and precisely position parts between mechanically activated welding presses.

Three Measures of Equipment Development. Trends in the use of mechanized transfer, equipment specialization, and mechanization at the assembly-plant level are indicated in Table 6.5. These data refer only to body construction in the assembly plant. The build-up in the ability to perform multiple welds (developed gradually throughout Ford) appears as a developmental surge in the 1950s, when welding presses were shifted from central operations and introduced in the assembly plant.

The three measures of equipment development are the same as those used for engine plants (see Chapter 5):

(1) *Transfer Span*

The maximum number of automatic stations through which a part is automatically transferred, indexed, and *automatically* processed. A rating of 1 is equivalent to no transfer.

(2) *Number of Grouped Operations*

The minimum number of simultaneous mechanically performed operations carried out at one station without extra operator intervention.

† For example, in late 1970 Pinto and Mustang bodies were built up and framed in a series of large integrated framing and spot-welding fixtures called pivoting-pillar bucks. Body pieces are fed into these machines, hydraulic clamps grip the pieces, and multiple welding heads are automatically sequenced to make a series of welds ("Mechanized Spot Welding at Ford," *American Machinist*, December 28, 1970, pp. 23–33).

(3) *Level of Mechanization‡*

The level reached on Bright's scale of machine mechanization. The active range of the scale is described in Chapter 5: 4—power tool, hand control; 5—power tool, fixed cycle, single function; 6—power tool, program control, sequence of fixed functions; 7—power-tool system, remote control; 8—activated by introduction of work; 9—measures characteristic of work; 10—signals preselected measurement; 11—records performance; and 12—changes speed, position, and direction according to measurement signal.

The final index, the level of mechanization, suggests equipment complexity—the extent to which the equipment has developed along a historical pattern of evolution. Its use here does not presume that machines at any level have developed through all preceding levels or that the machine necessarily supports a capability indicated by subordinate levels. For example, the servo-controlled door-hanging fixture uses feedback to position the door automatically, a level-12 rating. It does not carry out a series of fixed functions, however (level 6), although it does perform functions at levels 11, 10, 9, 5, 4, and below. The mechanization index is helpful in indicating the general level of machine complexity for this device.

These data specify peak conditions at a plant, but the peak incidence generally indicates a broader underlying trend. The capability for performing multiple operations is an important form of equipment specialization that yields increased efficiency. In general terms, the larger the number of grouped operations, the greater the labor savings, but the equipment becomes more susceptible to obsolescence from product change. Automatic transfer also reflects specialization, but at an even higher degree than grouped operations, since it carries the implicit assumption that assigned products must generally move through the same fixed sequence of machines and operations. The greater the transfer span, the greater the specialization, efficiency, and risk of obsolescence.

The flatness of the trends confirms that the level of assembly-plant specialization was very low until the 1950s, but began to increase after that. The maximum level of the transfer span and mechanization for the typical small-car plant is currently lower than in engine plants. This supports the concept that an assembly plant accommodates a wide range of product change with low risk of equipment obsolescence.

The abrupt change in the 1950s parallels the change in the management and organization of the Ford Motor Company discussed previously. The sequence starts with a large increase in grouped operations, then in the 1960s mechanized transfer began to be used,* and following this the level

‡ See Table 5.3 in Chapter 5 for a more complete description of mechanization level.

* One knowledgeable technical manager at Ford noted that, as far as he knew, the first significant use of in-line transfer in body assembly occurred in 1965 and involved the use of transfer among seven stations. This advances the build-up rate but not the general trend.

of mechanization started to rise, much as was the case with engine plants. All three measures indicate that the increase in specialization has accelerated in the 1970s.

Parallels with Engine Plants. Some intriguing parallels between these trends and those of engine plants before 1952 are suggested. The joint development of all three indices is the same as that in engine plants. First a build-up in grouped operations took place; then came a few automated transfers, followed by an increase in transfer span; and finally the level of mechanization rose. As may be recalled from Chapter 5, the rather complete transition to extensive in-line transfer in engine plants during the 1950s took place at approximately the point of development that has currently been reached in the assembly plant. If an analogy can be drawn between the productive units, it might be assumed that the assembly plant is presently poised for a major transition state in equipment technology.

These technological developments have caused the same specialization of the process to a particular model that we observed in engine plants. The evidence here, however, is elusive. Assembly plants at Ford and the other major producers vary considerably in the degree of equipment specialization, depending upon the type of car involved. The assembly plants for the smaller unit-construction cars have more often been equipped with specialized equipment than others. The plants for the main-line Fords and other body/frame cars are not yet so heavily equipped.

Model Changeover Implications. An appreciation for the effect of equipment-development trends on the cost of model change can be obtained by contrasting model changeover costs presently and in the 1920s. Specifically, the 1927 change from the Model T to Model A and a recent changeover in an assembly plant from a main-line Ford car to a compact Maverick can be compared.

The changeover from Model T to Model A came shortly after closed steel bodies were introduced in 1925. The change was dramatic, in that it closed down all Ford car production for about nine months and turned over market leadership to General Motors. The impact on process technology was very substantial at the Rouge plant. Many machines were scrapped, forty-five hundred new ones bought, and over 50 percent of all machine tools were rebuilt. The assembly plants were affected very little, however, in either equipment or process.[19]

In contrast, the conversion of the Wayne assembly plant to Mavericks in early 1974, following the shift in demand that accompanied the Mideast oil restriction, was reported in much different terms. The conversion, reported as a "move to stay in business," took fifty-one days, and, as one Ford official described it: "Everything in the body shop is new—assembly lines, weld lines, solder grind booths—everything." Dollar figures were not given, but Lee Iacocca, Ford's president, termed it: "The greatest industrial conversion in history, at least in peace-time. . . . I didn't know they could spend that much money in 51 days."[20] The point is that assembly plants are no longer the flexible labor-intensive plants they were during the prewar period. They have become specialized and capital-intensive.

Comparability with Other U.S. Firms. These trends are not unique to Ford. If anything, evidence suggests that body production at Volkswagen, Fiat, and the General Motors Lordstown plant for the Vega would each have ranked higher than Ford on the three measures for most years (see Table 6.5). In 1964, Volkswagen's Wolfsburg plant incorporated an automated body-assembly line in which 15 or more linked, in-line automated transfers were reported to be used in the process flow. As many as 108 welds were performed automatically at two of the stations. This would be equivalent to a transfer span of 15 and 108 grouped operations for 1964, as depicted in Table 6.5. Volkswagen's 18-second cycle time was more than three times faster than Ford's rate and double the Lordstown rate.[21] The General Motors Vega plant in 1970 used 11 Unimate robots along a moving body line to perform welding operations automatically. Approximately 20 welds were performed per robot. This represents an equivalent transfer span of 11 stations and 20 grouped operations. Of all 3,900 body welds, 95 percent were performed automatically.[22]

Although the specifics of the equipment specialization differ considerably between Europe and the United States and between Ford and General Motors, several common aspects are evident. Since World War II the trend has been toward higher levels of mechanization or the specific state in terms of our model. The most rapid progression is in the small standardized car. The equipment of these plants is highly specialized to a particular car, thereby increasing the cost of change, and in these aspects of process technology for small cars, Europe has been ahead of the United States. Engine plants in the United States, however, are apparently more advanced.[23]

Changing Task Characteristics

In contrast with engine plants, the task of the direct work force in assembly plants has not changed radically from an operative to a monitor function. The task duration and division of labor during peak demand periods have remained at a relatively stable level since the moving final-assembly line was introduced in 1914. The output rate of the assembly plant provides a good indication of the division of labor because the typical work assignment in final assembly involves a fixed work location and a work unit that moves to the operator at the output rate of the line. Table 6.6 shows that in periods of peak output, the division of labor for typical main-line Ford assembly plants has been around one minute since 1914.

The early transition from the craftsman's tradition of team build-up is

TABLE 6.6. Assembly Task Duration (Cycle Time per Station) *

1908–9	*514 Minutes*

No specific division-of-labor data for this period are available for Ford's final car assembly, but approximations can be inferred from two accounts: Sward's account of general production methods at Ford in 1908 and a more detailed 1909 account of methods in a nearby plant, the Chalmers-Detroit Motor Car Company of Detroit.

In describing Ford's assembly methods Sward notes: "There were . . . now several assemblers who worked over a particular car side by side (as a team), each one responsible for a somewhat limited set of operations.†

At the Chalmers-Detroit Company: "In ten hours 30 men completed 35 cars . . . [for each car] three men now devote their entire time to assembling two chassis . . . it is here the advantages of 'team work' are exhibited . . . each man knows just what he is to do."‡ Given these data, the average task duration is $\frac{30}{35} \times 10 = 8.57$ hours $= 514$ minutes.

1913	*2.3 minutes* (before September)

Chassis were stationary, and specialized teams, such as axle teams, motor teams, etc., moved from chassis to chassis completing their special tasks.** The lowest labor content achieved by this method was 748 minutes. The output rate for one row of cars (100 units in assembly) was one car per 2.3 minutes. If this is the assembly time of the last team, this can be taken as the task duration.

1914	*1.19 minutes*

Output rate for the new moving assembly line was 404 cars in 8 hours or a car every 1.19 minutes††

1926	*1.06 minutes*†† Edgewater, New Jersey, plant
1930	*1 minute*†† Chester, Pennsylvania, plant
1949	*1 minute*‡‡ Dearborn Assembly (Ford)
1953	*0.9 minutes*‡‡ Dearborn Assembly (Ford)
1966	*0.9 minutes*‡‡ Dearborn Assembly (Mustang)
1970	*1 minute*‡‡ Dearborn Assembly (Mustang)
1974	*1 minute*‡‡ Dearborn Assembly (Mustang)
1974	*1 minute**** Wayne Assembly (Maverick)

* Available evidence indicates that the moving assembly line was used exclusively as the process method at Ford from its date of introduction. Since cycle time per worker is effectively determined by the line's output rate for many workers, the task duration is given in these terms from 1914 and on.

† Sward, *Legend of Henry Ford*, p. 32.

‡ H. W. Slauson, "Efficient System for the Rapid Assembly of Motor Cars," *Machinery* (October 1909): 114–45.

** Arnold and Faurote, *Ford Methods and Ford Shops*, pp. 128–58.

†† Branch Assembly Accession, Ford Archives, Henry Ford Museum, Greenfield Village, Dearborn, Michigan.

‡‡ *Ford Motor Company Facts and Figures*, respective years.

*** "Large/Small Switch at Wayne," *Automotive Industries*, March 1, 1974, p. 20.

shown by the data in this table. Conditions that supported craft skills had largely disappeared by 1910 because of the introduction of progressive manufacturing methods. The introduction of the moving assembly line did not of itself have a major impact on task durations. A high division of labor had already been adopted through the use of teams that would move among stationary build-up stations and perform specialized tasks. The effect of the moving assembly line was further to shorten and freeze this division of labor and task duration. Future change in labor tasks is promised by further technological developments in equipment along the lines that occurred in engine plants.

The Changing Nature of Capacity

Since the period of rapid change in the 1910s, when assembly plants were built, subsequent periods have been marked by relative stability from year to year. Although change has not been revolutionary in nature, it has been cumulative, so that the total effect has been large, altering assembly functions more basically than during the earlier period of radical change.

Method of Analysis. Let us use the same approach as in Chapter 5 to consider specialization, concentration, and backward integration in the assembly plant. Changes in the process stages and the methods of producing a sample of eight components provide the primary source of comparative data. The components are: external body shell, body support members, window glass, upholstery fabric, frame, transmission, radiator, and engine. Two parts, that were used in engine plant calculations (in Chapter 5), the radiator and engine, are also included here to provide comparability. For each component the process steps have been ordered along the same nine-step scale that was used in Chapter 5, Figure 5.1, to determine roughly the degree of backward integration.

The nine generalized steps are shown in Table 6.7 in order of increasing steps of backward integration from final assembly "upstream" to raw material extraction.

Two measures, backward integration and centralization, are developed from these data. (Specialization as defined for engines is not developed here, for it would display the development of the same feeder plants that the index reflected in Chapter 5.) The first, the index of backward integration, is the average number of backward steps for the corporation as

TABLE 6.7. Steps of Backward Integration

Generalized Step	Flow
1. Final assembly	1
2. Preparation of module or component for final assembly	2
3. Module or component finishing (for example, painting, polishing)	3
4. Fabrication or assembly of component	4
5. Part making—finish dimensions	5
6. Part making—form to rough dimensions	6
7. Make material for part (for example, steel making)	7
8. Produce raw material (for example, iron making)	8
9. Extract raw material (for example, mining)	9

TABLE 6.8. Aggregate Assembly Plant Changes

	1910–12	1914	1925–26	1927–28	1935–36	1946–47	1955–57	After 1970
Purchases	All bodies Wood chassis parts Glass Leather and cloth Radiator Rolled steel Frame members	Bodies Wood Glass Cloth and leather Sheet steel Steel frame stock All forgings 90% of painting	Sheet steel Steel frame stock Cotton fiber	Most body components Laminated safety glass Rolled steel sheet Upholstery fabric	Upholstery fabric Zepher Unit construction bodies	Glass Some steel Upholstery fabrics Some body parts Some entire bodies	Some steel Upholstery fabrics Some body parts Some bodies	Some steel Some body parts Some bodies
Changes since prior period: corporatewide backward integration changes — LOSES				Windshield glass production Cloth weaving Some body production capacity	Most wood production	Tire production Soybean plastic production	Paper board	
ADDITIONS		Spring forming Fender presses Radiator	Logging and sawmill Glass plant Body parts production and components assembly Cloth weaving Artificial leather production Steel frame production Paper board production Blast furnace operation	Open-hearth steel plant	Safety glass production Rolled steel Steel-rolling plant Tire production (1937) Soybean plastics (1933)	Glass production resumed	Greater centralized trim kit production Automated stamping and frame plants (1948 and 1949) Plastic plant	Vinyl fabric production

140

Changes since prior period: assembly plant operation vis-à-vis other Ford plants	DELETIONS	Body finishing	Body framing and assembly from components; Multicolor painting			Reduced Trim and upholstery fabrication through use of trim kit	More of the body components built by welding in assembly plant	Automated welding to build up some major body components
	ADDITIONS							
Average no. backward-integration steps corporatewide	3.2	4	7.4	6.6	7.7	7.1	7.7	8
Average no. backward-integration steps, assembly plant only	1.7	1.6	2.0	2.7	2.3	2.3	1.7	1.7

SOURCE: Appendix 3.

a whole. For the eight parts, the value of the index was 7.4 for the 1924–26 period. The concentration index reflects the degree to which many operations were concentrated in one productive unit. This index is the average number of steps that are included in the one assembly plant. For the 1924–26 period the index has a value of 2.

These indices are tabulated for all periods in Table 6.8. Descriptive information is also provided for changes in the sample of eight components and for other materials and components as well. The use of averages causes the trends to be somewhat misleading in respect to cost, for the body shell, engine, and transmission cost more than other components. Nonetheless, the indices are useful in illustrating overall trends in the physical features of backward integration and centralization.

The method of presentation highlights changes that were made from period to period in the assembly plant apart from changes made throughout the company. For example, during the ten years preceding the 1925–26 period, extensive backward-integration steps had been taken. The backward-integration index increased from 4 to 7.4. Companywide, these changes involved backward-integration investments in logging, iron production, body production, glass manufacturing, and many other components. At the assembly-plant level, however, the index increased only from 1.6 to 2.0. The only major operations added to assembly were the framing of body components built at the Rouge plant and the multicolor painting capability.

Backward Integration. As pictured in Table 6.8, backward integration is very dynamic at the companywide level. In the early years, each major model change had the effect of eroding the degree of backward vertical integration that had been achieved throughout Ford, in support of the prior model. As shown in Table 6.8, for example, between 1914 and 1926, Ford achieved extensive backward vertical integration in steel bodies, upholstery fabrics, car glass, wood body supports, and iron production. Then, following the introduction of the Model A in 1927, a more complex body was introduced, which Ford was reportedly unable to produce in necessary volume. More than half of the Model A bodies were purchased from the Briggs Manufacturing Company.[24] Similarly, the newly introduced laminated safety glass was purchased for the Model A, as were upholstery fabrics, even though Ford had been extensively integrated into materials for both components in manufacturing the prior model. Of course, in subsequent periods, the previous degree of backward integration was reestablished through the introduction of new production processes for glass making and, in later years, for making vinyl plastic materials.

The pattern established has the same origin as that of engine manufacturing. The difference is that for the car as a whole, major product innovations have affected backward integration more severely by eroding the previous base of manufacturing efficiency. Major productive units that supported final assembly were both created and destroyed by the important product innovations. Large financial and technological investments have been needed throughout the years in initiating new productive units, just to stay even. The struggle between product innovation and backward integration is shown by fluctuations in the average number of companywide backward-integration steps at the bottom of Table 6.8.

Concentration: Assembly Technology. Process technology has been stable and homogeneous over a very long period. The stability of the concentration index and the types of operations that are included indicate little change in the narrow range of final assembly operation. These were very little affected by the turmoil throughout Ford, at least until the late 1950s. The figures in Table 6.8 are averages, however, and they fail to show a systematic change in the composition of operations because additions and deletions of particular operations cancel one another, but when averages are considered, the figures conceal the extensive additions made in support of body build-up functions in recent years. Aside from body-building operations, other changes have made assembly-plant operations more homogeneous. The early assembly plant's feeder departments were once filled with seamstresses making seat covers, glass-polishing operations, and trim operations that have since been eliminated by the use of prefinished components and the invention of mass-produced components that do not require finishing functions. The use of centrally prefabricated trim panels, formed seats, prewired instrument panels, and cables have made assembly plants more homogeneous in respect to included process technologies—now largely those of assembly, automated welding, and painting.

Organization. The changing role of assembly plants can be detected in the interplay among three variables: the number of active passenger-car plants, the average annual output per plant, and the extent of capacity replication at different locations throughout the United States. Capacity replication is defined here as the extent to which assembly-plant capacity is allocated to produce the same vehicle at different locations. For example, in 1930, the thirty-three Ford assembly plants were allocated so that both the Model A car and the Ford truck were produced together at thirty-two different assembly plants. The other plant produced the Lincoln. In this case there is a capacity replication of 31.3, indicating that, on the average, assembly capacity was replicated in about thirty-one locations.*

These three variables are plotted in Figure 6.5 for selected years. The average output per plant is based on high-volume years, since the intent is to reflect effective capacity. All plots are smoothed so that sharp dips, caused

---

* The weighting method and data sources are described in Appendix 3. The replications are weighted on the basis of capacity utilization rather than product lines because assembly capacity better reflects total sales volume.

FIGURE 6.5. Number of Plants, Scale, and Production Replications

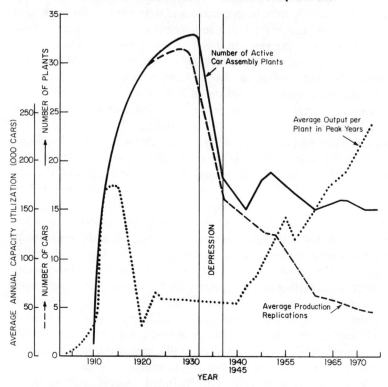

SOURCES: Ford Archives—Assembly Plant Accession; Appendix 3.

by the Great Depression when only eight assembly plants were in operation, are not shown.†

As shown by the three curves, a large systematic shift has occurred in the way the assembly plants are used in producing cars. Before World War II, the replication of capacity was approximately equal to the number of assembly plants. The apparent intent of the allocation was to produce all Ford car and light truck models in all assembly plants (except the one Lincoln plant). Although each plant could produce at a two-shift rate of 240,000 vehicles per year,‡ the average capacity utilized was around 60,000 units per year. This means that only 25 percent of the available assembly capacity was utilized in peak years. In effect, the assembly plants were devised as regional staging facilities containing little costly specialized

† Assembly-plant production records show that all but eight plants were shut down during the period around 1932.

‡ At one car per minute, the peak maximum capacity for many years; then 240,000 vehicles could be produced if two eight-hour shifts were worked for a normal work year.

equipment. Apparently the underutilized capacity was not of concern, since the plants provided transportation economies, sales advantages, and other benefits.

Following World War II, however, there was a major change, as indicated by the steep rates of change in capacity replication and scale. New plants were built at strategic, more central locations; more tooling was used; and the total number in use, relative to demand, was decreased. Through these changes, capacity utilization has been increased in peak years to the two-shift limit. At the same time, cars have been allocated to plants in a much different manner, changing the assembly plant as a productive unit from a general-purpose facility to one that is specialized to a particular vehicle. This is shown by the steep and continuing trend in replications. This pattern parallels the shifts that are apparent in all other aspects of assembly-plant operations, and it traces out a major systematic change in the nature of the assembly plant's role in automotive production.

COMPARISONS WITH THE ENGINE PLANT CASE

The sweep of change in assembly plants distinguishes this productive unit from the engine-plant example. Assembly plants were in a stable midstage of development for many years, and then, under the threat of foreign price competition from small cars, movement toward the specific state came rapidly. The possibility of a very significant reverse transition now seems possible.

Looking across the several aspects that have been considered, we see that the assembly plant's development has been much different from that of the engine plant, but within the common framework suggested in Chapter 4. The evolution of the product line, the characteristics of product change, task and labor characteristics, process equipment, changes in the type of capacity and in vertical integration have all followed a common pattern, but with a different timing. The long period in which the stage of development remained flexible shows that a productive unit need not progress toward either extreme unless the overall competitive environment requires such a change.

Ford's product lines have been formed through an evolutionary progression from a highly diverse product line to one that is rationalized and more nearly standardized. The rate of change slowed through steps and stages, and with this the effect of change has localized, so that the entire product is no longer altered by a component innovation. A slow and cumulative trend in equipment development has built up, and it has exercised a pervasive influence on the cost of product change. With these changes, capacity has evolved so that more homogeneous technologies are now included in productive units, and individual plants are more specialized to particular products.

Looking to the future of this productive unit in the new energy environment, the trends will increasingly be shaped by government regulation, the rising price of fuels, and the action of management in guiding innovation to meet this challenge. The real question is whether the car will become a commodity. Against the present pressures, management in a stagnant industry would probably not be able to avoid this extreme. The major automobile producers have historically responded rigorously to market-related change, however, and given this fact, a more likely forecast is that the recent trend toward the specific state will be reversed.

The concept of a productive unit does not provide answers to these important questions. It does, however, provide a framework wherein many implications surrounding the issue can be related one with another. In this sense it helps to identify consistent patterns of management action in response to the issues.

7 SOME IMPLICATIONS

The precursory but tentative ideas about innovation and process change that stimulated this inquiry fit well with the account of actual events in the automobile industry. Initial ideas about subtle links between innovation, product-line characteristics, production capabilities, and management organization, as presented in Chapter 4, are nicely borne out by the historical course of change in engine and assembly plants. The analysis of actual events does more than support the initial hypotheses, however; it offers a rich source for practical interpretation.

THE MODEL REVISITED

From the more detailed data given in Chapters 5 and 6 the ideas in Chapter 4 can be enriched and recast to reflect the development of both automotive units. At this higher level of abstraction some details of the historical analysis can be grasped more clearly.

Table 7.1 recasts and summarizes the model in a form similar in format and intent to Table 4.1. In contrast to the more limited number of aspects considered in the earlier table, seven are included in Table 7.1 over the full course of evolutionary transition from the fluid to the specific boundaries. The body of the table contains events for each of the seven aspects, and Exhibit 7.1 abstracts the sequence of transition.

EXHIBIT 7.1. The Productive Unit: Direction and Key Events in Transition

A. *Product Characteristics*

Direction. Overall, there is progress toward a "dominant design"—a broadening of appeal beyond a narrow market niche. Initially, a productive unit accommodates substantial product variety, and each product is specialized in the sense that it has limited breadth and duration in market appeal. It is virtually produced to customer order. Evolutionary progression ultimately leads to a high-volume, functionally standardized product.

Events. The transition is marked by a series of steps. The first step is the

TABLE 7.1. Productive Unit Characteristics

	A Product Characteristics (Main Line)	B Mode of Product and Process Change	C Process Configuration	D Task and Labor Characteristics	E Process Equipment	F Sourcing of Inputs	G Capacity
Central tendency in development	From: Custom product, specialized for appeal to specialized markets To: Standard product with appeal to aggregate markets.	From: Fluid change To: Incremental improvement.	From: Flexibility and independence among included operations To: continuous machine-paced line flow.	From: High trade craft skill and manual tasks To: Operative skills To: System overseer and maintenance skills.	From: General-purpose equipment To: Specialized integrated systems.	From: Components and materials available through common supply channels To: Devoted channels, back to raw material sources.	From: Small scale; assembly with ill-defined output limits To: Well-defined processes that are specialized to particular products.
Fluid 1.	Produced to customer order and specification.	Frequent major and novel product change. Prior models made obsolete.	Job Shop: Adaptable, fluid flow configuration	Craftsman or artisan skills required.	General-purpose equipment predominates.	Commonly available grades, through normal distribution channels.	Capacity limits ill-defined. Scale is small, many components purchased.

148

2.	At least one model "sold as produced" in substantial quantities (with or without options).	Major but cumulative changes made to successive product models across product line.	Progressive flow configuration around particular product(s).	Semiskilled workers; long task durations, training on job important.	Some specially designed machines for key tasks.	Override of common distribution channels and pricing policies.	General-purpose plant of moderate scale. Capacity increased by paralleling similar plants.
3.	Dominant product design (one type design gains major market share, forcing competitive reaction).	Incremental changes introduced during production, with periodic major model redesign across product line to increase functional product performance.	Line-flow configuration with separate production process for each standard product.	Operative skills and short task duration (minimum skills and training).	Frequent use of machines that perform multiple operations at one station.	Commands especially designed input materials and components and product development services by suppliers.	General-purpose plant organized and controlled by product/market categories. Includes production of most components. Capacity increased by investments to break bottlenecks.
4.	Highly standardized product. Options for different market segments formed as peripheral variations	Long periods between major model changes. Refinements emphasized. Changes no longer made across all models in line but are introduced selectively by model.	Closely balanced, commonly paced tasks organized and controlled by component.	Mixed skills and tasks. Some operatives and others monitoring.	Integration of special machines at some stations to form islands of automation	Substantially devoted input sources either through backward integration or other forms of close supplier control.	Capacity organized by process types. Separation of dissimilar or uncommon production processes from segment.
Specific 5.	Functionally standardized product(s).	Incremental product change implemented through process improvement, emphasizing greater product consistency and standardization.	Technologically controlled continuous or near-continuous flow.	Predominant tasks are equipment monitoring and intervention when equipment fails. Predominant skills are process maintenance.	Extensively integrated and direct linked process designed and procured as system.	Extensive integration into raw materials.	Large-scale plant specialized to particular process function, capacity well defined, increased only by designing new facilities.

149

development of a model that has sufficiently broad appeal to be produced in long runs and promoted and sold as a standard rather than a made-to-order product. The second and decisive step is the achievement of a dominant product design, one that attracts significant market share and forces imitative competitive design reaction. This induces product standardization throughout the industry. Finally, the dominant design is exploited to achieve a highly standardized product that is changed only incrementally from year to year, with emphasis on cost in competition.

B. *Product and Process*

Direction. The nature of change evolves from frequent, fluid, and novel product change toward conditions of stability.

Events. Early in the life of a unit, important functional improvements cannot be postponed. Then, as produced-to-order models are developed, improvements are incorporated in a more organized manner. The period between new model introductions is short, however; new models introduce major functional improvements; and in a competitive environment they cannot be withheld too long without serious loss of market position. The changes are introduced across the entire product line, imparting a simultaneity to the timing of model change. A dominant design, once achieved, decreases the urgency of product modification, and the character of model change shifts to become more that of design refinement and cost reduction than of major functional improvement. Then, with successive refinement, the interval between major design changes lengthens, although the frequency of incremental change may increase. The impact of change is localized as each component is separately standardized and produced.

C. *Process Configuration*

Direction. As a productive unit develops from initial conditions to those of the later stages, the configuration of the production process is altered from one that affords a high degree of independence among included operations and tasks to one with a high degree of integration and balance among these operations. Characteristics of the process configuration in the beginning stage of development are similar to those of a "job shop." That is, subordinate operations include diverse technologies that are loosely organized and independent of one another so that they can be flexibly applied to produce a wide variety of products under conditions of change. As a consequence, the flow of work is erratic, output rates are unpredictable, much management attention is required, and inventory levels are high; but change is readily accommodated at minimum cost.

Events. By successive redefinitions the flow of work in process and the subordinate operations are redefined and rearranged to achieve an intermittent line-flow movement. That is, changes are made so that operations are performed as the work moves forward, without retracing, typically in batches that are processed intermittently. With further development the flow becomes more continuous. Intermittent processing of batches gives way to continuous product flow with mechanical pacing keyed to final product output. Control comes to be based on rate-flow adjustments. With subsequent development, subordinate operations are redesigned to provide tight balance among included operatives. Heterogeneous and disruptive technologies are eliminated from the process flow as necessary to achieve continuity. Inventories are introduced where needed to buffer the outputs. Finally, the flow configuration is mechanically linked to form a single continuous line-flow system that is managed on a rate-flow control basis, affording few options in the product output.

D. *Task and Labor Characteristics*

Direction. Task characteristics and the skills sought in the work force shift with development, so that there is less skilled-labor input in direct work tasks and more skilled-labor input to process overseer functions.

Events. The transition from the initial to the later stage of development involves an evolutionary progression. Tasks are first reduced in duration and content, so that only semiskilled workers are required, and then are redefined even further, until they require only the manual dexterity of the operative. As tasks are broken down into smaller and smaller elements, better specified, organized, and made more predictable, they become more susceptible to automation. Islands of automation are created as a sequence of related tasks are mechanized, first by analogy to manual methods and then by reengineering the methods to make them more appropriate to automation. Ultimately, then, as these islands are linked, the predominant task of the work force becomes that of the systems overseer.

E. *Process Equipment*

Direction. As the productive unit develops, the type of equipment changes from general-purpose, independent equipment to equipment that is designed, integrated, and purchased as a system.

Events. In the beginning stage, when the economic future is uncertain, general-purpose process equipment is used. A type of equipment is used that can be procured from conventional suppliers. Only in cases where technical feasibility of production requires special-purpose equipment is it specially developed. Then, as confidence and market acceptance of the product grow and the demand for output increases, special equipment is designed to overcome particular bottlenecks. Because the process is new, because a large supplier industry does not exist, and because requirements are uncertain, special-purpose equipment is likely to be developed by the organization itself. With increasing demand for output, growing economic success, greater stability in product design, more predictable process flows and task definitions, there is a corresponding increase in the development of special-purpose machines. Islands of automation in the process grow through an increase in the number of multiple operations that are performed at one work station. Subsequently, advanced development takes place through the linkage of adjacent stations into common units of equipment. As integration proceeds, machines become more reliable and complete, so as to support unattended operation. It finally becomes possible to join major elements of the process into a common large system that operates as a single machine. At this stage, equipment is purchased and integrated as a specially developed system from special suppliers. By linking equipment in this manner, however, it becomes highly specialized to a particular product design.

The effect is to link product and process so that both are costly to change, but highly efficient.

F. Sources of Material Inputs

Direction. As a productive unit develops, change takes place in the types of material input that are utilized and in the sources for these inputs. Initially, materials are used that are commonly available through traditional supply sources. In highly developed stages the materials are special, and supply sources are wholly devoted.

Events. Initially, when product design, market needs, and process configuration are all uncertain and in flux, the type and sources of inputs vary widely, precluding the major commitments in time, equipment, and money that would be required to obtain the ultimately most appropriate and efficient types of inputs. With development, suppliers seek to compete through innovation in materials and services. Successful innovation forges tighter, more specialized linkages and dependencies between the unit and its suppliers, with implications for further cost reduction and improved efficiency. To seek economic returns and ensure predictability of inputs, control over supply sources is achieved through backward vertical integration by new facility construction, merger, acquisition, or long-term contract.

G. Capacity

Direction. The aggregate characteristics of a productive unit's capacity change with transition. Initially, the capacity is centralized, it includes heterogeneous technologies, and capacity limits are ill-defined since the process itself is unstructured. In a highly developed state, capacity is very specific, it includes homogeneous technologies, and it is provided by a decentralized and independent facility.

Events. Through horizontal and backward integration, the scope of included operations is first rounded out to encompass those operations that affect the basis of competition. At first this increases the heterogeneity of included process technologies and imparts a general purpose as opposed to a specialized quality to capacity. Capacity limits remain ill-defined, and increases in capacity are achieved by paralleling existing general-purpose segments. As development advances, subprocesses take definite form. To increase capacity, bottlenecks are eliminated in particular processes. With still further development, individual units and subprocesses are organized and managed independently. Heterogeneous technologies are separated, and the processes become specialized to particular components. Finally, in a highly developed state, capacity is explicit, composed of tightly balanced homogeneous operations and organized in units synonymous with product components (engine plants, rolling mills for sheet steel, body-building lines, and so forth). Increases in capacity are achieved by designing entirely new plants.

The events are ordered in Table 7.1 so that milestones included in a given row are judged to be at a comparable stage of development. At any given time, however, it would not be expected that the characteristics of an actual productive unit would be evenly aligned across a row. Development is expected to be somewhat uneven in specific detail at specific times but to proceed overall with a definite degree of evenness.

DYNAMICS OF TRANSITION

Although a certain degree of evenness among the major elements of the productive unit is evident over the long run, the timing of progress is ragged, and it varies considerably among the different elements. For example, the product line can be highly standardized as a matter of market conditions and management policy, corresponding to an advanced stage in column A of the table. Until equipment is advanced to a comparable stage, however, the evenness of progression will be out of balance. A product-line policy that embraces standardization will facilitate equipment advances, but until such advances are realized and until parallel advances in other elements are also realized, the overall productive unit cannot be considered to be at the same stage as the one element, product line. The full economic benefits of this higher stage will not be realized until, among other things, labor tasks are altered to achieve the gains in efficiency that are possible through higher division of labor; more efficient equipment is used; and backward integration lowers input costs. At the same time, until these other developments come about, there will not be an accompanying loss in flexibility. Consequently, a reversion back to an earlier stage in product-line policy will be relatively cost-free. In other words, the productive unit will still be flexible in response to product innovation.

This means that product-line characteristics may move through a cycle of development and revert back to an earlier stage with comparative ease. In contrast, the development of equipment and changes in labor or management task characteristics tend to be cumulative in nature and persistent in effect. Once these aspects are advanced, reversals occur less frequently and carry higher costs.

Reverse Transition—An Illustration

These concepts of uneven development—transition and reversal—are illustrated in Figure 7.1.

This figure uses changes in product-line and equipment characteristics in the early years of Ford's engine plant to illustrate different relationships among the various elements that affect progress. The scale of development on the left can be identified with the five successive steps that are shown respectively for product-line and equipment development in Table 7.1. Note, however, that the use of these stages causes the scale to be inverted, with the most advanced stage near the origin. Years are indicated along the bottom. The shape of the two curves depicts trends described by the data and historical accounts of development in Chapter 5.

This figure contrasts the relatively volatile quality of product-line changes with the steady cumulative advance in equipment characteristics. Although equipment trends are shown to lag behind product-line changes, they act like a ratchet to limit or constrain a complete return in product-line conditions to the early fluid state. Equipment development acts like a steadily rising lower limit that presses the productive unit's overall development. Practically, this represents the pervasive impact of equipment advances on the cost structure, the way labor can be used, minimum economies of scale, and equipment flexibility itself, as well as the associated effects on the organization and management.

Innovative product change, as represented by the introduction of engines for the models T, A, and V-8, is shown to reverse temporarily the trend in equipment development only if the stage of equipment development had advanced beyond the lower limit of variation in the stage of product-line development. For example, even though the Model N engine was being produced, the introduction of the Model T did not cause a reversal; yet the other two engines did at a later time. (We noted these same interactions in prior chapters for equipment-development trends in the assembly plant and the engine plant.)

It would be expected that developments in productive units of other industries have differed significantly from those in the automobile engine plant in respect to convergence between the states of equipment and product-line advancement. For example, although the product characteristics of the DC-3 were rather standardized,[1] there is no indication that

FIGURE 7.1. Interactions in Ford Engine Development: Product Line and Equipment Developments in Transition

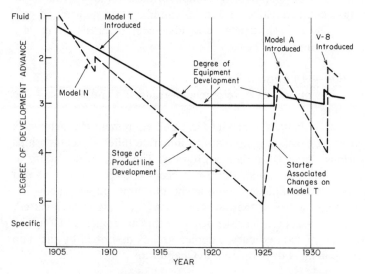

process equipment evolved as extensively as in automobile engines. Neither did equipment developments in automotive assembly plants keep pace with the opportunities posed by the product standardization of the early car models.

Conceptually, the convergence of the two curves to a common advanced stage of development represents the linking of major product innovation with process innovation. When both aspects reach an advanced stage, product and process innovation become highly interdependent.

PRODUCTIVITY CHANGE BY STAGE OF DEVELOPMENT

Productivity improvement comes about when a product unit undergoes transition to a more advanced stage. This important relationship warrants careful consideration.

A profile of the productive unit's course of development in aggregate, as illustrated in Figure 7.1 for product-line and equipment characteristics, can be extended to illustrate the tie between productivity, innovation, and the overall stage of development. The average stage of all seven aspects in Table 7.1 may be used to gauge each productive unit's overall degree of development at different times. The profiles of aggregate development obtained in this way can be used to see how changes in stage of development are related to changes in both technological innovation and labor productivity.

Figures 7.2 and 7.3 each relate productivity and stage of development through two curves: one curve is the development of engine plants and assembly plants; the other curve presents data showing the labor hours per product that were actually used by the respective productive units in various years.* As in Figure 7.1, above, the stage of development uses an inverted scale, so that the origin represents an advanced stage. The profiles are derived from published data, and better information is available about the earlier years than about the years since World War II.† The stage changes are more sharply defined in the earlier period because of this and because conditions have stabilized in later years. Tables 7.4 and 7.5, at the end of this chapter, indicate the events or circumstances in various periods that underlie the assessments. The data on labor hours are summarized in Tables 7.6 and 7.7. It should be noted that total nonsalaried labor hours

---

* Note that the labor hours are those of all nonsalaried employees, approximated from other sources. Direct labor hours per engine are now only a fraction of one hour, although total hours are seven to nine hours per engine.

† Although financial data were not disclosed until Ford became a publicly held company in the 1950s, there are numerous personal accounts, books, articles, and so on, about prewar conditions. The Ford archives contain little material from the postwar period.

FIGURE 7.2. Stage of Development and Labor Hours per Engine

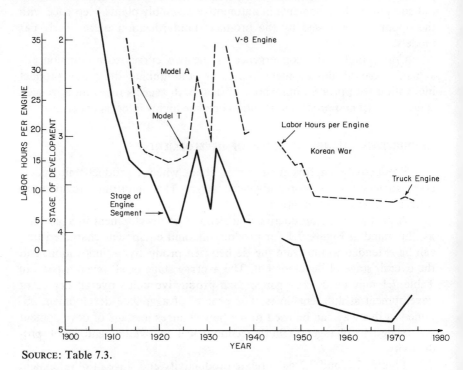

SOURCE: Table 7.3.

are reported rather than just direct labor hours. Direct labor hours would be much lower for engine plants.

Transition and Productivity Improvement in Engine Plants

The curve at the bottom of Figure 7.2, the profile of development stages, suggests there were two periods of rapid development: the initial years of the Model T era and the immediate postwar period that led up to the integration of engine plants with transfer lines. Between these periods, conditions were on a plateau in the sense that Ford was reacting defensively to product advances by other manufacturers. A strong relationship between the labor hours per engine and the assessed stage of the engine segment is evident in the figure. Although there might be some disagreement about the exact stage rankings, there should be little contention about the overall shape of the profile, and it is from the overall fit between the two curves that the major conclusions arise.

The *change* in the stage of development ties closely to labor productivity gains. The periods of major improvement in labor productivity occur with large and rapid advances in the stage of development. Such rapid advances took place in two periods when engines were relatively standardized and demand was strong. The first period was the production build-up phase of the Model T and the second was market expansion following World War II.‡ When the postwar expansion took place, the same basic V-8 engine had been in production since 1932.

Evidently the direction of transition reversed during the 1930s and with it the trend in labor productivity. During the periods of rapid change, labor inputs increase or remain high. This is evident as both a short-run disruptive spike and a longer-run trend. The introductions of the Model A and V-8 engines provide two conspicuous illustrations of the short-run effect. Massive increases in labor inputs per engine were required when they were introduced. More significantly, however, the base line of the trend shows that the labor content per engine increased from about 1924 until the end of the prewar period. The upward sloping base line is not surprising, for many design changes were made to improve the engine throughout this entire period. Design changes increased the number of required operations and the overall complexity of the product. The upward trend began with the addition of the starter while the Model T engine was in production.* Before the starter was introduced, the curve showing labor hours per engine reached its lowest level, in the early 1920s, and climbed steadily upward from there. This period can legitimately be interpreted as a reversal in the normal direction of a productive unit's development.

Since 1955, however, the overall trend in labor content per unit seems to be smoother, and rates are still decreasing, but progress is no longer rapid. The structure of this productive unit has apparently already reached a highly advanced state, and there is little opportunity for further progression. These trends support the concept that productivity changes are associated with structural changes in the productive unit.

Different Sources of Productivity-Improvement. Productivity improvement during the two periods of rapid increase came from different sources. In the first period, during the Model T build-up, productivity improvement came about smoothly in association with total production volume growth. These are the relationships of an experience curve or learning curve, and they are dynamic in the sense that productivity improvements depend directly on innovations that take advantage of volume growth. As identified in Chapter 3, many of the important innovations in engine plants during

‡ Some of the apparent improvement is explained by the changes in the scope of operations that are included. Changes in scope generally correspond with the concentration index changes given in Chapter 5. Based on an analysis of detailed cost data for the Model T, it is concluded that the effect of these structural changes on labor content was less than proportional. Decreases in scope probably account for less than 10 percent of the overall reduction in labor content. The types of operations that were separated from the engine segment include foundry and iron making. Although these weigh heavily in the concentration index, they do not contribute nearly so heavily to labor content as do engine assembly, testing, and machining (in earlier years).

* The effect of adding the starter was of considerable consequence in the design of many engine components. Cost data on Model T engine components show a ripple effect of cost increase in many components after the starter was first added.

this period originated in the automobile firms themselves, and they involved changes in process organization.

The second period of rapid improvement in productivity came about through the mode of designing and purchasing an entirely new integrated plant. In this case the mode of productivity improvement could be called static, for a given level of improvement was obtained by purchasing a plant of a given capability.

The two modes are entirely different insofar as both internal management and the entry of new firms in the industry are concerned. In the latter case, a competitive level of productivity could be purchased by a new firm at time of entry through capital expenditures. In the first case, however, a competitive position requires innovation, and this in turn requires volume growth, so entry by a new firm would be more difficult. Such difficulty of entry seems highly consistent with two modern industries, computers and semiconductors. In these industries a strong experience-curve pattern of productivity improvement, like the early automobile pattern, has been apparent. The successful entrants have been small firms that evolved into larger companies rather than large established firms that gained entry through head-on competition in established product lines.[2]

The modes of productivity improvement depend upon the stage of development. Concepts like the experience curve and learning curve are only parts of a larger framework that must be considered in discussing productivity issues.

Productivity Comparisons for Assembly Plants

A close relationship is also evident between labor-hour rates per car and the profile of development for assembly plants. The profile of development in Figure 7.3 is consistent with the notion that assembly plants are less developed than engine plants, although one might be misled in a visual comparison of the two figures because the scales are different.

The major changes that followed the introduction of closed steel bodies, the Model A, and the V-8 produced peak cost increases, as was the case in engines. During the postwar period, major short-term peaks that might have followed new model introductions are not evident. This partly results from data limitations but, more generally, in recent years, new model change in assembly has been better planned. Greater reliance has been placed on modular component lines, as discussed in Chapters 5 and 6, so that new model introduction is more smoothly handled.

The remarkable evenness in labor content per vehicle since the 1920s stands out as a major feature of this graph. It understates real productivity improvements, however, because many body operations that were once performed centrally, outside of the assembly plant, are now performed in the plant, and, of course, the car has grown in complexity.

The overall picture is consistent with the model and the discussion in

FIGURE 7.3. Stage of Development and Labor Hours per Car

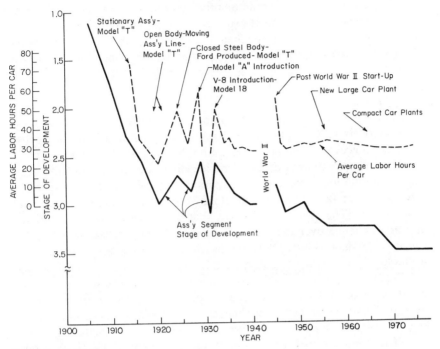

SOURCES: Table 7.4.

Chapter 6. The assembly plant is a productive unit that has remained relatively flexible, and consequently the labor content per vehicle has remained constant and has not developed like that in the engine plant. It is somewhat surprising, however, that rates of labor input have not varied a little more during the last decade, as would be anticipated from the changed stage of development as discussed in Chapter 6. Of course, the data extend only through 1974. It may also be that all of the necessary enabling conditions for a stage change (product standardization and design stability) are not yet present, so that the full consequences of recent changes have yet to be realized.

INNOVATION AND THE AGGREGATE STAGE OF DEVELOPMENT

In Chapter 4 the hypothesis was presented that patterns of innovation would change with stage of development in type, frequency, and locus of innovation. In respect to type and frequency, it is expected that major product innovations will be more frequent initially, relative to process innovation, but that process innovations will increase in relative importance as development advances. In respect to the locus of process innovation, process-equipment innovations are initially expected from the using firm, in this case the major automotive producers. For more advanced stages, innovative equipment is expected to be purchased as major process systems from special producers. Stated alternatively, the originating source of important process innovations is expected to shift from within to outside the firm.

Types of Innovation

The cases, as analyzed in Chapter 3, generally confirm these ideas about innovation. The anticipated changes in type of innovation are better analyzed, however, from data on one firm, here the Ford Motor Company.

Two simple sources of data provide direct evidence about the questions: "Ford Firsts" for the initial period and patents for later periods. Neither covers the entire period alone, for patent data are inadequate before 1920. The types of advances that are reported in "Ford Firsts" appear to change over the years. In later years they reflect largely sales-oriented product changes,* while in earlier periods very substantative technological innovations of all types were reported.

Table 7.2 lists all "Ford Firsts" that relate to the two productive units of interest from 1901 to 1915. These represent innovations of four types: overall chassis design (product changes), process innovations in assembly, engine-design innovations, and innovations in engine manufacturing.

The frequency of product and process innovations in this table changed over time, as we might expect. The first innovations pertained exclusively to product designs, for both engines and chassis. They constitute major conceptual changes in the organization and relationship of major car components. By 1906, however, process innovations began to appear, and the nature of product innovations began to shift, reflecting technological improvements in existing components or the addition of new ones. By the time the Model T was in production, 1908, the relative frequency of innovation had shifted, as expected, in favor of process innovations. These data nicely illustrate the ideas about changes in the type of innovation.

The Locus of Process Innovation

Patents are not necessarily equivalent to innovations, but data on patent applications can be expected to indicate how technical activity is

---

* It is surprising that a search of both company names and principal employees revealed few Ford patent applications for these early years. The type of advances Ford documents also change in a curious way. For the early years company chronologies of important events or "Ford Firsts" make frequent reference to notable technological achievements. In recent years, however, even significant contributions recognized industry-wide are omitted in favor of less significant sales-oriented firsts. For example, the major postwar contributions in cast cam and crankshafts, thin-wall cast-iron engines, and electrocoating are not listed.

TABLE 7.2. Ford Firsts to 1915

Chassis and Assembly		Engine and Transmission	
P 1901	Left-hand steering	P 1903	Adjustable spark advance
P 1904	Mount engine longitudinally	P 1906	Unitary engine and transmission
P 1904	Torque-tube drive	P 1907	Separate removable cylinder head
P 1904	Bevel-gear drive	P 1907	Magneto for ignition
M 1906	Wiring harness	M 1907	Simultaneous machining operations on cast parts
M 1907	Electric resistance welding	P 1907	Vanadium steel crankshaft
M 1908	Moving assembly line tried	P&M 1908	One-piece cast vanadium-steel crankshaft
P 1908	Left-hand steering on production model	P&M 1908	Planetary transmission and single-casting 4-cylinder block
P 1909	Steel running boards	M 1913	Moving assembly lines on motor, axle, and magneto
M 1911	Industry's first branch assembly plant (Kansas City, Mo.)		
M 1914	Endless chain-power-driven final assembly line for chassis		

SOURCE: Ford Motor Company Chronology of Important Events, Ford Archives, Henry Ford Museum, Greenfield Village, Dearborn, Mich.
NOTE: P = Product-design innovation; M = Manufacturing or process innovation.

directed within a company. On average, more patents would be anticipated in areas of greater technical activity and vice versa.

To use patent statistics in this way in analyzing activities at Ford, a few periods were selected for consideration. Ford patents pertinent to the engine plant as a productive unit were classified from their description as product, process, or other. For the assembly plant, however, no attempt was made to define the broad class that would represent product patents for the car as a whole. Instead, only process patents were classified. The necessary inferences can be made without data on product innovation for assembly.

Table 7.3 shows results in the form of percentage changes among

TABLE 7.3. Ford Patents by Application

Period	Engine Patents		Assembly Patents		All Ford	All Process Patents as a
	Product and Design	Process	Product	Process	Product and Process	Percent of all Ford Patents
1926–36	15	9	—	13	195	23.7
1946–52	6	2	—	4	162	26.7
1957–62	30	0	—	6	433	8.7
1970 and 1972	14	0	—	26	323	17.8

product and process patents for four different periods. All Ford patents were classified in this way. As a control, the percentage of process patents to total patents is also shown.

The concept that the originating source of innovation will shift outside the firm as the productive unit matures is supported by the patent statistics. The engine plant reached an advanced stage of development around 1952, as previously shown. Table 7.3 indicates there were only two process patents in the period ending in 1952, and afterward there are none. These data complement the case data in Appendix 1 and Chapter 3, which show that engine lines were purchased after 1950 and strongly confirm the ideas about originating sources of innovation at Ford.

A shift has come about in all Ford productive units. Patents that pertain to the assembly plant are still frequent, and some of these correspond to major process innovations that Ford originated for this unit. Since the 1950s, Ford has originated innovations in the electrocoating process for reducing corrosion of car bodies, welding, and others (see Chapter 3). Throughout the corporation the percent of process patents to all patents increased in the period of revitalization at Ford following World War II. The late 1950s and early 1960s reflect a slump. Then, since 1970, an increased rate is apparent. Because significant product innovations are linked to process innovations, as discussed in Chapter 3 and later in this chapter, this percentage may reflect an overall tendency toward maturity and then renewal in the industry. To the extent that this is such an indicator, an increase in the rate of significant innovation has occurred since the 1960s. In any event, the overall direction of technical activity in the company has not turned away from efforts that would lead to process patents. A fact that supports our hypothesis is that process patents in assembly seem to have led the corporatewide trend in numbers of patents, indicating a more fluid response to industrywide innovative stimuli, the engine plant has not followed the trend. The engine plant is a special case, which is nicely explained by its advanced stage of development.

The shift in originating sources does not mean that Ford stopped contributing to innovation in engine-manufacturing processes altogether. Contributions in concept and in process organization and method have apparently been made and implemented through purchasing policy. The Cleveland engine plant is an example, for this plant itself is considered an innovation.* In this plant Ford established the concepts, organization, and equipment specifications and absorbed most of the risk of the equipment producer. Process equipment in this plant was designed and purchased as a system and not by individual equipment units.

---

* The extensive integration of engine plants with transfer lines was identified in Chapter 3 as one of the major industrywide process innovations in engines in the 1945 to 1954 period. Ford's Cleveland engine plant is identified as the first plant to be so integrated.

Our model would predict that Ford will again originate an increasing percentage of process innovations for engine manufacturing if the recent emphasis on fuel economy causes this productive unit to reverse its historical direction of transition. Recent work at Ford on the Stirling and the Dual Displacement engines leads me to believe that such a change is promised. Whether it actually occurs, however, remains a question for future research.

Other Evidence on Shifts in Innovation. The shift in type and locus of innovation with stage of development is not just an idiosyncrasy of Ford. The importance of stage of development in the shift is borne out by differences between U.S. and European automobile firms and by innovative patterns in other industries.

Along with Ford, other U.S. producers turned to the machine-tool industry for innovative process equipment for engine plants after World War II, as observed above, but this was not the case with European automobile firms. European manufacturers, whose engine plants were not developed to such an advanced stage as U.S. plants, retained their capability for internal innovation.[3] This is consistent with the idea that the locus of innovation depends upon the stage of development, and not just the passage of time.

The change in type of major innovation, from product to process, as illustrated for Ford in Table 7.2, has also been studied for firms in other industries. James Utterback and I analyzed patterns of product and process innovations for seventy-seven firms in four different industrial sectors: railroad-equipment suppliers, computer firms, computer-components producers, and housing-contractor suppliers.[4] Among these firms, their stage of development seems to explain significant differences in their innovative potential, much as observed in engine and assembly plants at Ford.

The change in the locus of process innovation is much more than a matter of idle curiosity. George Stigler's work on the birth of industries[5] predicts that process-equipment sources will develop external to the firm, as has been observed. But the explanation he proposes is not successful in accounting for the differences between engine plants and assembly plants in the United States some fifty years after the automobile's birth, nor between those in Europe and in the United States.

IMPLICATIONS FOR MANAGEMENT IN THE AUTOMOBILE INDUSTRY

The automobile producer manages a portfolio of different productive units whose products are the components of the final product—the car. The present general model specifies the set of trade-offs that affect each productive unit, but individual units cannot be managed independently;

rather, the entire portfolio must be considered as a whole in order to realize both short-run and long-run competitive advantages.

For individual productive units, we have seen that conditions for innovation and efficiency are strongly linked, but in an inverse manner. The conditions that support a high level of efficiency are entirely different from those that support a high rate of innovation. Decisions that determine equipment development, product-line standardization, labor-force charac- teristics, and vertical integration simultaneously influence capabilities for innovation and productivity improvement.

Many variables are involved, but the present findings suggest that the path of progress can be changed and directed to achieve desired objectives. The objectives must be set, however, taking account of all the productive units in the portfolio.

Corporate Perspective

From a competitive standpoint, the mix in stage of development among the included productive units is absolutely critical. If all productive units were at an early, fluid stage, then costs would be prohibitively high for the customer. If, on the other hand, all units were highly advanced, then costs would be low but innovation would be eliminated as a competitive variable. This is what happened with the Model T: all productive units were allowed to advance together. The consequences were a great reduc- tion in price, but the loss of capability for change.

A better balance in stages of development among productive units would have all the productive units highly developed except one. The one would embody a competitively important feature, it would be in the early stages, and it would be in transition.

Such a controlled rate of innovation in deference to cost is essential with a high-priced consumer good like the car. Unlike an industrial product, such as a computer, the allowable price cannot increase with the real value of the product. At some price, not far above the present market price for cars, most of the market would be lost, no matter how excellent the product.

Cost control is the first requirement in managing the set of units. The essential trade-off between innovation and cost is illustrated by historical data for four productive units of the automobile. Figure 7.4 displays trends in price and volume* for the closed steel body, the Ford starter, power steering, and automatic transmission. These curves show that, as antici- pated, prices generally decrease with advancing volume and diffusion fol- lowing a learning-curve formula. (The diffusion data for these innovations

---

* Power-steering and automatic-transmission graphs are based on industrywide volume and, as might be anticipated, price trends are more shallow than the Ford- starter graph, which uses exact Ford-starter volume.

were given in Chapter 3.) The automatic-transmission graph is the exception, and it is here that the present concepts about a productive unit deviate from the traditional wisdom about the learning curve (or experience curve). The learning curve predicts an absolute decrease in cost with cumulative volume. The present general model anticipates cost reductions only when product designs are stable and product innovation is incremental. The case on automatic transmissions indicates that designs were fluid for a long period, so prices rose and declined. As Figure 7.4 shows, a trend toward reduced prices did, in fact, not begin until the late 1950s.† These

† Ford automatic-transmission trends after 1963 are not given because of difficulty in following the quoted price of this feature. Changes in the base price of the car to include this as an option package obscure prices.

FIGURE 7.4. Price-Volume Trends for Selected Features (1958 Dollar Value)

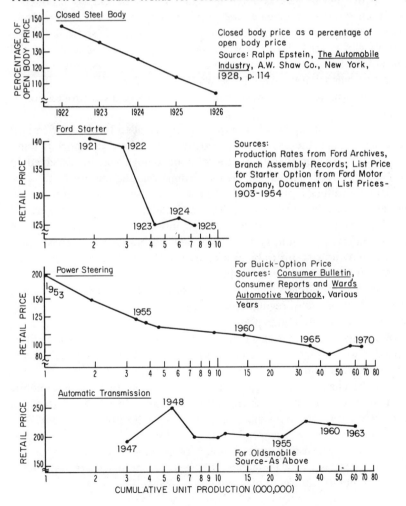

data are quite consistent with the observed changes in engine labor content during the 1930s, as previously shown in Figure 7.2.

Taken collectively, these curves reinforce the ideas discussed above about managing technology at the corporate level for a costly and complex consumer product. Strategy can be viewed in terms of managing a portfolio of productive units that are continuously changing. Innovation to create new features is essential, but the cost must be controlled to keep the total price of the product within reach of the consumer. Once the feature is perfected, costs are reduced, the technology is packed down, the diffusion is rapid, and all competitive advantage is lost. Another innovation is needed, or the basis of competition will shift to cost competition, and profit margins will be lost.

As this process continues over time, the final product comes to be made up of intermediate components from highly developed productive units. Such growth complicates the problem of cost control under conditions of change. The cost spikes in Figures 7.2 and 7.3 show that costs revert to earlier high levels when major change is introduced. Careful studies of the learning curve have shown that previous cost-reduction gains can be lost when innovative change occurs.[6] There is a reset, as it were, and cost returns to higher levels when the volume-growth progression is disrupted.

These relationships explain why it is important to localize the impact of change through the use of independent standardized component lines. Because of these considerations, the cost of change can be expected to increase as productive units become more numerous and mature.

Major product innovations for the car as a whole (as discussed in Chapter 3) were less frequent in the last decade. Recently, however, the rate of innovation has increased, although most innovations have not yet diffused. Safety, pollution, and fuel economy have added new constraints. Fuel economy now seems to be desired by the U.S. public, but this in itself is another form of an efficiency emphasis.

The long-term trends have greatly increased the cost of further change, and the effect of many regulations has raised the cost even higher. Only large firms are viable under present conditions. If firms were smaller, the rate of change would be even slower or prices would be higher. Large firms are needed to run highly advanced technologies to meet our society's desire for product innovation.

All the changes discussed might seem to imply that the automobile has matured as a product, but this is not the case. In the first place, the automobile is not the relevant unit of analysis: the productive unit is a better focus. As long as new productive units are being added, or as long as existing ones are resisting extreme states of development, the car has not matured. There is every indication that new technologies are now being introduced, notably in electronics and engine controls.

Second, maturity must be defined in relation to the market's preferences. If the product line matches market needs, the product would be mature. This is not the case presently in automobiles. Recent regulations and the consumer's interest in fuel economy have changed the competitive environment. After years of progress in perfecting the U.S.-produced automobile for the established market environment, the environment has suddenly changed. There are now new targets for innovation. Until the product again fully satisfies both market and regulatory requirements, the industry will not mature. And with ever more stringent regulation and uncertain energy supplies there is certainly no match between future needs and the product. There is now reason to believe that the direction of evolution has reversed in several important productive units. This suggests that severe government action can be used to manage technology in industry. It does not guarantee, however, that all of the consequences will be positive.

CONCEPTUAL IMPLICATIONS

The ideas underlying the model have been illustrated by the changing characteristics of automobile engine and assembly plants. Product and process innovation are not isolated events; they are linked together and to the characteristics of the productive unit where they occur. The mainstream of technological progress occurs through evolutionary changes in the major characteristics of a productive unit, changes that are difficult to reverse and that normally move from the Fluid toward the Specific condition.

This model applies two ways, to the productive unit that creates an industrial good and to the productive unit that may adopt it either as process equipment or as a new component for its product. It is important to recognize that a product innovation in one productive unit may be viewed alternatively as a process innovation for the adopting unit.[7] The characteristics of both the creator and the adoptor require serious consideration if technological innovation is to be better understood. By representing the different types of innovation that such related productive units can accommodate in their respective stages of development, the present model offers a new way of examining the potential for innovation between supplier and adoptor.

Prior research findings about variations in innovative behavior in different settings and firms and from different disciplinary perspectives are not unrelated or independent phenomena. They may be reinterpreted as factors in this larger picture of technological progress.

Conditions for Innovation within the Firm

The management of innovation within the productive unit and the firm goes far beyond the problems of creating an environment that is favorable to radical innovation. Because radical innovations are interesting of themselves, they may have received undue attention, perhaps obscuring management requirements for technological progress in other forms. Special, but different, conditions are required for steady cumulative progress in high-volume established products and production processes: to reduce costs, improve productivity, perfect product features, and assure quality. These capabilities are found in a productive unit's more advanced stage of development. They are much different from those needed to achieve a high rate of major product innovation—characteristics akin to the fluid stage. Both types of capabilities are needed in our economy. Effectiveness in either form of technological progress involves balanced and matched characteristics, or capabilities, of different types. Consequently, there is a real danger that if both types of innovative capability are sought in one productive unit, effectiveness will not be realized in either. The conditions in a productive unit need to be internally consistent or matched with one another at different stages of development.

These ideas fit nicely with findings from earlier studies that have examined particulars of innovative behavior and technological progress, like organizational characteristics, or degree of concentration and capital intensity, or labor and automation relationships. They contrast, however, with recommendations that are sometimes drawn from the very same studies. The notion that the effective capability for innovation can be practically altered through the arbitrary introduction of innovative traits in any single characteristic, like a changed organizational structure, does not fit the observed requirements for balance. This would be equivalent to changing any one column in Table 7.1 without varying the other necessary characteristics.

The implication is that a given productive unit cannot respond well to all types of demands. It cannot be both highly efficient and support a high rate of innovation. Of course, a given firm can manage a portfolio of productive units, theoretically at different stages of development. Even for management at this level, however, there are problems, and the ideas of match and balance may extend in some degree to corporate management.

There is some evidence that corporations are limited in their ability effectively to manage several productive units (or business lines) that are in widely different stages of development. Very little systematic research has been done in this area but, as a practical matter, firms that are effective at one stage are seldom successful at the same time with productive units at an opposite extreme. Corporations such as the major automobile firms, petroleum refiners, or steel producers, that stand out as the most competitively successful in making mass-produced, standardized products are not frequent sources of radical new products. Conversely, successful "high-technology" organizations often experience difficulty competing successfully in high-volume commercial markets. This model of balanced and matched capabilities helps to represent the different environments which managers in firms face at different stages of development.

Evenness of Progression

As a productive unit progresses from the fluid toward more advanced stages, its respective characteristics are modified through evolutionary and parallel development. There is a certain degree of evenness in this progression, and the movement is difficult to reverse. Explained in terms of Table 7.1, this can be seen as a parallel movement down the columns.

Transition from stage to stage is related to the experience or learning-curve phenomenon, in which spectacular rates of productivity improvement have been observed in products like the Model T Ford, rayon, incandescent light bulbs, and, more recently, pocket calculators. While the productivity improvement that accompanies this transition is vital to national progress, it is achieved with attendant losses. Productivity gains are realized through an associated change in stage of development with ramifications for innovative capability. While evidence from the present study suggests that productive units sometimes regain (or revert to) their earlier stage of development, the problems that arise are difficult to manage. They often depend on major changes in the environment that are beyond the control of managers in an individual firm. The strategic problems of managing productive units hinge on the issues of trading the possible gains in productivity against possible losses in innovative capability.

External Stimuli for Innovation

The nature of technological innovation takes on much different characteristics as the productive unit progresses from Fluid to Specific on the spectrum of development. There is no one best way to encourage technological innovation through external action or government policy, for the appropriate types of stimuli, the coupling between scientific advance and innovation, and the barriers to innovation all vary depending upon stage of development. The concept of innovation as a linear process, in which scientific advance stimulates innovation and ultimately broad commercialization, can mislead the selection of policies that would be most appropriate to encourage innovation in every stage.

Several factors change with the stage of development in addition to the particular types of innovation (product versus process and incremental versus major as discussed above). The locus of process innovation (where innovation originates) tends to move outside the firm that uses the process, and the role of scientific and engineering advances as a stimulating factor also changes (see below).

Fluid State Stimuli. Radical innovations underlying the creation of successful new businesses are seen to occur as an entrepreneurial act, corresponding to the fluid stage of development. The impetus is typically provided by individuals and organizations that are either users of the new product or have intimate insight about latent market needs. New Technologies or scientific advances are used as available to satisfy these new insights about user needs. Evidence from a variety of different viewpoints suggests that such innovations do not frequently occur through a process wherein advanced technologies seek out new needs, but instead a new understanding about needs draws in the best available technology. This is consistent with evidence that shows that radical innovations initially arise from without established large firms and industries. Advanced technologies may lie fallow until market conditions are correct and the necessary stimuli are present to nurture this type of innovation. It is true that advanced technological capabilities must be available to support major new technology-based products. This condition is far different, however, from that implied by the traditional linear model of innovation, which implicitly suggests that greater inputs of R&D offer an output of greater economic benefit. At this stage of development, actions to encourage the development of new market niches for high-performance products, and incentives to stimulate entrepreneurial action in desired areas of technological innovation, seem to offer better prospects for rapid progress.

Shifting Locus of Process Innovation. As a productive unit evolves from early Fluid condition toward a more advanced stage of development, the originating source of major process innovation shifts outside the unit. With automotive engines, for example, the present study shows that the major automobile firms were once the originators of major process innovations. The machine-tool industry has now become the major source of advanced process technology. Such a shift in locus is apparent in other industries like computers, where the rate of transition in development is rapid and capital equipment supplier firms have increased their contribution to major process innovation.

In terms of process innovation, it is significant that productive units that might be classed as "mature" or less innovative, such as coarse weaving mills in textiles or shoe producers or oil refineries, are the very same industries that look almost exclusively to other firms, their capital goods suppliers, for advances in manufacturing-process equipment. Those productive units that might be classed as innovative, like jet engine manufacturers, semiconductors manufacturers, and even Japanese automotive engine producers, contribute directly in process as well as product innovations.

These changes that occur in the evolution of an industry cause the linkage between scientific advance and ultimate economic application to shift and change in a corresponding way. For mature productive units the potential for innovation will depend heavily on technological progress by capital equipment suppliers, while this linkage will typically be less important nearer the Fluid stage. These types of dependencies are particularly evident in textile weaving and shoe manufacturing, where the characteristics of a few equipment producers have played a large role in innovation and productivity, or the lack of it, throughout the industry.

Science and Innovation

Several indicators suggest that the most direct link between science and innovation occurs for productive units in the midranges of transition, in the technologically active stage of development. At this stage the economics appear most favorable, and empirical evidence suggests that investment in R&D is indeed at a peak.

The economic justification would seem to be most favorable in such cases for three reasons. First, the markets are still volatile though already aggregated. Second, for this reason and because adequate profit margins can still be realized, the economic benefits from applying the results from a relevant R&D breakthrough are large and relatively sure. Finally, the cost of change will not have risen to the prohibitive levels that are likely to attain in the specific stage.

Data are not available to pinpoint actual R&D investment by productive unit, but evidence from several sources suggests that the largest investments in R&D are made by successful firms whose main lines of business depend on productive units in these middle ranges. According to a recent National Science Foundation survey, a handful of companies, twenty in all, spend more than half of all their funds for R&D within industry.

From his review of economic research on innovation, concentration, and R&D investment, Jesse Markham describes these firms that make high rates of R&D investment. The characteristics of such firms also suggest the nature of their major business lines, or productive units: "Data are beginning to suggest that large vertically integrated companies with relatively large market shares have a greater incentive to invest in R&D than other firms have." He goes on to cite specific research findings that show that "R&D spending is negatively associated with profits for companies having small 'relative market shares.' "[8]

Too much attention may have been given to radical innovation as a mechanism for exploiting the fruits of R&D investment. The mainstream of our economy and the United States position in crucial international markets require competitive success in high-volume established products. It is here that our scientific and engineering capability may have its greatest advantage. This would also seem to be the lesson from the Japanese experience. They have succeeded in applying technology to improve major products in established industries like automobiles, cameras, consumer electronics, and steel. Perhaps national R&D investments should seek their major benefits in existing major productive units. This concept is likely to be controversial, for it is contrary to other recommendations calling for more R&D investment to encourage innovation in new industries.[9]

For productive units that have evolved to a highly advanced, or Specific, state of development, advanced technology still fills an important role. Here innovation is more incremental in nature, however, and it is often stimulated by competitive pressure on prices and the need for greater efficiency and quality standardization in the product and manufacturing process. Changes in the environment, shortages of materials, and the threat of government regulation provide the greatest stimuli for major innovation in productive units at this stage of development. Stated another way, in this case government regulations or changes in the competitive environment that act to fragment mass markets and create niches for new products may encourage innovative product designs. Such disruptions are not achieved without attendant cost, however, and can be expected to cause dislocations and to raise costs as economies of scale are lost and the conditions supporting efficiency are disrupted.

The model predicts that productive units at different stages of development will respond to differing stimuli and undertake different types of innovation. This idea extends to the question of barriers to innovation and probable patterns of success and failure in innovation for units in different situations. For productive units in an early stage of development, factors that impede product standardization, or market aggregation, or lack of capital are barriers to innovation. Conversely, for those nearer the specific state, disruptive factors like uncertainty over government regulation or labor demands are the most important barriers to the normal direction of technological progress. At the same time, these same factors that reverse the normal direction of technological progress may evoke more radical innovation, although with attendant productivity consequences.

In sum, then, the effects of alternative government policies and management action will vary, depending on the productive unit's stage of development. Actions that encourage standardization or market aggregation may increase the rate of technological progress in one case, while actions that disrupt markets may be associated with another type of progress in other circumstances.

FINAL QUESTIONS

The ideas presented in this study outline a framework for evaluating the cluster of conditions that support technological change. The descriptive model will not represent every case or, perhaps, even most cases. Only future investigation will show which situations do or do not fit the model. It does fit some important cases, however, and by highlighting regularities that are important in these cases it can help to focus attention on exceptions in other situations. It may be more important to understand why a regular pattern of progress is not realized than to seek a universal explanation.

A model or framework of this type can be helpful if it can clarify consistencies or inconsistencies among policies in widely different areas that must be coordinated as a condition for progress. Answers to four different questions raised in chapter 1 help to illustrate the variety of issues that are encompassed by the model:

(1) Can a firm decide to increase the variety and diversity of a product line while it simultaneously realizes the highest possible levels of efficiency?

(2) Is a policy that envisions a high rate of product innovation consistent with one that seeks to reduce costs substantially through extensive backward integration?

(3) Is government policy action that would enforce a low level of market concentration in technologically active industries consistent with a policy that envisions a high rate of effective product innovation?

(4) Would a firm's action to restructure its work environment for employees so that tasks would be more challenging, require greater skill, be less repetitive, and embody greater content be compatible with a policy that proposed to eliminate undesirable direct labor tasks through extensive process automation?

"No" is the answer prompted by the model to each of these questions. On the basis of current hypotheses, each question suggests a pair of actions that are mutually inconsistent in respect to either forward or reverse transition.

The model clarifies the ramifications that follow from actions that accompany a regular pattern of technological development. It is not assumed that progression toward a more advanced state of development is always beneficial or inevitable. To the contrary, it may be argued that management can and should control both forward and reverse transition. If a typical path of transition can be described, then better judgments can be made about the advantages and disadvantages of reaching a new stage of development.

Neither extreme state, Fluid or Specific, would be attractive to the firm or to the economy as a whole. In the Fluid state, the future is uncertain, productivity is low, and any particular unit is apt to experience economic and personal failure for those involved. In the other extreme, Specific condition, continued transition may first be slowed and then halted in the economic stagnation or even death of a productive unit. This may take the form of a geographic migration of production to less-developed areas or countries, where the factor prices of production are low enough to support continued economic vitality. Or it may take the form of absorption and restructuring of product and process, as was the case with the demise of the gaslight companies at the turn of the century. Or it may be a case of attrition, as with the slow death of telegraph services, provided initially from a dominant position by Western Union, following its strategic decision in the early 1900s to limit its communication interests to nonvoice media.

A sustained policy of product innovation and of constantly reconceptualizing market needs and opportunities can provide the mechanism for avoiding these extremes. In planning such a policy, the present framework seeks to make the unfavorable as well as the favorable implications of continued technological advance more obvious.

TABLE 7.4. Events Highlighting Stages of Development of the Engine Plant

		Factor*	Stage* Change to
1905	Program to improve manufacturing process undertaken. Concept of progressive flow in process configuration placed in application.	C	2
1905–7	Horizontal and vertical integration into primary engine parts manufacture to round out manufacturing capacity—pressed parts, machining operations, etc.	G	2
1907	Systematic purchasing policies introduced to reduce cost of inputs and stimulate suppliers to develop new components (vanadium steel innovation, forward planning of requirements, and competitive bidding).	F	2
1908	Tasks largely deskilled, but division of labor not extensive.	D	2
1910	With move to Highland Park plant and large expansion in facilities:		
	Program initiated to support development of efficient special-purpose machine tools	E	2
	(by 1913)	E	3
	Started further backward integration (by 1915) into engine parts, foundry operations, forging, etc.	F	4
	Start of program to put broad-based (by 1915) manufacturing capability in place in one facility with a variety of relevant process technologies	G	3
1911–13	Most tasks redesigned to reduce division of labor; begin use of moving conveyors and progressive assembly in engines.	D	3
1913–14	By 1914, extensive use made of conveyors, gravity feeds, or moving assembly and other methods of line-flow management in process organization.	C	3
	Following settlement of Seldon patent suit (which struck down claim on broad concept of internal-combustion	A	4

TABLE 7.4. (Continued)

		Factor*	Stage* Change to
	auto), uncertainty over commitment to Model T design was reduced and market was pursued.	B	3
1914	Renewed emphasis placed on cost and price reductions through standardization in all components. By 1916 prices in some cars reduced by 41 percent over late 1913 prices, but functional and cost-reducing changes still being made.	A B	4 3
1917–18	Refinements continue but increasingly on incremental basis (for example, cooling-system improvements).	A	5
1920–24	Period of extreme standardization, very high volume, and little change (2 million cars a year produced, higher than any rate at Ford until 1950s).	A B	5 5
1920–24	Tightly balanced, near-continuous line-flow configuration in manufacturing and assembly; lathe beds cut short so they would fit in line.	C D	3½ 3
	Extensive backward integration into iron mining, blast furnace operation, etc.	F	5
1925–26	Competitive advances caused obsolescence in engine design and major loss of market share and volume (overheating of engine, vibration, manual starting, planetary transmission rather than shift, etc.). Attempts still made to continue policy of product standardization through cost reduction and minor change.	A B	3 4
1927–28	Complete shutdown and new crash start-up with experimental development of new Model A power train, new engine, transmission, carburetor, etc., but still on basis of prior 4-cylinder engine concept. Initial period of introduction and start-up (1927–28) marked by design improvement.	A B	3 3
	New components and materials used, replacing some sources (aluminum pistons).	F	4
	Most prior specialized machine tools scrapped.	E	2½
1929	New process equipment developed and purchased.	E	3
1930–31	With wide market acceptance of Model A, overtaking Chevrolet, policy of product standardization, allowing only minor change, resumed.	A B	4 4
	Further backward integration undertaken.	F	5
1932	Experimental development and introduction of V-8 engine; first low-cost, single-cylinder block-casting engine in industry; extensive disruption.	A	3
1932	Improvements continued to be introduced during mid-1930s.	B	3
	Much prior process equipment rendered obsolete by new design; new equipment developed.	E	2½
	New materials and components required.	F	4
1934–39	Refinements and improvements to engine continue to be made but basic design remains standard for twenty years (cast-iron crank and camshafts added and variation in CID made).	A B	4 4
1945–46	Major investments made in developing new process equipment; introduction of multiple-transfer machines begun.	E	4

TABLE 7.4. (Continued)

		Factor*	Stage* Change to
	Backward integration into materials—steel manufacturing, rolling mills, casting facilities, etc.	F	5
	Major disruption in materials sources due to World War II shutdown and postwar material and component scarcities.	F	2
	V-8 and IL6 engines are dominant types.	A	4
	Move toward new product division organization started, ultimately giving product divisions their own production facilities.	B	3
1947–48	Engine plant and engine foundry placed under management separate from other manufacturing units.	G	4
	Backward integration position reestablished.	F	5
1952–53	Cleveland engine plant placed in operation, representing major advance in extensive integration of process through introduction of transfer machines and automation, separation of engine and foundry capacity into separate, decentralized facilities managed as a separate plant, focused to a particular engine.	E	5
		G	5
		C	5
	Predominant characteristic of labor task changed to process overseeing and system maintenance.	D	5
1954–59	Horsepower war starting, causing increase in size of engine.	A	4
		B	4
1961–67	Decrease in frequency of model change and end of horsepower race causes greater standardization in engines.	B	4
		A	5
1968–70	Management of engine plant separated from that of foundries because management problems differ.	G	5
	Environmental controls increase rate of design change in engines.	B	4
1971–72	Small 4-cylinder engine introduced into line, and environmental requirements raise uncertainty about dominance of existing engine design.	A	4
		B	4

*The factor refers to the column heading and the stage refers to the row in Table 7.1.

TABLE 7.5. Events Highlighting Stages of Development of the Assembly Plant

		Factor	Stage Change to
1907	Systematic purchasing policies introduced.	F	2
1905–7	Horizontal and vertical integration into production of chassis parts, rounding out capacity.	G	2
1905–6	Move toward progressive manufacturing initiated with successful standard model—Model N.	C	2
		A	2
		B	2
1910	Backward integration into some material (foundry, wood, etc.) started with move to new Highland Park facility, some suppliers absorbed.	F	3

TABLE 7.5. (Continued)

		Factor	Stage Change to
1910–11	One dominant chassis design adopted (Model T), bodies still varied; 20 percent market-share increase.	A	2½
1910–18	Periodic incremental improvements introduced in chassis; bodies changed frequently.	B	2½
1912–14	Division of labor increased in assembly.	D	3
1914–15	Moving assembly-line innovation for final assembly.	C	3
	Assembly operations begin to be decentralized in regional assembly plants.	G	3
1918	Extensive decentralization of assembly into regional assembly plants achieved.	G	4
1920	Period of high standardization in chassis production begins. Bodies continue to vary.	A B	3½ 3½
1924–25	Chassis configuration made obsolete by market trend to closed body. Chassis changes and new closed body line tried experimentally, then adopted; 15 percent market-share loss.	A	2
1925–26	Change in body still frequent, but chassis standardized.	B	2½
1925	Body production incorporated in assembly plants; stationary body framing mixed with moving final assembly in same assembly plants.	C	2½
1925	Extensive backward integration into bodies and materials achieved (wood for frames, fabric weaving, glass manufacturing, body parts, etc.).	F	5
1926–28	Model T design rendered obsolete by market trend, market position lost to GM. Experimental development of new model undertaken (Model A) and introduced; 30 percent market-share loss.	A	2
1927–28	One-half of bodies purchased, many other prior chains of vertical integration rendered inappropriate as inputs to new model.	F	3
1929–31	With market success of Model A, prior policies of standardization resumed. Backward integration in bodies and other components reestablished.	A B F	4 4 4
1932–33	Model A rendered obsolete by market trends and entirely new model experimentally developed; new bodies' chassis and V-8 engine; 15 percent market-share loss.	A B	2 2
	Model change made some prior sources arrangements inappropriate.	F	3
1932	Introduction of some special-purpose process equipment begun.	E	1½
1933	Start of competitive annual-model-change era by Ford. Car bodies evolved rapidly through changes made during remaining years of decade. (Appendix 2).	A B	3 2
1936	Further backward integration achieved in steel and other materials and components.	F	4
1939–41	Successful streamlined body designs are in place (Appendix 2).	B	3
1941–46	Shut down during World War II; supply sources unreliable following war.	F	2
1945–57	Backlogged demand after World War II encourages product standardization; period of increasing market share.	A B	3½ 3

TABLE 7.5. (Continued)

		Factor	Stage Change to
1947	Normal sources and backward integration reestablished following World War II.	F	4
1950–60	Move toward organization and management of assembly capacity by type of product line (Ford-Mercury) rather than functionally by type of body. Returned to functional, centralized control after 1960s (Appendix 2).	G	3½
1955	Beginning of trend introducing special automated process equipment in assembly plants (welding presses, multiple nut runners, etc., integrated into line-flow process).	E	2½
		C	3
1958–60	Frequent model change—short-duration models (Mercury, Edsel changes); 2 percent market-share loss.	A	3
		B	2
1960	Successful, compact unit-construction car introduced. Rate of model change reduced.	A	3
		B	3
1965	Start of sharp trend toward specialization of assembly plant to particular car, for example, Mustang.	G	4
1967	Beginning of trend toward slowed model change, extensive use of common body/chassis designs spanning several market segments, and long-lived small-car models.	A	3½
		B	3½
1970	Integration of machines at some stations to form transfer lines.	E	4

TABLE 7.6. Labor Content Data for Engine Plants

Year	Labor Hours per Engine	Model		Data Sources*
1913	35	Model T		a
1914	23.1	Model T		a
1916	17.3	Model T		a
1917	16.5	Model T		a
1918	16.3	Model T		a
1922	14.3	Model T		a
1924	14.9	Model T		a
1926	16.0	Late Model T		b
1928	29.0	New Model A		b
1931	18.0	Late Model A	Extrapolated from direct	b
1932	19.5	Model B, IL-4	time study data, engine	b
1932	59	Model 18, V-8	assembly, wage rates, and	b
1938	19.5	V-8	accounting data, giving	b
1939	20	V-8	direct labor for chassis	b
1949	14.2	V-8 car and truck	components.	c&d
1950	15.1	V-8 car and truck		c&d
1953	9.0	V-8 car and truck		d
1966	8.5	V-8 truck (old plant)		d
1970	8	V-8 car and truck (high-volume plant)		d
1972	10	V-8 truck engine (low volume)		d

TABLE 7.6. (Continued)

Year	Labor Hours per Engine	Model	Data Sources*
1972	8.2 overall	For plant engine mix (9.4 large V-8, 6.7 hrs. IL-4)	e
1974	9.5	Large V-8 engines (low volume)	d

NOTES:

Data through 1939 include labor costs of manual transmission, which represents approximately 20 percent of the labor hours given above, based on 1924 records.

From 1953, labor content excludes direct foundry labor included in earlier statistics. It is estimated that this introduces no more than a 5 percent difference.

Data are approximations of direct and indirect labor hours. Pre-World War II data are based on accounting records; post-World War II figures are based on total employees per plant.

* DATA SOURCES:

a. Model T Cost Books, Ford Archives, Henry Ford Museum, Greenfield Village, Dearborn, Michigan.

b. Cost Studies Accession 250, Ford Archives.

c. Allan Nevins, and Frank Hill, *Ford: Decline and Rebirth* (New York: Charles Scribners, 1963), pp. 345–76.

d. Ford Motor Company, *Facts and Figures,* respective years. The necessary assumptions as to number of shifts covered in stated employment rates, from 1 to 3, were based on estimates of output rates for engines produced.

e. D. N. Williams, "NEP Evaluation Speeds Pinto Engine Naturalization," *Iron Age,* January 20, 1972, p. 27.

TABLE 7.7. Labor Content Data for Assembly Plants

	Assembly Plant Labor Hours/Car			
Year	Including Body Assembly and Finishing	With Preassembled and Painted Bodies	Vehicle Type and Plant Location	Data Sources
1914	73		Model T before moving assembly line (N.J. Branch)e	d
1916	38	17	With moving assembly line (Mass. and Tenn. Branch)e	a
1917		16	Open car (Mass. Branch)	a
1920	21	14	In plant finish, closed car versus finished open car (Mass. Branch)	a
1924 (Sept.)	47		New Tudor closed body, introducing standard assembly plant body (assembly and painting) (Ave. of Branches)	b
1926	34		Closed Tudor bodies, Late Model T (Ave.)	b
1926	33		Mix of bodies, Late Model T (N.J.)	d
1928	66		Closed Tudor body, New Model A (Ave.)	b

TABLE 7.7. (Continued)

Assembly Plant Labor Hours/Car

Year	Including Body Assembly and Finishing	With Preassembled and Painted Bodies	Vehicle Type and Plant Location	Data Sources
1929	29		Closed Tudor body, Model A (Ave.)	b
1931	26		Mix of bodies, Late Model A (N.J.)	d
1933	47		Mixed Ford bodies, New model —body, frame and engine (Ave.)	b
1934	37		Mixed Ford bodies V-8 (Ave.)	b
1935	38		Mixed Ford bodies V-8 (Ave.)	b
1936	27.8		Mixed Ford bodies V-8 (Ave.)	b
1937	28–29.5		Mixed Ford bodies, comparative data for 60-hp Delux Ford (Ave.)	b
1938	28		Mixed Ford bodies (Ave.)	b
1939	27.5–28.8		Mixed Ford bodies (Ave.)	b
1945	60		100 hp, Super Delux Tudor Sedan (Ave.)	b
1946	31		Average for four locations	b
1947	28.8		Data average for four locations	b
1951	33		Station wagon (Michigan)	d
1952	32		Station wagon (Michigan)	d
1956	34–37		Large Mercury car, San Jose assembly plant (proposal) (Calif.)	d
1966	28		Compact car, UBC 7 body (Michigan)	d & c
1970	26		Compact car, UBC 7 body (Michigan)	d & c
1972	27		Compact Car, UBC 7 body (Michigan)	d & c
1974	29		Compact car, new body introduction, UBC 10 (Michigan)	d & c

DATA SOURCES:

a. Accounting Data, Ford Archives.

b. Cost Study, Ford Archives.

c. *Ford Facts and Figures*, respective years.

d. Employment and Operating Rates Data, Ford Archives Assembly Plant Records.

e. Location of Assembly Plant N.J.: Edgewater, N.J.; Mass.: Cambridge or Somerville, Mass.; Michigan: Dearborn (Central Ford Facility); Illinois: Chicago; Tenn.: Memphis; Calif.: San Jose, Calif.; Ave: Average of several locations.

APPENDIXES

APPENDIX 1 / ABSTRACTS OF TWENTY CASE STUDIES

CASE 1 / THE CLOSED STEEL BODY

The closed steel body was the culmination of two trends: the rise in popularity of closed cars and the increasing use of steel in car bodies.

Until the 1920s, closed cars were handcrafted and expensive. In 1921, Hudson Essex used standardized, simpler parts and subassemblies to produce the first inexpensive closed car. Other manufacturers followed this example, and closed car production increased dramatically through the 1920s. However, these early, inexpensive closed cars, which used wood extensively, lacked durability and stylishness.

The all-steel car promised strength with less weight, greater styling possibilities, and mass-production economies. Because of the greater temperature tolerance of steel, paint could be "baked" on, thereby permitting a faster finishing process. However, several disadvantages of steel bodies prevented rapid adoption by the industry. Sheet steel had properties that made finishing difficult, steel bodies often caused annoying noise and vibration, and expensive new dies and presses would have been practical only for large-scale production, making numerous models and styling changes impractical.

Several manufacturing innovations in the 1920s removed these obstacles. Box annealing, normalizing, and loose rolling processes developed by the steel industry improved the quality of sheet steel. Automatic welding machines, improvements in sound-deadening materials, and the monopiece body, all developed by the Budd Manufacturing Company, led to quieter and stronger steel bodies. The increasing demand for closed cars made expensive equipment practical. The success of the Ford Model T taught manufacturers that the public would accept fewer style changes if costs were also reduced. Although Budd was the innovative leader during this period, other manufacturers such as Ford and Hayes Body Corporation also made contributions.

The first all-steel open car was produced by Budd in 1912 for Oakland and Hupmobile and in 1914 for Dodge on a large-scale production basis. In

William H. Rodgers, a research assistant at Harvard University, who was involved with this study when it started, did much of the research and writing in developing these twenty cases under my general supervision. He also assumed important responsibilities in directing the work of other Research assistants, including William Berger and Peter Francis, for those cases which he did not personally develop. His contributions added significantly to this study, and they are gratefully acknowledged.

183

1922, Dodge announced the first closed steel body. Pullman Packard, Ford, Essex, Chrysler, and Cadillac had followed by 1928. Until 1935, however, cars did not have steel roofs. GM's "turret top" on 1935 models had a one-piece steel roof supported by wooden rails, and the 1935 Studebaker used an all-steel roof made by Budd. By 1940, diffusion of the closed steel body was widespread.

The rise of the closed steel body contributed to the decline of small manufacturers, who could not afford investments in expensive equipment. In 1928, fifteen makes of cars had annual unit sales of less than twenty-five thousand. At the beginning of World War II, there was only one: Cadillac. The high cost of body-making equipment also centered mass production on a few different models, with an annual style change, a pattern that has continued to the present.

CHRONOLOGY OF EVENTS

1905	Appearance of first closed automobiles.
1912	Budd Manufacturing Company designs an all-steel open body for use on the Hupmobile.
1914	The first successful all-steel open body is developed and patented by Budd Manufacturing Company. Dodge adopts the body and begins quantity production.
1915	Closed bodies of wood and steel composite construction begin to appear.
1910–20	The steel industry introduces several improved processes, including box annealing.
1921	Hudson's Essex introduces an inexpensive closed model constructed of wood and steel.
1922	Dodge builds the first all-steel closed body for its 1923 model car.
1925	Automatic resistance welding is introduced into automotive industry. Ford introduces all-steel closed bodies for the Model T.
1926	Essex and Jordan switch to all-steel closed bodies.
1934	GM introduces the turret top as the first all-steel outer shell top.
1935	Studebaker uses Budd-built monopiece all-steel roof with no wooden inner supports.

REFERENCES

"All-Steel Body." *Motor*, January 15, 1958, p. 935.

"All-Steel Business Sedan Being Produced by Dodge." *Automotive Industries*, September 14, 1922, p. 539.

"Bodies of Steel." *Motor*, January 1926, p. 96.

"Body by Briggs." *Special Interest Autos*, November–December 1973, p. 24.

"Chicago Salon Shows Present Trends in Body Designs." *Automotive Industries*, February 7, 1924, p. 274.

Denham, Athel F. "All Metal Construction Almost Attained in Building Austin Bantam Bodies." *Automotive Industries*, September 27, 1930, p. 452.

"Fisher Announces the Turret Top." *Automotive Industries*, December 15, 1934, p. 289.

"G.M. Describes Rise of the Closed Car." *Automotive Industries*, December 11, 1924, p. 1025.

"Growing Demand for Low-Priced Closed Car." *Automotive Industries*, November 24, 1921, p. 1001.

"Half-hour History of Unit Bodies." *Special Interest Autos*, August–October 1973, p. 26.

Hersey, Irwin. "Stepping Stones to Modern Styling." *Motor*, November 1953, p. 290.

Hogan, William T. *Economic History of the Iron and Steel Industry in the United States*. Vol. 2. Lexington, Mass.: D. C. Heath and Co., 1971.

Huntington, Roger. "Engineering Evolution: Development of Automotive Styling." Parts II and III, *Car Life*, August 1964, p. 38, and September 1964, p. 38.

Lane, Charles. "Body Design." *Automobile Engineer*, February 1945, p. 60.

Meadowcroft, Joseph W. "All-Steel Automobile Body as a Manufacturing Problem." *American Machinist*, January 5, 1928, p. 9.

Mercer, George M. "Closed Bodies for Low-Priced Quantity Output." *Automotive Industries*, July 8, 1920, p. 56.

———. "Four Passenger Town Car Design." *Automotive Industries*, November 29, 1917, p. 950.

Nevins, Allan, and Hill, Frank. *Ford: Expansion and Challenge: 1915–1933*. New York: Charles Scribners, 1957.

Schipper, J. Edward. "Closed Body Production Costs Minimized in Essex Coach." *Automotive Industries*, November 17, 1921, p. 956.

———. "Improved But Cheaper Closed Bodies Are Predicted." *Automotive Industries*, July 20, 1922, p. 127.

Stillman, K. W. "All-Steel Bodies Now Possible with Moderate Production." *Automotive Industries*, November 5, 1925, p. 778.

Tarbox, John P. "Chronological Commentary of Budd Patents." Philadelphia: The Budd Company, 1948.

Thum, E. E. "Many Advantages Realized in Body of 5-Piece All-Steel Design." *Automotive Industries*, September 15, 1928, p. 370.

"Wagon Market." *Car Life*, August 1964, p. 48.

"Welding All-Steel Automobile Bodies." *American Machinist*, November 12, 1925, p. 773.

CASE 2 / WELDING IN BODY AND CHASSIS ASSEMBLY

The welding innovations of the 1920s were closely connected to the rise of the closed steel body. Competition and the need for mass production spurred a search for assembly techniques that were fast, economical, and reliable. Automatic welding satisfied all of these requirements. It produced strong and neat joints with greater speed and uniformity than previous assembly methods. The assembly consumed less material, and the resulting body was lighter.

Welding had been used in other industries in the early 1900s, and as early as 1914 Budd Manufacturing Company had used welding in automobile body assembly. At that time, welding was a time-consuming, expensive manual process; manual welds could not be made uniformly, so grinding and filing added to expenses. The occasional failure of welds, the unavailability of proper alloys for welding, and the nonuniformity of sheet steel also prevented the widespread use of welding. The alternatives, however, had disadvantages. Rivets were not uniform in size, and riveted joints became shaky under prolonged stress. Nuts and bolts left unsightly projections that had to be covered. Both riveting and bolting were slow processes and therefore expensive.

As more steel bodies were produced in the 1920s, the quality of sheet steel improved. Automatic machines were developed to overcome many of the disadvantages of welding. In 1923, the Thomson Electric Welding Company introduced an automatic spot-welding machine. In 1924 they made an automatic welder that produced six hundred automobile rims per hour. Taylor-Hall Welding Company developed a process for welding cast-iron valve heads to steel stems in 1925. Beginning with Budd in 1925, automatic welding equipment was designed and used in body assembly. In 1928, Ford used welding extensively on the Model A. Almost all of the five thousand welding operations on major assemblies at Ford's River Rouge plant were machine-assisted, and many of the machines and processes were developed by Ford.

Automatic welding reduced the cost of assembly and improved the quality of the product. A welding machine designed by Ford, for example, produced fifty to sixty uniform rear-axle housings per hour with one operator. Using earlier techniques, three men could produce only twenty-five to thirty non-uniform housings per hour.

Other manufacturers in the United States and Europe quickly adopted automatic welding techniques for subassemblies and for final assembly work. By 1931, all-steel auto bodies were almost universally fabricated by welding.

CHRONOLOGY OF EVENTS

1877	Resistance welding invented by Dr. Elihu Thomson.
1880	Arc-welding process developed.
1900	Oxyacetylene welding introduced in France.
1912	Budd Manufacturing Company uses electric-spot welding on its all-steel car.
1914	Budd Manufacturing Company extends use of electric-spot, oxyacetylene, and arc welding; however, it is all manual.
1914–25	Use of welding increases in auto industry, but it is manual. Most construction is still done with rivets and bolts.
1923	Thomson Electric Welding Company introduces an automatic spot-welding machine.
1924–25	Various welding companies automate their welding machines.
1925	General advent of closed steel body automobile on mass-production basis (see Closed Steel Body case chronology for more detail on integrating the two innovations).
1925	Budd begins development of automatic welding equipment for production of its closed steel bodies.
1928	Ford makes extensive use of automatic electric welding at River Rouge, often designing their own welding machines.
1928	Chrysler, Dodge, and Fisher Body are using automatic welding extensively.
1928	Ford final assembly is still a "nuts and bolts" operation.
1931	All-steel auto bodies are almost universally fabricated by welding.
1935	Ford assembly plants are using oxyacetylene welding extensively.

REFERENCES

"Acetylene Welding in Automobile Body Production." *Automotive Industries*, November 24, 1928, p. 754.

"An Automatic Spot Welder." *Automotive Industries*, November 13, 1924, p. 858.

"Arc-Welding Sheet-Metal Parts." *American Machinist*, March 20, 1924, p. 426.

"Automobile and Aircraft Production Get Attention from Welders." *Automotive Industries*, October 1, 1927, p. 518.

Barclay, Hartley W. *Ford Production Methods*. New York: Harper and Brothers, 1936.

Calvin, Fred H. "Sheet Metal Work for Automobiles." *American Machinist*, December 23, 1920, p. 1165.

Chase, Herbert. "Cast Iron Valve Heads Can Be Welded to Steel Stems at Rate of 400 Per Hour." *Automotive Industries*, March 19, 1925, p. 533.

Eksergian, C. L. "Welding Automobile Wheels." *American Machinist*, September 17, 1931, p. 459.

Faurote, Fay Leone. "Equipment Makes Possible the Ford Model A." *American Machinist*, May 17, 1928, p. 805; July 5, 1928, p. 15; and August 16, 1928, p. 269.
———. "Welding Ford Rear Axles." *Iron Age*, June 21, 1928, p. 1739.
"Five Machines Devised to Meet Various Needs of Car and Parts Manufacturers." *Automotive Industries*, November 13, 1924, p. 858.
Heldt, P. M. "Electric Welding Becomes Important Production Aid." *Automotive Industries*, November 17, 1928, p. 709.
"Intricate Welding Operations Vital Parts of Ford Production." *Automotive Industries*, July 21, 1928, p. 86.
Lane, Charles. "Body Design." *Automobile Engineer*, February 1945, p. 60.
"Many Automotive Production Problems Solved by Welding Process." *Automotive Industries*, September 24, 1925, p. 507.
Meadowcroft, Joseph. "Mass Production Welding Operations." *Iron Age*, November 8, 1928, p. 1154.
———. "Welded Automobile Bodies and the Oxyacetylene Torch." *American Machinist*, March 27, 1930, p. 521.
———. "Welding All-Steel Automobile Bodies." *American Machinist*, November 12, 1925, p. 773.
Schipper, J. Edward. "Special Body Welding Methods Cut Labor Costs to a Minimum." *Automotive Industries*, April 9, 1925, p. 652.
"Welding." *Encyclopedia Britannica*, 23:491.
"Welding: A Feature of Ford Production." *American Machinist*, October 2, 1930, p. 537.
"Welding Effects Economies of Construction of Jigs." *Automotive Industries*, October 17, 1931, p. 591.

CASE 3 / THE ALUMINUM ALLOY PISTON

The development and diffusion of aluminum alloy pistons has extended over a sixty-year period, from the earliest automobiles to the present. This innovation illustrates the effects that small changes in design, manufacturing methods, or material costs can have on the acceptance of an innovation.

The piston of a reciprocating engine performs two basic functions. It converts heat energy from burning fuel into mechanical energy and provides a path for excess heat to escape the combustion chamber. To perform these functions, the piston should be light in weight, gas-tight, fit the cylinder within close tolerances, and conduct heat without becoming so hot that it preignites fuel in the cylinder.

Aluminum alloys offer two major advantages over cast iron or steel as material for pistons. Aluminum is much lighter and therefore reduces inertia as the piston continually reverses direction. It also conducts heat more effectively than cast iron; unlike most metals, aluminum conducts more heat as it becomes hotter. Both of these advantages become more important at higher engine speeds, when temperatures and inertia problems increase.

The major disadvantage of aluminum is its rate of thermal expansion, which is 50 percent higher than cast iron over engine temperature ranges. This makes it difficult to maintain close tolerances when an aluminum piston is used in a cast-iron cylinder.

Aluminum pistons had been used by 1900 both in the United States and in France, and the first airplane, flown by the Wright brothers in 1903, used an aluminum engine. Much of the early development of aluminum pistons was by the aviation industry, where saving weight was critical. The development of stronger aluminum alloys after 1910, better control of casting operations in aluminum foundries, and the continuing emphasis on speed and acceleration in automobiles also stimulated the development of aluminum pistons between 1910 and 1920. The earliest American cars to use aluminum pistons, Duesenberg and Stutz, were successful racing cars.

Design improvements, such as reinforcing ribs, split skirts, and strut pistons, reduced the problems of thermal expansion and made aluminum pistons more reliable. In the 1920s aluminum pistons rose to over half of unit car production. Even at this time, however, other materials seemed promising. Cast-iron, cast-steel, and tin-plated pistons were experimented with and seemed to have some advantages over aluminum. After World War II, all automakers began shifting to aluminum pistons. When Pontiac switched to aluminum in 1955, the diffusion was complete. All of the pistons at this time were cast aluminum. The 1963 Corvette was the first car to use impact-forged aluminum pistons, which were lighter and stronger than cast aluminum. This innovation has since been adopted for other high-performance engines.

CHRONOLOGY OF EVENTS

1807   Davey (Britain) establishes existence of aluminum, but is unsuccessful in producing it.

1825   Oersted (Denmark) produces small pellet of aluminum by chemical process.

1845   Wöhler (Germany) makes enough aluminum by modification to Oersted's chemical process to determine aluminum's low density and other important properties.

1854   Sainte-Claire Deville (France) reduces aluminum chloride with sodium and lays the foundation of the aluminum industry.

1856   Sainte-Claire Deville and others start aluminum works at Glaciere, France.

1886   Hall (U.S.) and Héroult (France) invent the first commercially successful electrolytic reduction process and found the modern aluminum industry.

1888   Pittsburgh Reduction Company (now Alcoa) founded to produce aluminum by the electrolytic reduction process. Other companies using this process founded in Switzerland and France.

1895   Engine of aluminum, with the exception of the cylinder, is produced by the Haynes-Apperson Company, Indiana.

1900   Use of aluminum pistons by Clerget (France).

1903   Use of aluminum pistons in the Wright brothers' first airplane.

1908   First manufacture of production aluminum alloy pistons for automobiles by Corbin and Cie in France.

1911   First U.S.manufacture of production aluminum alloy pistons for automobiles by the Levett Company.

1915   Stutz racing car with aluminum alloy pistons is first in the United States to average over 100 mph in a major racing event.

1922   Several popular American makes using aluminum alloy pistons.

1928   Ford Model A begins to use aluminum alloy pistons.

1930   Diffusion of aluminum alloy pistons in the United States at 61 percent of car production.

1936   Cadillac, Buick, and Oldsmobile on the GM line switch to aluminum alloy pistons.

1954   Pontiac switches completely to aluminum alloy pistons, making diffusion in American automobiles complete.

REFERENCES

Aluminum Panorama. Montreal: Aluminum, Ltd., 1953.

Carr, Charles C. *Alcoa: An American Enterprise.* New York: Rinehart and Co., 1952.

Claydon, A. Ludlow. "America's First Engineering Triumph." *The Automobile*, October 14, 1915, p. 697.

DeFleury, M. R. "Classification des doctrines constructives et des allaiges en matiere de pistons en metaux legers et ultra legers." *Journal de la Société des Ingenieurs de l'Automobile*, December 1932, p. 1980.

Denham, Athel F. "Chevrolet for 1928." *Automotive Industries*, December 31, 1927, p. 965.

Edwards, J. D. *The Aluminum Industry: Aluminum Products and Their Fabrication.* New York: McGraw-Hill, 1930.

Geschelin, Joseph. "Forged Aluminum Pistons." *Automotive Industries*, June 1, 1966, p. 67.

"Haynes and Apperson at Work on a New Model." *Horseless Age*, July 1896, p. 10.

Jehle, Ferdinand. "The Use of Aluminum in the Present and the Future Motor Car." *Journal of the Society of Automotive Engineers*, June 1920, p. 367.

Jones, M. Glyn. "Aluminum in the Automobile." *Motor Industry*, November 1962, p. 62.

Leopold, Joseph. "Early Days of Aluminum Pistons." *The Automobile*, October 7, 1915, p. 650.

Levett, Walker M. "Predicts Adoption of Aluminum Pistons as Standard by Majority of Cars." *The Automobile*, September 2, 1915, p. 421.

"Many Automobiles Now Have Tin-Plated Cast-Iron Pistons." *Iron Age*, May 12, 1932, p. 1063.

"1926 Models: What's New in Design?" *Automotive Industries*, December 31, 1925.

Schipper, J. Edward. "Aluminum—A Feather Weight." *The Automobile*, March 26, 1914, p. 673.

―――. "Aluminum Piston Development." *Automotive Industries*, June 13, 1918, p. 1139.

―――. "The Status of Aluminum in the Automobile Engine." *Automotive Industries*, September 2, 1920, p. 468.

"Specifications." *Automotive Industries*, February issues, various years.

CASE 4 / CEMENTED CARBIDE CUTTING TOOLS

Cemented carbide cutting tools were introduced in the United States in 1928, at a time when the automobile industry was rapidly expanding. Substantial performance advantages, such as extended tool life, faster cutting speeds, and greater precision, made the tools economical for mass-production systems. By 1930, such tools were widely used throughout the automobile industry. Through 1935, continued improvements in materials and in tool design contributed to wider acceptance.

Tungsten carbide (TC) was first produced in Europe in 1898, but was a brittle material whose commercial value was doubtful. During and after World War I, the Osram Lamp Works in Germany developed cemented tungsten carbide, in which tungsten carbide powder was cemented by cobalt. The first commercially available TC was "WIDIA," produced by the Krupp Steel Works in Germany in 1926. By 1928, Krupp had licensed American manufacturers, including General Electric, Firth-Sterling Steel Company, and Thomas Prosser and Son. American research, especially by General Electric, was responsible for much of the commercial development of the material.

The primary advantage of TC was its hardness—2100–2500 on the Brinell scale compared to 850 for high-speed steel, the traditional cutting-tool material. High-speed steel also required special heat treatment to develop hardness, but TC was hard after it was cemented and could be reheated and cooled rapidly or slowly without losing hardness. The greatest disadvantages of TC were its lack of strength and its high cost. The cost of TC, $450 per pound in 1929, could often be recouped through cost savings in machining processes. Costs were reduced further in 1929, when a GM subsidiary began "tipping" tools, attaching a cutting edge of TC to a steel tool. The weakness of TC prevented it from making heavy steel cuts, where it would break under the high pressures and slow speeds. Many machines were redesigned to be more rigid because comparatively weak TC tools would break from excess vibration. Grinding wheels were also redesigned with harder grinding surfaces, such as silicon carbide carborundum.

Even before these problems were solved, TC produced remarkable results. A high-speed steel drill had produced about 155 holes per cycle; a TC drill increased this to 10,700 holes. An aluminum-silicon alloy, previously considered unmachinable, was machined with TC to produce pistons. TC produced a smoother cut than high-speed steel and permitted greater precision in machining.

By 1930, the use of TC was well established in the automobile industry. Continued research, led by GM, developed different grades of TC suited for different purposes and developed other materials such as tantalum and titanium carbide. By 1935, all major carbide manufacturers furnished a wide line of carbide products, each adapted to a specific use and market. In the automobile industry, emphasis shifted from a few uses that produced great economies to a wide variety of more ordinary applications. Cemented carbide cutting tools continue to be widely used today.

CHRONOLOGY OF EVENTS

1898   Moisson produced carbide of tungsten having unusual properties of hardness.

1904   Just and Hanaman of Budapest invent the tungsten carbide lamp filament.

1914   Patents for tungsten carbide issued to Voigtlander and Lohmann of Germany.

1914–26   Karl Schroeter of Germany begins research on uses of tungsten carbide as a diamond substitute.

1926   Krupp Steel Works, under license from Osram Lamp Works, introduces WIDIA, a commercial cemented tungsten carbide.

1928   Cemented tungsten carbide marketed in United States by Krupp and various licensees of Krupp.

1928   GM uses tungsten carbide cutting tools.

1929   Major industries, including automobile industry, adopt tungsten carbide cutting tools. Diffusion rapid and complete sometime in period 1929–30.

1929   GM's Brown-Lipe-Chapin Company begins tipping cutting tools with carbide tips, using copper brazing technique.

1931   GM and others experiment with various alloys of tungsten carbide in efforts to improve properties.

1931   Tantalum carbide introduced.

1935   Titanium carbide in use under German patent.

REFERENCES

"Appraisal of Carbide Tools." *Iron Age*, November 21, 1929, p. 1367.

Barclay, Hartley W. *Ford Production Methods.* New York: Harper and Brothers, 1936.

"Cutting Alloys Affect Tool Design." *Iron Trade Review*, December 6, 1928, p. 1442.

Eddy, Paul W., Jr., and Long, Henry J. "Production Results with Tungsten and Carbide Tools." *American Machinist*, June 6, 1929, p. 901.

"Firth-Sterling Acquires U.S. Rights to Produce 'Cutanit,'" *Iron Age*, July 13, 1939, p. 119.

Gerken, T. H. "Tantalum Binder Improves Quality of Hard Cutting Tool Alloy." *Iron Age*, March 10, 1932, p. 600.

Geschelin, Joseph. "Cutting Materials." *Automotive Industries*, December 18, 1937, p. 866.

———. "Uses of Cemented Tungsten Carbide Extend Beyond Expectations." *Automotive Industries*, February 15, 1930, p. 227.

Hoyt, Samuel L. "Carboloy and Tungsten—Carbide Tools." *American Machinist*, January 10, 1929, p. 48.

———. "Tungsten Carbide—New Cutting Tool Material—Scratches Sapphire." *Iron Trade Review*, October 11, 1928, p. 912.

"Kennametal—A New Cutting Alloy." *Iron Age*, September 7, 1939, p. 45.

"Krupp Works Develops New Low-Priced High-Speed Steel." *Iron Age*, March 17, 1927, p. 798.

"Machine Tool Construction Reflects Rapid Development in Employment of Cemented Tungsten Carbide." *Automotive Industries*, October 12, 1929, p. 553.

McCoy, W. H. "Regulation of Particle Size Promises Added Strength." *Steel*, October 16, 1930, p. 48.

"Mechanical Engineers at Rochester." *Iron Age*, May 23, 1929, p. 1418.

Prosser, Roger D. "Development and Application of WIDIA." *American Machinist*, April 11, 1929, p. 588.

———. "Variety of Grades Opens New Fields for Cemented Carbides." *Automotive Industries*, October 29, 1932, p. 552.

Schroeter, Karl. "Inception and Development of Hard Metal Carbides." *Iron Age*, February 1, 1934, p. 27.

"Status of Tungsten Carbide as a Cutting Material." *Iron Age*, May 16, 1929, p. 1349.

Wells, J. P. "Modern Machine Cutting Tool Requirements." Paper presented before the Society of Automotive Engineers, April 22, 1936.

Wells, John E. "The Use of Tungsten Carbide Tools Results in Holding More Uniform Limits on Machined Parts." *Automotive Industries*, October 17, 1931, p. 574.

CASE 5 / INDEPENDENT FRONT SUSPENSION

Independent front suspension (IFS) began to appear on mass-produced U.S. cars in 1933 and was adopted quickly by most manufacturers. IFS was probably the most important product innovation of the 1930s. It came at a time when American auto production was substantially depressed, and it may have been an effort to generate consumer interest and stimulate car sales. The rapidity with which manufacturers adopted suspension innovations suggests that competitive pressures were an important stimulus for change.

IFS is the elimination of a common axle connecting the two front wheels, substituting half-axles or other connecting devices. Using this suspension, movement of one wheel causes no direct movement of the other wheel; handling, riding comfort, and safety are improved.

Many aspects of IFS had been developed and used before World War I. The delay in developing IFS can be traced to several factors. A series of innovations in the 1920s aggravated suspension problems. Low-pressure tires, front wheel brakes, shock absorbers, and soft springs contributed to the problems of "tramp" and "shimmy," the oscillation of the front axle and the wobbling of the front wheels. Increasing horsepower and speed made such problems more dangerous. IFS was not the only possible solution, however. Chrysler, for example, improved riding and handling (and created more passenger space) by moving the engine eighteen inches forward. Other companies reinforced frames and changed steering linkages. The adoption of IFS required a substantial capital investment. Large numbers of machine tools had to be purchased, and parts had to be produced within close tolerances. At a time when car sales were low, this investment was risky. The ultimate success of IFS indicates the change in the automobile industry from providing basic transportation to making driving easier, safer, and more comfortable.

The first modern IFS was introduced by Mercedes in 1931. By 1932, thirty-five European models used IFS, independent rear suspension, or both. In the United States, GM began developing IFS in late 1930. Development centered on two designs, one similar to the Mercedes system and another developed by a French inventor, Dubonnet, in 1927. Beginning in 1934, Buick, Oldsmobile, and Cadillac used the first design. Chevrolet and Pontiac used the Dubonnet system because there were not enough machines available in the United States to produce parts for the Mercedes-type design. The Dubonnet system proved inadequate, but it was not until 1939 that Chevrolet switched. Some Chrysler cars used IFS in 1934, but then dropped it until 1939, moving the engine forward instead. Smaller manufacturers quickly adopted IFS systems similar to GM's. Apparently because of Henry Ford's opposition, Ford did not have IFS until 1949.

Other suspension improvements have been developed since; torsion bars, air suspension, and the replacement of king pins with ball joints have met with varying degrees of acceptance. Independent rear suspension has been widely used on European cars, but only the Corvette has used it in the United States. Apparently, wide, smoother roads and different driving habits have made independent rear suspension only marginally attractive for American drivers.

CHRONOLOGY OF EVENTS

United States	Europe	
	1878	Amedee Bollé (Fr.). Steam car. Transverse-leaf spring IFS.
	1909	Morgan (Br.). Pillar IFS.
1920 Pavanti Motors transverse-leaf spring IFS. Only a few cars produced.	1922	Lancia Lambda (It.). First production car with IFS.
	1930	Mercedes Benz (Ger.). 1931 6-cyl. model with transverse-leaf IFS.
1933 General Motors A-bracket-type IFS. Used first on 1934 Buick. Other U.S. makers introduce IFS subsequently.	1932	Thirty-one European makes using IFS.
	1932	Mercedes Benz 1933 model has A-bracket IFS—precurser to modern-day IFS.
	1939	Volkswagen (Ger.). Large-volume production car using torsion bar IFS.
1949 Ford is last major U.S. automaker to introduce IFS.	1950	Introduction of McPherson strut on English Fords.

United States
1955 Packard is first U.S. production car to use torsion bar IFS. Followed later by Chrysler and others.
1958 U.S. car makers introduce air suspension.

Europe
1956 Air suspension on Citroen (Fr.).

REFERENCES

"Baker Front Suspension System Requires Few Changes in Conventional Car Design." *Automotive Industries*, December 23, 1933, p. 764.

"British and Continental Car Specifications." *Automotive Industries*, February 23, 1935, p. 289.

Denham, Athel F. "Hudson-Terraplane 1935 Models." *Automotive Industries*, December 15, 1934.

———. "1934 Hudson 8 and Terraplane 6 Models." *Automotive Industries*, January 6, 1934, p. 18.

Fahnestock, Murray. "Evolution of Spring Suspensions." *Automobile Topics*, December 1952, p. 19.

"Features of 1940 Nash Lines." *Automotive Industries*, September 15, 1939, p. 254.

Geschelin, Joseph. "How Chrysler Makes Coil Springs." *Automotive Industries*, March 31, 1934, p. 394.

Heldt, P. M. "Thirty-five Cars Use Independent Springing as Suspension Design Sweeps Europe." *Automotive Industries*, July 30, 1932.

———. "What, No Springs?" *Automotive Industries*, August 6, 1932, p. 164.

Huntington, Roger. "Suspension Systems." *Car Life*, October 1964, p. 77.

"Lafayette in New Price Field with $595 Model." *Automotive Industries*, April 21, 1934, p. 498.

Lanchester, G. H. "Evaluation of the Car Chassis." *Automobile Engineer*, June 1960, p. 225.

Ludvigsen, Karl. "End of the Swing Axle." *Motor Trend*, January 1969, p. 71.

"1935 Dodge Has Semi-Elliptic Front Springs." *Automotive Industries*, December 22, 1934, p. 764.

Norbye, Jan. P. "Independent Front Suspensions." *Special Interest Autos*, November–December 1973, p. 40.

———. "Short History of Air Suspension." *Special Interest Autos*, June–July 1973, p. 54.

Sloan, Alfred P. *My Years with General Motors*. New York: MacFadden, 1963.

Wakefield, Ron. "Suspension and Handling." *Road and Track*, post 1968 issue, p. 5.

CASE 6 / UNIT BODY CONSTRUCTION

Unit body construction is an automobile design feature and a method of manufacture in which a single structure, built on one assembly line, serves as both body and chassis of the car. Conventional design and assembly uses two structures, the chassis and the body, built on separate assembly lines. Two basic designs have been used on unit bodies. In the "monocoque" or stressed-skin design, the outer skin bears most of the stress. In the space-frame design, a stress-bearing framework is covered by nonstructural sheet metal. Most unit body construction today uses the space-frame design.

The most important advantage of unit body construction is its greater rigidity-to-weight ratio. The design allows a strong body with a larger seating capacity for a given weight than the conventional body-on-chassis assembly.

Unit body construction also had disadvantages, both in performance and manufacturing. The design cannot insulate the body from resonant vibrations, which cause body "drumming." It is inherently noisier than chassis designs. A switch to unit body construction requires a considerable commitment of manufacturing resources and would be expensive to reverse. Unit body assembly lines are longer because frames are much shorter than bodies and can be spaced closer together on the line. Significant styling changes are more expensive than on frame construction, in which body design can be changed without affecting chassis design.

Unit body designs were used on some horse-drawn carriages and on some of the earliest automobiles, but were not widely used until the 1930s. The rise of the closed steel body and related advances in metal stamping and welding made unit bodies more feasible and desirable. Joseph Ledwinka, an engineer for Budd Company, was instrumental in the development of the closed steel body and later designed and patented unit body designs. The first mass-produced unit body passenger car was the 1934 French Citroen, which used Budd patents. Hupp and GM were investigating unit body construction at this time, though neither produced such a car in the United States. Other American companies, such as Essex, Chrysler, and DeSoto, developed bodies that carried much of the stress but retained a separately assembled frame. The 1936 Lincoln Zephyr, designed by Ford and Briggs Manufacturing Company, was the first American chassisless car.

Over the next twenty years, several small manufacturers experimented with the design. In the late 1950s, the Big Three introduced unit body designs. By 1961, over 45 percent of production used the design, but Ford and GM gradually switched back to body-on-chassis construction. The chief reason for the switch seems to be the greater flexibility of body-on-chassis design, both in producing different models on the same assembly line and in reducing the cost of change from one year to another.

CHRONOLOGY OF EVENTS

United States

1912 Budd sells steel bodies to Oakland and later to Dodge (not unit body).

1928 First Ludwinka (Budd) patent for steel frame and body assembled as one unit.

1932 Hudson "Essex Terraplane" with some unit body features.

1933 Chrysler "Airflow" cars have some unit body features.

1935 Lincoln "Zephyr" is first fully unitized U.S. production car.

1940 Nash "600" with unitized body introduced for the 1941 model year.

Europe

1903 Vauxhall (Br.) two-seater with stressed skin.

1913 Lagonda (Br.) stressed-skin design.

1921 Lancia (It.) space frame.

1933 Citroen (Fr.) 1934 model is first mass-produced unit-bodied passenger car.

1937 GM's Vauxhall Ten (Br.) and Opel Olympia (Ger.) using unit body construction.

1940s and 1950s Many European cars adopt unit body construction.

United States   *Europe*

1948 Hudson "Monobilt" with unit body construction.

1960 High point of unit body construction in the United States—over 40 percent of production. All American Motors cars, all Chrysler cars except the Imperial, and some GM and Ford use unit body construction.

REFERENCES

"Body by Briggs." *Special Interest Autos*, November–December 1973, p. 26.

Bourdon, M. W. "Unit Body and Chassis Construction Features British Lagonda." *Automotive Industries*, July 12, 1923, p. 62.

Huntington, Roger. "Monocoque." *Car Life*, February 1965, p. 27.

Lanchester, G. H. "Evolution of the Car Chassis." *Automobile Engineer*, June 1960, p. 226.

McLintock, J. Dewar. "Considerations of Unitary, Semi-Unitary and Separate Body Construction." Automotive Body Engineering, July 1965, p. 6.

Nagler, L. H. "American Motors' Unitized Body Design: The First Quarter Century." Paper presented to the Society of Automotive Engineers meeting, April 13, 1965.

Norbye, Jan. "Half-hour History of Unit Bodies." *Special Interest Autos*, August–October 1973, p. 24.

"Pioneer without Profit; Edward G. Budd Built the First All-Steel Auto Bodies." *Fortune*, February 1937, p. 82.

"Safety Trends in Body Design." *Automotive Industries*, June 13, 1963, p. 848.

Shank, J. W., and Kushler, R. H. "Chrysler Unit Construction Story." *SAE Journal*, January 1960, p. 1.

"Why G.M. Dropped Unit Bodies." *Commercial Car Journal*, October 1963, p. 17.

CASE 7 / THE AUTOMATIC CHOKE

The function of the choke is to regulate the mixture of air and fuel that is carried to the cylinders of the engine. In order to provide maximum efficiency, the air-fuel ratio must be changed as the engine is started, as it warms up, and as engine speed increases.

A manually operated choke was inherently less convenient than an automatic choke, and the driver had to know why, when, and how to effectively operate it. Improper operation could result in carboned valves, piston rings, and spark plugs and poor engine performance.

The adoption of the down-draft carburetor in the early 1930s provided a major impetus for switching to automatic chokes. With an up-draft carburetor, located underneath the engine, excess fuel resulting from improper choking could drain to the ground. With the down-draft carburetor, above the engine, excess fuel collected in the manifold. Distribution of fuel to the cylinders was uneven when the car was on a grade, and heat from the cylinders caused excess fuel to evaporate and smoke. The down-draft carburetor was made possible by the mechanical fuel pump, introduced by A.C. in 1926. The down-draft carburetor increased air and fuel flow to the engine, thereby increasing its power.

The first automatic choke was introduced by the Pierce Governor Company in 1928. It used two controls: an electrical control activated by pressing the starter pedal and a thermostatic control that changed choking action as the engine warmed up. In 1931, Stromberg introduced an automatic choke with thermostatic and vacuum controls. This choke was first used on the 1932 Oldsmobile and was adopted rapidly on other models. Automatic chokes were common on 1934 cars, especially in medium- and high-priced models. Since then, manual chokes have gradually disappeared. By 1953, Ford was the only major automaker using manual chokes. Although manual chokes have re-appeared since then on some inexpensive cars, the automatic is now used on all American cars.

CHRONOLOGY OF EVENTS

1926 AC introduces mechanical fuel pump.
1928 Pierce Governor Company introduces Sisson-type automatic choke.
1929 Stromberg down-draft carburetor used on 1930 model Chryslers.
1931 Stromberg automatic choke used on 1932 model Oldsmobile.

REFERENCES

Crouse, William H. *Automotive Mechanics.* New York: McGraw-Hill, 1970.

Denham, Athel F. "Chrysler Models for 1930." *Automobile Industries*, August 10, 1929, p. 183.

Heldt, P. M. "Car Makers Mobilize for 1933 Drive." *Automotive Industries*, December 24, 1932, p. 791.

Mock, Frank C. "Highlights in Carburetion." Paper presented before the Society of Automotive Engineers meeting, February 4, 1938.

"New (Zenith) Carburetor Is Designed for All Automotive Needs Except Aircraft." *Automotive Industries*, November 1, 1930, p. 661.

"Pierce Governor Company is Making an Automatic Choke." *Automobile Topics*, October 20, 1928, p. 975.

Shepard, E. H. "Downdraft Carburetion." *SAE Journal*, February 1930, p. 153.

"Stromberg Automatic Choke Opens as Engine Warms." *Automotive Industries*, December 27, 1930, p. 939.

"Wheeler-Schebler Develops Carburetor." *Automotive Industries*, December 27, 1930, p. 939.

CASE 8 / CAST CRANKSHAFTS AND CAMSHAFTS

Cast crankshafts were first used on a production basis by Ford in 1933, but all other manufacturers continued to use forged crankshafts until 1956. Automakers were reluctant to abandon established forging processes until castings offered a substantial advantage.

After several years of research, Ford used cast crankshafts on its V-8 models in 1934. These crankshafts were comparable to forged crankshafts in mechanical performance—they had adequate hardness, strength, and fatigue resistance—while offering engineering and manufacturing improvements. Cast crankshafts allowed counterweights and gravity centers to be located where mathematical calculations indicated they should be. They weighed less than forged crankshafts, so material costs were reduced. Casting molds were less expensive than forging dies, making design changes easier. Heat treatment and machining costs were reduced, as were losses from defective parts.

These advantages were at least partly offset by subsequent developments in forging processes. In 1936, Ohio Crankshaft Company introduced an electrical-induction hardening process. This process reduced material, machining, and hardening costs for forged crankshafts. Beginning in 1938 with Chevrolet, automakers began to automate forge shops. These two developments had complementary effects. They reduced the competitive advantage of castings over forgings and made manufacturers reluctant to scrap their investments in forging processes until casting processes offered substantial advantages.

The development of nodular iron after World War II changed this situation. The material, introduced in the United States by International Nickel, proved very desirable in casting crankshafts. In 1952, Ford estimated a savings of several dollars per unit using the new material. In 1956, Pontiac began casting crankshafts with ArmaSteel, a nodular alloy developed by GM. Buick, Oldsmobile, and Cadillac followed in 1961 and 1962. By 1962, 45 percent of U.S. auto production used cast crankshafts; information on subsequent diffusion is unavailable.

Cast camshafts were also developed in the 1930s. In 1934, Ford produced cast camshafts, using a controlled chill method of hardening cam tips. Machining operations were reduced from sixty-one to forty-eight. In 1941, only Buick, Chevrolet, and Pontiac were forging camshafts. These models had switched to cast camshafts by 1956.

CHRONOLOGY OF EVENTS

United States	*Europe*
CRANKSHAFTS	
1929 Ford begins experimentation with cast crankshafts for cars.	
1931 Industrial Steel Company of Toledo casts crankshafts for pumps.	
1932 Two thousand Ford V-8s equipped with cast crankshafts on an experimental basis.	1933 Cast crankshafts used in slow engines and pumps in Britain.
1934 Ford introduces the cast crankshaft on its new V-8 models for that year.	
1936 Tocco process of electrical-induction hardening is developed. Greatly reduces fabrication time for forged crankshafts and camshafts.	
1938 Chevrolet automates its forge shop.	1941 Midland Company of England announces development of Cromol and extensive experimentation with cast crankshafts for automobile uses.
1945 GM experiments with ArmaSteel, a pearlite malleable iron.	
1949 International Nickel introduces nodular iron on a production basis.	1947 First British patent for nodular iron is applied for.
1952 Ford begins using nodular iron in its cast crankshafts.	1954 Several British automakers have been using cast crankshafts for several years.
1956 Pontiac switches from the forged	

United States	Europe
crankshaft to a cast crankshaft, incorporating ArmaSteel.	

1956 Packard uses cast crankshafts on its V-8 engines.
1961 Buick and Oldsmobile switch to castings.
1962 Cadillac switches to cast crankshafts.

CAMSHAFTS
1924 Campbell, Wyant & Cannon begin experimenting with cast camshafts
1927 CWC introduces Proferall, a ferrous alloy with improved castability.

United States	Europe
1932 Hudson introduces Proferall camshafts on a 100 percent basis.	1933 Cast camshafts are being used on production basis in some British engines.
1934 Ford develops controlled chill method for hardening cam tips on cast camshafts.	
1934 Ford incorporates cast camshafts on its automobiles for that year.	1938 Midland Company of England announces use of Monikrom for cast camshafts in light engines.
1941 Cast camshaft use is nearly universal in automotive industry.	1941 Cast camshaft diffusion in Britain follows U.S. trend.
1954 Chevrolet converts.	1944 Volkswagen is using cast camshaft.
1955 Pontiac converts.	
1956 Buick converts and diffusion is complete.	

REFERENCES

"Alloy Cast Irons." *Automobile Engineer*, November 6, 1941, p. 384.
"Announce Process for Selective Surface Hardening of Crankshafts." *Steel*, September 21, 1936, p. 27.
"Ausco Method for Casting Packard V-8 Crankshafts." *Automotive Industries*, June 15, 1955, p. 68.
"Automotive Engineers' Production Meeting." *Iron Age*, April 30, 1936, p. 47.
"Cast Materials for Crankshafts." *Automobile Engineer*, February 1939, p. 63.
"Crankshaft Production." *Automobile Engineer*, January 1953, p. 23.
"Crankshafts with a Future." *Steel*, June 4, 1956, p. 117.
Currie, E. M., and Templeton, R. B. "Manufacture of High Test Iron Crankshafts." *Iron Age*, May 21, 1942, p. 46.
Dwyer, Pat. "Making the Ford Alloy Crankshafts." *Steel*, March 19, 1934, p. 25.
"Ford Improves Quality and Cuts Costs by Casting Crankshafts." *Iron Age*, August 15, 1935, p. 22.
"German War Vehicle." *Automobile Engineer*, July 1944, p. 260.
Geschelin, Joseph. "Ausco's Diversified Production Facilities." *Automotive Industries*, March 1, 1951, p. 38.
———. "Cast Crankshafts." *Automotive Industries*, March 1, 1951, p. 38.
———. "Crankshaft Production." *Automotive Industries*, August 1, 1939, p. 123.
———. "Essex Slashes Camshaft Costs with Electric Furnace Alloy." *Automotive Industries*, November 12, 1932, p. 620.
———. "Mechanized Foundry Set-up for Shell-Cast Pontiac Crankshafts." *Automotive Industries*, April 15, 1956, p. 48.
Heyn, H. M. "Crankshafts Are Cast from Alloy Steel." *Steel*, July 9, 1931, p. 31.

"High Output Forging Line at Opel Plant." *Automotive Industries*, March 1, 1963, p. 53.
"High Strength, Toughness Shown by Cast Steel Crankshafts." *Steel*, August 13, 1931, p. 31.
"Induction Hardening." *Steel*, May 2, 1938, p. 57.
LeGrand, Rupert. "Dodge Automates Press Forging." *American Machinist*, September 29, 1952, p. 123.
Mealy, Michael. "Robots Take Over Forging." *American Machinist*, November 12, 1973, p. 77.
"Modern Foundry Methods." *Automobile Engineer*, February 1938, p. 49.
"Modernization Miracles." *Mill and Factory*, January 1936, p. 100.
Morral, F. R. "Nodular Iron." *Foundry*, March 1950, p. 135.
Nealy, J. B. "Automatic Production." *Steel*, June 13, 1938, p. 50.
Nevins, Allan, and Hill, Frank E. *Ford: The Times, The Man, The Company*. New York: Charles Scribner, 1954.
"Nodular Cast Irons." *Automobile Engineer*, May 1954, p. 187.
"Production of Crankshafts." *Automobile Engineer*, October 1968, p. 441.
"Summary of Design Changes on 1941 Automobiles." *Automotive Industries*, November 1, 1940, p. 474.
"Traditional Methods Discarded." *Automotive Industries*, July 18, 1936, p. 88.
Walls, Fred J. "Cast Camshafts and Crankshafts Possess Many Advantages." *Foundry*, March 1937, p. 25, and April 1937, p. 60.
Wickenden, Thomas H. "Cast Iron Crankshafts." *Automobile Engineer*, November 1933, p. 419.

CASE 9 / AUTOMATIC TRANSMISSIONS

The purpose of the automatic transmission is to simplify operation of the automobile by eliminating manual clutching and gear shifting. In meeting this purpose, it should also be reliable, quiet, safe, efficient, and reasonably priced. Because of these requirements, the automatic transmission is one of the most complex product innovations in the industry.

The importance of the automatic transmission was recognized in the early years of the auto industry. Numerous designs were adopted and dropped, when their performance was inadequate. Two innovations, fluid coupling and torque converters, were eventually combined to produce the modern automatic transmission. Both were invented in Germany in the early 1900s for marine engines.

The 1940 Oldsmobile Hydra-Matic was the first fully automatic transmission, using a fluid coupling and a four-speed planetary gear box. The Buick Dynaflow, produced briefly before World War II and reintroduced in 1948, was the first automatic to use the torque converter. Other manufacturers quickly introduced automatic transmissions on their own models.

By 1955, 70 percent of new cars had automatic transmissions. Many of the early designs, however, lacked smooth performance or fast acceleration. The performance of the transmission became an important competitive factor. Development continued through 1964, when GM began phasing out fluid coupling transmissions and replacing them with torque converted transmissions. Further refinements are no longer a major engineering challenge, since all makes offer satisfactory performance.

The diffusion of automatic transmissions was influenced by factors other than performance. During recessions, cheaper and more efficient manual transmissions become more popular. In Europe, fuel economy, smaller cars, and different driving habits have limited the acceptance of automatics. The most successful automatic transmissions in Europe are American-designed and are more prevalent in larger cars.

CHRONOLOGY OF EVENTS

United States
1904 Sturtevant centrifugal transmission —the first automatic transmission.
1907 Carter car-friction transmission.
1908 Ford first uses planetary gears.
1910 Pneumatic Transmission and Clutch Company develops pneumatic transmission.
1914 Owen magnetic car with Entz electric drive.
1933 Reo Self-Shifter. A semiautomatic transmission.
1934 Borg-Warner automatic overdrive.
1937 Oldsmobile 1937 model semi-automatic transmission.
1938 Chrysler introduces Fluid Drive.
1939 Oldsmobile introduces Hydra-Matic automatic transmission. First production automatic transmission. Cadillac introduces Hydra-Matic the next year.
1941 Packard introduces Electromatic drive.
1942 Buick introduces Dynaflow automatic transmission utilizing a torque converter. Reintroduced after World War II in 1948.
1942 Mercury and Lincoln offer Liquimatic Drive. Hudson offers Drivemaster and Studebaker offers Turbo-Matic.
1957 Automatic transmission used on 80 percent of new U.S. cars in year before 1958 recession.

Europe
1904 Foettinger (Ger.) invents torque converter for ships.
1906 Renault (Fr.) hydraulic transmission.
1910 Thomas (Br.) electric drive.
1912 Hele-Shae (Br.) hydraulic transmission.
1912 Dr. Bauer (Ger.) designs and builds first fluid coupling.
1925 Delavaud (Fr.) variable-crank drive.
1926 Sinclair's (Br.) fluid flywheel used on English buses.
1927 Constantinesco (Fr.) inertia drive.
1928 Lysholm-Smith (Sweden) torque converter; later used in buses.
1930 Daimler (Br.) fluid coupling and Vickers-Coates (Br.) torque converter.
1937 Rieseler torque converter and hydraulically activated planetary gearing in Mercedes.

REFERENCES

"Automatic Transmission in Olds Has Hydraulic Control." *Automotive Industries*, May 29, 1937, p. 807.
Chayne, Charles A. "Automatic Transmissions in America." *Motor* (Britain), November 19, 1952, p. 587.
"Chronological History of Automatic Transmission Developments." *Automotive Industries*, August 15, 1951, p. 36.
Crouse, William. *Automotive Mechanics.* New York: McGraw-Hill, 1970.
Hayes, Cecil. "European Designers Going for More Automatic Transmissions and Disc Brakes." *SAE Journal*, September 1962, p. 77.

Huntington, Roger. "Putting the Automatic in Transmissions." *Car Life*, February 1965, p. 76.

————. "Transmission and Drive Line." *Car Life*, January 1965, p. 57.

Lamm, Michael. "Birth Pangs of the Automatic." *Car Life*, October 1969, p. 99.

McFarland, Forest. "Automatic Transmissions, Past, Present, and Future." Paper presented before the Society of Automotive Engineers meeting, Buffalo section, January 1956.

"Olds Offers Special Transmission." *Automotive Industries*, May 22, 1937, p. 734.

"Oldsmobile for 1940." *Automotive Industries*, October 15, 1939, p. 441.

Pond, James B. "Borg-Warner Tools Up for New Transmissions." *Automotive Industries*, September 15, 1972, p. 29.

Scott, David. "New Automatic Transmission Developed for British Cars." *Automotive Industries*, July 1, 1954, p. 68.

" '64 Engineering Highlights of U.S. Cars, Trucks." *Automotive News*, 1964 Almanac Issue, p. 10.

"Transmission Developments." *Automobile Engineer*, November issues, various years.

"Twenty-five Years of Chrysler Automatic Transmissions." *Car Life*, June 1964, p. 18.

CASE 10 / ELECTRONIC-ASSISTED SCHEDULING CASE

Computer-assisted scheduling in assembly plants is a particularly illusive innovation because the benefits are realized in many different areas of management decision making and the advances themselves are incremental. During the postwar period, advances have contributed to improvement in at least five areas: (1) an increased number of car models that can be produced from common sets of major components (body designs, engines, transmissions, and so forth); (2) reduced component inventories in assembly plants; (3) better work-force scheduling within assembly plants; (4) higher rates of assembly plant utilization overall through central control; and (5) more effective planning and control of components going into the assembly plant.

The advances that contributed to these improved capabilities developed incrementally from manual means of information processing that were used prior to World War II. Attempts to implement major stepped advances (radical changes) through optimized computer-based systems or mathematical models have been notable as failures. In particular, attempts by several car producers in the late 1950s and early 1960s, during the computer revolution, to implement "optimal systems" led to significant failures.

Improvements began with the introduction of teletype within assembly plants after World War II to coordinate and control the incorporation of optional components on particular cars as they traveled down the long assembly line. Teletype was also extended to feeder plants to control the shipment of components. Computers were added, beginning in 1950, first to take over manual data processing and then to extend the number and range of information-processing functions included within the scheduling function. Where previously separate groups were needed to handle sales and distribution, internal scheduling of products on the line, and material ordering, these functions came to be consolidated.

Through the changes that were introduced, Chrysler in just four years increased the number of car-line/price-class/body-style combinations from 67 in 1962 to 107 in 1966 and the number of end items fed to the assembly plant from 12,000 to 20,500; Ford more than doubled assembly plant utilizations during the postwar period; and General Motors greatly extended the number of options that could be obtained from a relatively constant number of standardized major component groups. By 1970, General Motors' Vega plant at Lordstown, Ohio, also included line balancing and product mix scheduling on the assembly line.

The largest gains have been realized since 1970 in truck plants, where the options that must be accommodated per order are the greatest. In truck plants, such as Ford's Louisville, Kentucky, Truck Plant (1969) and General Motors' Truck and Coach Division Plant (1973), the application of computer-based operations has reached the highest state of development. By coupling automatic warehousing and part retrieval with computer scheduling, almost complete flexibility was obtained in customizing the product with minimum loss of labor productivity. The capital and management costs were high, however.

As a result of continuous incremental progress, the computer has become critically important in scheduling some plants (truck) and highly valuable in others. The history of these innovations shows that progress can be realized through evolutionary progress where radical change is rejected.

CHRONOLOGY OF EVENTS

1945   General Motors introduces teletype within assembly to coordinate schedules along production line.
1950   Computer applied to assembly plant scheduling at General Motors Buick plant.
1966   Separate functions of distribution (sales commitment), plant loading (scheduling), and component inputs planning were consolidated as single computerized function at Chrysler.
1973   Automatic assembly line stocking from warehouse, GMC truck plant.

REFERENCES

DiCicco, J. J. "Computer Organized Data Flow Smooth Chrysler's Assembly Operations." *Control Engineering*, September 1966, pp. 139–41.
Eshelman, R. H. "Automation Plus at Lordstown." *Automotive Industries*, October 1, 1970, p. 43–47.
————. "How Computers Keep GM's Materials Flowing." *Business Week*, May 19, 1973, pp. 44d–44k.
Geschelin, Joseph. "Tailor-Made Cars by Teletype." *Automotive Industries*, July 15, 1947, pp. 32–33.
————. "Major Operations and Scheduling of Huge Dodge Truck Plant." *Automotive and Aviation Industries*, September 1, 1946, pp. 22–27.
————. "The Complexities of Scheduling Car Production Today." *Automotive Industries*, December 15, 1949, pp. 32–34.
Horrigan, George. "Systems in the Seventies: Ford's Better Idea Is an Automated Assembly Plant." *Material Handling Engineering*, January 1970, pp. 80–86.

CASE 11 / HIGH-COMPRESSION V-8 ENGINE

The short-stroke, high-compression V-8 engine, on 1949 Cadillacs and Oldsmobiles, was probably the most significant engine development since World War II. Since its introduction, this V-8 has been the dominant engine design in the United States.

The first V-8 engine was used on a French racing car in the early 1900s.

Cadillac introduced a V-8 in 1914, and other models, both in the United States and in Europe, offered V-8s in the next few years. In 1934, Ford began producing three thousand V-8 engine blocks per day, using a monoblock casting process. Numerous design changes in the 1920s and 1930s improved the performance of the engine. Cadillac introduced the 90° counterweighted crankshaft in 1923, reducing engine vibrations. The two-barrel carburetor, popularized in the 1930s, improved fuel distribution to the cylinders. Rubber engine mounts improved engine smoothness and helped V-8s compete with inherently smoother engine designs. The most important changes in V-8 design, however, came after World War II.

The 1949 Cadillac engine incorporated numerous design changes, none of them drastic, but together they significantly improved the horsepower-to-weight ratio. The slipper piston, which had two halfmoon sections cut out of the piston skirt, allowed connecting rods to be shortened. This reduced cylinder height and made the engine much lighter. Fuel improvements during World War II permitted a higher-compression engine without knock. Overhead valves, rather than L-lead valves, further increased compression while reducing engine size. The short stroke and wide bore of the piston increased thermal efficiency, so the size of the radiator could be reduced, saving fifteen pounds. A five-main bearing crankshaft improved engine balance and allowed additional weight savings. All of these changes improved the horsepower-to-weight ratio of the engine, from 7.15 pounds per horsepower to 5.52 pounds per horsepower. This resulted in 12–17 percent better gas mileage.

In a competitive atmosphere that demanded greater acceleration and speed, other models quickly incorporated these changes in their own V-8s. By 1955, 79 percent of U.S. auto production had V-8 engines. The popularity of the V-8 has been affected by recessionary periods and high gasoline prices (as in Europe), when the economy of smaller engines is more important.

CHRONOLOGY OF EVENTS

United States

1914   Cadillac introduces type 51 V-8 engine. First production V-8 in United States.
1923   Cadillac V-8, the "V-63" with 90° counterweighted crankshaft.
1926   Pontiac has L-6 engine, starting low stroke-to-bore ratio trend.
1934   Ford mass-produced V-8 engine with monoblock and dual carburetor.
1947   Kettering L-6 high-compression engine.
1948   Short-stroke, high-compression ratio V-8s introduced on 1949

Europe

1876   Dr. Otto (Ger.) invents four-stroke engine.
1903 or 1904   First V-8 engine in racing car (Fr.). Rolls Royce (Eng.) has V-8 passenger car.
1910   DeDion Bouton has first production V-8.

United States

    model Cadillacs and Oldsmobile.
1951 Chrysler hemihead V-8 engine.
1952 Studebaker V-8.
1953 Ford introduces wide-block V-8
      for 1954 model.
1955 Lightweight Chevrolet V-8
      engine.
1957 V-8 is used in 83 percent of U.S.
      car production—the high point
      prior to the 1958 recession.

Europe

1952 Pegaso (Spain) over-square V-8
      followed by Fiat the next year.

REFERENCES

Bond, John R. "Milestone Engines." *Special Interest Autos*, May–June 1971, p. 27.
Hendry, Maurice. "Half-hour History of V-8 Engines." *Special Interest Autos*, September–October 1974, p. 36.
Huntington, Roger. "Engine Layout." *Car Life*, April 1965, p. 92.
Lamm, Michael. "1948 and 1949 Cadillac Fastbacks." *Special Interest Autos*, June–July 1972, p. 13.
"Overhead Valve V-8 Powers 1949 Cadillac." *Automotive Industries*, November 1, 1948, p. 34.
"Power Output." *Automobile Engineer*, May 1953, p. 176.
Venk, Ernest. *Automotive Engines*. Chicago: American Technical Society, 1951.

CASE 12 / EXTENSIVE INTEGRATION OF ENGINE PLANTS USING TRANSFER LINES

The typical U.S. automobile engine plant is more highly automated than any other production process for a highly complex product. The development of this automation was spurred in 1951 by Ford's Cleveland engine plant, which integrated major machining operations into a single machine-controlled production sequence. The Cleveland plant extensively used in-line transfer machines that automatically moved parts from one operation to another to form a line-flow operation. Forty-one in-line transfer machines, built by several machine-tool companies, were linked by automatic transfer lines.

The use of transfer machines in the auto industry began in 1922, when the A. O. Smith Company used mechanical transfer in building auto frames. Morris Engines in England tried to apply the concept to engine manufacturing in 1924, but was unsuccessful. In 1932, Ford built a hydraulic transfer machine to connect two boring operations on a V-8 engine. The number of stations linked by transfer gradually increased. A 1947 Ford plant linked eight stations, and a 1948 GM plant linked nineteen.

The Ford Cleveland plant was significant because it integrated machines that were not designed to be compatible and because of the plant-level systems analysis in integrating product design and the production process. The automation reduced the number of laborers from 8,253 to 6,399 for a comparable production volume. Ford's objective was not merely to reduce labor costs, but to increase the efficiency of capital by increasing line output. Subsequent advances have increasingly sought improvements in capital-equipment utilization.

Ford's innovation was accompanied by a loss in flexibility. Before the Cleveland plant was begun, Ford produced all engines in one plant. By 1974,

Ford had six specialized engine plants. One engine design change in the 1960s caused an entire line to be shut down for six months.

Engine plants built since 1951 have carried automation further, first in the United States and later in foreign countries. Subsequent advances have attempted to reduce equipment downtime, improve machining precision, and increase flexibility in modifying engines. Ford's newest engine plants have used higher-order feedback-control devices, including closed-circuit TV monitoring and routing of parts and extensive information-processing techniques through programmable controllers.

CHRONOLOGY OF EVENTS

1922   Integration using automatic-transfer machines. Extensive automation of car-frame production (A. O. Smith for GM).

1924   Attempted application in England that failed (Morris Engines).

1932   Two stations; first engine plant automatic in-line transfer (developed and applied by Ford).

1936   Seven-station return to start transfer machines for drive-train components (Baird Machine Company, applied at Ford).

1947   Eight stations in engine machining line (Excello, applied at Ford).

1948   Nineteen stations in cylinder-block machining (Greenlee, applied at Buick).

1952   One hundred fifty stations in equivalents of stand-alone machine tools (various machine-tool manufacturers; systems design and initiation by Ford).

1955   Segmented transfer lines, 555 operations performed in long line that could be operated as five independent units (Cross Company, applied at General Motors).

1972   Transfer of complete modern U.S. engine plant to Germany (U.S. machine-tool companies, applied at Ford, Cologne, Germany).

REFERENCES

"American Methods Fitted to German Conditions at Volkswagen." *Automotive Industries*, April 15, 1955, p. 54.

"At France's Renault It's 'Vive l'Automation.'" *American Machinist*, May 4, 1959, p. 112.

Bright, J. R. *Automation and Management*. Boston: Division of Research, Graduate School of Business, Harvard University, 1958.

"Ford Retools." *Automotive Industries*, February 1, 1948, p. 38.

"Ford Revamps for New Engine Production." *Iron Age*, June 29, 1967, p. 12.

"Ford's New Cleveland Facilities." *Automotive Industries*, December 1, 1955, p. 64.

Geschelin, Joseph. "Buick Cylinder Blocks Now Standardized on First Unitized Transfer Line." *Automotive Industries*, February 1, 1947, p. 20.

Hoffman, Peter. "Building the Pinto Engine." *American Machinist*, November 16, 1970, p. 75.

"Japanese Auto Maker Pushes Automation." *Steel*, August 9, 1965, p. 112.

LeGrand, Rupert. "How Ford Automates Production Lines." *American Machinist*, March 17, 1952, p. 136.

Nevins, Allan, and Hill, Frank. *Ford: Decline and Rebirth*. New York: Charles Scribners, 1963.

"Newly Designed Transfer Machines in Ford's Engine Plant." *Automotive Industries*, December 1, 1955, p. 64.

Scott, David. "Advanced Production Methods for Daimler-Benz Cars." *Automotive Industries*, June 15, 1959, p. 76, and July 15, 1959, p. 87.

"Sectionized Automation Applied to Huge Transfer Machines." *Automotive Industries*, December 1, 1954, p. 48.

Smith, L. R. "We Build a Plant to Run Without Men." *Magazine of Business*, February 1929.

"Vauxhall Plant Uses American Equipment." *Automotive Industries*, May 15, 1959, p. 70.

Woollard, F. C. *Principles of Mass and Flow Production*. London: Iliffe and Sons, 1954.

CASE 13 / DISC BRAKES

The earliest disc brakes appeared on automobiles in the early 1900s, and reappeared sporadically for the next forty years. The major development of the modern caliper disc brake began in the aircraft industry in the 1940s. After World War II, Chrysler and Crosley introduced disc brakes in the United States. The brake was first popularized in Europe in the early 1960s and has been adopted in the United States in the last decade.

Disc brakes have three basic advantages over drum brakes. They do not fade as much under severe braking conditions, they provide more consistent straight-line stops, and they do not tend to slip or grab if water or grease enter the braking system. Several factors limit these advantages. The performance improvement is not dramatic: under normal conditions, drum brakes performed adequately. Disc brakes are not well suited to use as a parking brake, so many cars have retained drum brakes on rear wheels. Balancing these performance factors, U.S. manufacturers were reluctant to scrap drum-brake manufacturing equipment and invest in disc-brake equipment.

The diffusion of disc brakes began on European racing cars in the early 1950s, where performance advantages were very important. The earliest passenger cars to use disc brakes included Citroen, Triumph, Jentzen, and Jaguar in the late 1950s. In the early 1960s, disc brakes became common on European cars. The European design was not well suited for larger American cars, which delayed diffusion in the United States. Americans began developing their own designs in the 1950s, and the Studebaker Avanti had standard disc brakes in 1963. By 1965, all major U.S. manufacturers offered disc brakes on some models. Today, front disc brakes are standard on most U.S. cars.

CHRONOLOGY OF EVENTS

United States	*Europe*
	1904 Lanchester (Br.) takes out first patent on disc brake.
1911 Metz uses eighteen-disc hub brake.	1914 AC Cycle Car (Br.) uses disc brakes. Other minor uses of disc brakes in British cars in the 1920s.
1930s Aircraft field begins to adopt disc brakes. Lockheed, Goodyear, and Bendix are important suppliers.	1930s Aircraft field begins to adopt disc brakes. Girling is important British supplier.
1949 Crosley Hotshot and Chrysler Crown Imperial are first applications of disc brakes on passenger cars. Programs are phased out within five years.	1953 Jaguar Le Mans victory with Girling disc brakes.
	1956 Citroen's (Fr.) models DS-19 and ID-19 are first successful long-term application of disc brakes in Europe.

United States	Europe
	1957 Triumph TR-3 and Jentzen Interceptor (Br.) use Girling disc brakes as standard.
	1960 English Ford is first mass-production application of disc brakes.
1963 Bendix-Dunlop disc brakes are standard on Studebaker Avanti.	1960s Rapid diffusion of disc brakes on European cars.
1973 Disc brakes, at least on front wheels, nearly universal in the United States—on 86 percent of production.	

REFERENCES

"About Those Disc Brakes Now." Bulletin published by Plymouth Division of Chrysler Corporation, Detroit, Michigan (no date).

Huntington, Roger. "What's Coming in Disc Brakes." *Motor Trend,* November 1964, p. 92.

Koehler, Walter O. "Costs Holding Back Disc Brakes." *Motor,* April 1963, p. 60.

Norbye, Jan P. "Short History of Disc Brakes." *Special Interest Autos,* February–March 1973, p. 22.

Starling, J. O. "Disc Brakes." *Automobile Engineer,* January 1959, p. 11.

CASE 14 / DIP PAINTING AND ELECTROCOATING

Automobile body painting before the 1950s was characterized by the development of different coating materials and the absence of process innovations in applying paint. The only significant process innovation was the introduction of spray guns in the 1920s. In the early 1950s, new methods of body assembly and the increased use of salt on snow-covered streets led to serious corrosion damage to automobiles. A series of innovations attempted to solve this problem, culminating in Ford's electrocoating process in 1963.

In the early 1950s, Chrysler introduced automatic spray guns and body assembly prior to painting. The second innovation made car color uniform, but made areas within the body inaccessible for painting. Corrosion problems increased, usually beginning on inner surfaces that were inadequately painted or in poorly ventilated areas that trapped humidity.

In 1957, American Motors began dipping the entire body in primer paint. This helped prevent corrosion, but had limitations. Trapped air prevented complete paint coverage, and drips and runs marred the body's appearance. Large painting tanks were expensive and sometimes required extensive changes in plant layout. Until 1964, AMC was the only U.S. manufacturer to totally immerse all bodies in primer paint. In the early 1960s, automakers began using galvanized steel and zinc-rich paints. This innovation provided significant corrosion protection at a reasonable cost.

The most important innovation, though, was Ford's electrocoating process. Ford used an electrical charge to attract paint particles to metal surfaces. The result was a uniform layer of primer on all metal surfaces. Water, grease, and dirt were forced away from metal by electro-osmosis. The process provided almost 100 percent paint utilization and almost completely eliminated serious corrosion problems. Ford used electrocoating extensively in 1964 at its Wixom assembly plant.

The advantages of the process were great; by 1970 it had been widely adopted in both the United States and Europe. The process highlighted a twenty-year trend, in which body painting changed from a manual process to a mechanically and electrically controlled process. The resulting corrosion resistance was a major improvement in automobile bodies.

CHRONOLOGY OF EVENTS

1953 Beginning of dramatic increase in use of sodium chloride to fight ice and snow.
1954 Installation of automatic spraying guns at Chrysler's Los Angeles assembly plant.
1955 Chrysler initiates complete body assembly before painting at Jefferson assembly plant in Detroit.
1957 AMC installs first U.S. application of full body dip.
1957 Partial body dip for Lincolns and Mercurys installed by Ford.
1957 GM begins converting sheet-metal painting from dip process to flow-coat spraying in its assembly plants.
1960 Chrysler converts to unitized body construction and installs partial body dip tanks in its assembly plants.
1960 Ford introduced zinc-rich primer application on Falcons.
1960 Chevrolet introduced zinc-rich primer application on Corvairs.
1961 Ford decides to dramatically increase galvanized steel usage on all of its bodies.
1962 Chrysler discovers increased corrosion protection with a combination of chemical salts and flourides.
1962 AMC develops method of zinc coating by impaction.
1963 Electrocoating introduced at Ford's Wixom plant.
1964 Ford extends electrocoating to its British operations.
1967 GM introduces electrocoating at its South Gate, California, and Kansas City, Missouri, assembly plants.
1968 Chrysler adopts electrocoating in its British operations.
1969 Thirty-four European assembly plants had introduced electrocoating.

REFERENCES

"AMC Using New Paint Technique for Improved Primer Coverages." *Automotive Industries*, September 1, 1957, p. 58.
"Bodies Assembled before Painting at New Chrysler Plant." *Automotive Industries*, December 15, 1955, p. 53.
Bush, G. Fred. "Progress in the Battle with Corrosion of Automobiles." *Metal Progress*, December 1966, p. 58.
"Corrosion War Boosts Zinc Use." *Iron Age*, March 7, 1963, p. 117.
Egeler, O. A. "Automatic Painting of Passenger Cars." *Automotive Industries*, June 1, 1955, p. 64.
"Electrocoating: Ford's Giant Step in Painting." *American Machinist*, May 11, 1964, p. 110.
"Flow Coat Paint for Ease and Safety." *Iron Age*, December 12, 1957, p. 136.
Ginsler, V. W. "Evolution of Automotive Finishes." *Automotive Industries*, September 15, 1957, p. 72.
Ransome, J. G. "Electropainting in Europe." *Metal Progress*, June 1969, p. 75.
Widman, John C. "Galvanized Steel Joins Fight against Auto Corrosion." *Metal Progress*, March 1962, p. 66.

CASE 15 / THE ALUMINUM ENGINE

Aluminum engines have never been widely adopted on American cars. The high point of diffusion was 1961, when 10 percent of new cars had aluminum engines. The innovation is important, however, because of the large amounts of resources devoted to its development and the intense interest in aluminum engines from 1958 to 1963.

Aluminum-alloy engines have three advantages over cast-iron engines: light weight, greater heat conductivity, and potentially lower machining costs. Their major disadvantages are higher raw material cost, lower wear resistance, and a greater thermal expansion rate.

Aluminum engines were used in airplane engines and a wide variety of cars from 1895 through the 1930s, but cast iron remained the dominant engine material. Excess aluminum production after World War II brought renewed interest in the material. Through the 1950s, Kaiser, Reynolds, Alcoa, Doehler-Jarvis, and all U.S. car manufacturers experimented with various casting techniques and aluminum alloys. In the late 1950s, several European cars introduced aluminum engines. GM's 1960 Corvair was the first mass-produced American car with an aluminum engine. Chrysler and AMC followed the next year.

The impact of the innovation was brief, however, Ford introduced the thin-wall cast-iron engine in 1960, which provided a lighter and cheaper cast-iron engine. By 1964, only Corvair had a standard aluminum engine.

The success of this innovation has been influenced by the value of aluminum's performance advantages and its cost compared to cast iron. When fuel economy is important, as in Europe and during American recessions, aluminum's light weight is more attractive. Similarly, variations in cost have been important. The Corvair engine plant, for example, was located less than a mile from a Reynolds aluminum foundry, making the cost of aluminum more competitive. The low wear resistance of aluminum has been a major problem, necessitating the use of cast-iron "liners" in cylinders and increasing production costs. The 1971 Chevrolet Vega reintroduced aluminum engines, this time with a high-silicon alloy that eliminated the need for liners. Finally, aluminum has competed with a technology that car companies, particularly Ford, are familiar with and have invested heavily in. GM, the company most interested in aluminum today, was also the most heavily committed to aluminum development in the past.

CHRONOLOGY OF EVENTS

United States

1895 Haynes and Apperson work on aluminum engine using steel tubing for cylinder liners.

1916 White Motor Company produces trucks with aluminum engines for U.S. Army.

1930 Marmon V-16 and Franklin 6 use aluminum engines.

Europe

1899 DeDion Bouton (Fr.) engine uses aluminum crankcase.

1903 Napier (Br.) produces 4-cylinder aluminum block with cylinder liners.

1920s Hispano Suiza (Fr.) Napier and A.C. Ltd. (Br.) produce aluminum cylinder blocks.

United States

1955 Doehler-Jarvis produces first die-cast aluminum engine block.

1959 Corvair 1960 model air-cooled rear-engine aluminum engine. First U.S. mass-production aluminum engine.

1959 Ford introduces thin-wall gray cast-iron engine on 1960 model Ford Falcons and Mercury Comets.

1960 American Motors' Rambler and GM and Chrysler compacts offer aluminum engines for 1961 model year. 10 percent of engine production is aluminum in 1961 model year.

1964 GM drops aluminum V-8s on Buick and Oldsmobile, Rambler goes to optional aluminum engine, leaving only Corvair with a standard aluminum engine.

1966–69 Phase-out of Corvair.

1970 GM introduces sleeveless aluminum engine on 1971 model Chevrolet Vega.

Europe

1957 Porsche (Ger.) using aluminum cylinder blocks—about five thousand per year.

Late 1950s Other European cars adopt aluminum engines.

REFERENCES

"Air-cooled V-4 Engine." *Mechanical Engineering*, October 1956.

"Aluminum Die-cast Engine Blocks." *Mechanical Engineering*, January 1956, p. 35.

"Aluminum Engines at a Crossroads." *Iron Age*, June 29, 1961, p. 57.

"Can Aluminum Engines Stage a Comeback?" *Iron Age*, October 24, 1963, p. 47.

Clayden, A. Ludlow. "Vast Progress in Motor Design." *The Automobile*, November 4, 1915, p. 823.

"Coming Aluminum Engines Bring to Light Engineers' Agreement on Problems, Divergence on Solutions." *SAE Journal*, September 1958, p. 38.

"Daimler Dart Engine Has Aluminum Heads and Oilpan." *Automotive Industries*, October 15, 1959, p. 81.

Edwards, J. D. *Aluminum Industry: Aluminum Products and Their Fabrication.* New York: McGraw-Hill, 1930.

Eshelman, R. H. "Vega 2300 Has No Iron Cylinder Liners." *Automotive Industries*, June 1, 1970, p. 26.

"General Motors Testing V-8 Aluminum Engines." *Modern Metals*, June 1958, p. 77.

Geschelin, Joseph. "Advancements in New Passenger Cars." *Automotive Industries*, November 1, 1959, p. 49.

———. "New Chevrolet Aluminum Foundry." *Automotive Industries*, July 15, 1960, p. 71.

Hankla, William B. *Aluminum in Automobiles.* Richmond, Va.: Reynolds Metals Co., 1959.

Harris, Andy. "Engines Go Aluminum." *Speed Age*, March 1957, p. 58.

"Haynes and Apperson at Work on New Model." *Horseless Age*, July 1896, p. 10.

"How Ford Sees Materials Trends." *Iron Age*, October 5, 1951, p. 57.

Jones, M. Glyn. "Aluminum in the Automobile." *Motor Industry*, November 1962, p. 62.

Levett, Walker M. "Predicts Adoption of Aluminum Pistons as Standard by Majority of Cars." *The Automobile*, September 2, 1915, p. 447.

"Lighter Cast Iron Engine Blocks Expected from New Process." *Automotive Industries,* July 15, 1952, p. 75.

Lloyd, Norman M. "Use of Aluminum Continues to Climb." *Automotive Industries,* June 1, 1962, p. 46.

Macklin, Harold M. "Anatomy and Development of the Aluminum Cylinder Block." *Automotive Industries,* May 1, 1971, p. 42.

McClelland, Graham. "How Problems Are Being Overcome in Modern Aluminum Engines." *Australian Motor Manual,* June 1961, p. 15.

Patton, W. G. "How Aluminum Engines Are Made." *Iron Age,* May 28, 1970, p. 104.

Pond, James B. "Materials: New Marriages in Design." *Automotive Industries,* December 15, 1973, p. 40.

"Six-cylinder Engine Block in Aluminum Die-casting." *SAE Journal,* January 1957, p. 26.

"Small Firms Have Aluminum Engines, Too." *Steel,* June 30, 1958, p. 63.

"Special Techniques Produce the Aluminum Corvair Engine." *American Machinist,* June 27, 1960, p. 105.

Swaboda, F. "Aluminum's Future in the Automotive Industry." *SAE Journal,* July 1956, p. 106.

"Use of Aluminum for Cylinder Heads Eliminates Excessive Deadweight." *Automotive Industries,* December 10, 1932, p. 749.

Ward's Automotive Yearbook. Detroit: Ward's Publications, various years.

CASE 16 / THE THIN-WALL GRAY CAST-IRON ENGINE

The thin-wall cast-iron engine, introduced by Ford in 1959, permitted engine weight savings of 10 percent or more and helped cast iron retain its position as the dominant American engine material.

Since the beginning of the automobile, the vast majority of engines have been made of gray cast iron. Cast iron has high strength, low thermal expansion, sound and vibration dampening qualities, and low cost. Gray iron contains more graphite than pure cast iron. The graphite serves as a natural lubricant and holds oil particles better than pure iron. Thin-wall casting reduced engine wall thickness from .20 inches to .15 inches, thereby reducing weight and increasing thermal efficiency. The innovation was made possible by improved metallurgical consistency of gray cast iron and more accurate mold fabrication for engine castings. Ford was instrumental in both of these developments.

Thin-wall engines were introduced on the 1960 Ford Falcon and Mercury Comet and on the 1962 Ford Fairlane and Mercury Meteor. The innovation was stimulated by consumer demand for smaller, lighter cars and the simultaneous introduction of aluminum engines by other manufacturers. For Ford, which had invested in iron and steel works, the development of a cast-iron engine to compete against aluminum was very important. The aluminum engine was never widely accepted, partly because of thin-wall casting. The familiarity of cast-iron technology, the investments of all companies in cast-iron equipment, the lower cost of iron, and the lack of market interest in aluminum engines preserved the dominance of cast gray iron.

CHRONOLOGY OF EVENTS

1903   Ford uses gray cast iron for production engines.
1916   White Motor Company makes first production aluminum engines for U.S. Army trucks.
1945   Shell molding technology comes to the United States from Germany.

1951   Ford uses shell molding for casting crankshafts, camshafts, and valves.
1959   Ford introduces 6-cylinder thin-walled gray cast-iron engine for 1960 model Ford Falcon and Mercury Comet.
1959   Chevrolet introduces aluminum engine in 1960 model Corvair. In following year aluminum engines appear on other makes.
1961   Ford introduces V-8 thin-walled gray cast-iron engine for 1962 model Ford Fairlane and Mercury Meteor.

REFERENCES

Bogart, Harold N. "Automotive Cylinder Block Material—Cast Iron." Paper presented before the Society of Automotive Engineers, November 6, 1961.

"Can Aluminum Engines Stage a Comeback?" *Iron Age*, October 24, 1963, p. 47.

Frey, Donald, and Goldman, J. E. "Applied Science and Manufacturing Technology: The Case of Thin Wall Iron Castings for Automobile Cylinder Blocks." In *Applied Science and Technological Progress* Washington, D.C.: National Academy of Sciences, 1967.

Geschelin, Joseph. "Oldsmobile 425 Cubic Inch Engine." *Automotive Industries*, September 15, 1964.

Herrman, Robert H. "Improved Casting Design." *Foundry*, November 1959, p. 82.

"How Coremaking Puts Precision into New Cast Iron Engine." *Iron Age*, October 19, 1961, p. 142.

"How Ford Sees Materials Trends." *Iron Age*, October 5, 1961, p. 57.

"Lighter Cast Iron Engine Blocks Expected from New Process." *Automotive Industries*, July 15, 1962, p. 75.

CASE 17 / ENERGY-ABSORBING STEERING ASSEMBLIES

The energy-absorbing steering assembly was a result of automobile crash research that began in the late 1940s and a rising concern to protect passengers in car accidents. Cornell University Medical College research, sponsored partly by Ford and Chrysler, indicated that steering assemblies were responsible for a large percentage of auto injuries and that injuries could be reduced if the assembly would collapse slowly upon impact.

Ford's 1956 models featured a "safety package" that included a "deep-dish" steering wheel in which a collapsible rim was six inches above the hub of the steering column. This design was similar to a British steering wheel patented in 1939. The deep-dish concept was adopted throughout the industry by 1957, and Cornell research indicated that the innovation was successful in reducing injuries. Auto manufacturers continued research through the 1960s and introduced other safety innovations, such as penetration-resistant windshields and dual braking systems.

Despite some evidence that the 1956 safety campaign had been a competitive factor, no U.S. company tried again to use safety as a major marketing effort. An important factor in increasing automobile safety was a gathering storm of public and government concern.

In 1966, Congress passed the Motor Vehicle Safety Act, concluding that voluntary safety promotion had failed and imposing mandatory safety standards for automobiles. The General Services Administration had previously issued safety standards for all cars purchased by the federal government. Both the congressional and GSA standards required collapsible steering assemblies. A GM-designed collapsible steering column was used by all manufacturers except Ford on 1967 models. Ford claimed that its existing steering assembly met initial safety standards. In 1968 models, Ford incorporated a collapsible column similar to GM's. The primary energy-absorbing component in this design was a column jacket made of steel mesh; the column would collapse a maximum $8\frac{1}{4}$ inches upon impact.

For 1969 models, GM developed a new design with superior engineering characteristics. This design could be easily modified to meet new energy-absorbing standards if continuing research showed that changes were necessary. Safety research has continued in areas such as flexible shafting, alternative materials, and air bags to protect passengers in accidents.

CHRONOLOGY OF EVENTS

1939   British patent issued for resilient flexible steering wheel.
1955   Ford includes deep-dish steering wheel as standard feature on 1956 model Fords.
1957   Diffusion of deep-dish concept complete throughout industry.
1965   GSA requires impact-absorbing steering column be included on all cars purchased by federal government, effective September 28, 1966.
1966   National Traffic and Motor Vehicle Safety Act of 1966 enacted. Standards promulgated therein include two dealing with energy-absorbing steering assembly. Effective date of initial standards: September 1, 1967.
1966   GM's Saginaw Steering Gear Division introduces the energy-absorbing collapsible steering column. GM, Chrysler, and AMC adopt the system for 1967 models.
1967   Ford introduces its version of an energy-absorbing column for incorporation into 1968 Ford models.
1968   Saginaw introduces second-generation steering column for use in 1969 models.

REFERENCES

Bickley, Bill. "Japan Retains Second Place." *Automotive Industries,* July 1, 1969, p. 84.

Biggs, Colver R. "Ford Progress in Safety." *Automotive Industries,* September 15, 1965, p. 78.

"British Patents." *Automobile Engineer,* May 1939, p. 175.

"Chrysler Changeover." *Automotive Industries,* March 1, 1971, p. 19.

De Wees, John. "Flexible Shafts for Steering." *Automotive Industries,* December 15, 1971, p. 64.

Eckhold, John C. "Ford's Safety Advances." *Automotive Industries,* March 1, 1968, p. 45.

"Energy-Absorbing Column Aids GI's." *Automotive Industries,* September 1, 1968, p. 190.

"Flexible Steering Link." *Automotive Industries,* November 15, 1961, p. 91.

"For '56: Safest Cars Yet." *Business Week,* September 17, 1955, p. 70.

Geschelin, Joseph. "Saginaw's Collapsible Steering Column." *Automotive Industries,* April 15, 1967, p. 76.

————. "Summary Features of Ford, L-M Line." *Automotive Industries,* September 15, 1966, p. 75.

Lawrence, Floyd G. "Detroit Starts Auto Race." *Steel,* September 19, 1955, p. 75.

"Manufacturing a Collapsible Steering Column." *Steel,* April 24, 1967, p. 54.

Marquis, Donald A. "Second Generation Energy Absorbing Column with Locking Feature." Paper presented before the Society of Automotive Engineers, January 12, 1970.

Nader, Ralph. *Unsafe at Any Speed.* New York: Grossman Publishers, 1972.

National Traffic and Motor Vehicle Safety Act of 1966, 15 U.S.C., sec. 1381 *et seq.* (1974).
"New Safety Feature." *Automotive Industries*, March 15, 1966, p. 312.
"News and Views." *Autocar*, November 26, 1954, p. 846.
"News Features." *Automotive Industries*, May 1, 1966, p. 43.
"Safety Rules Brake Foreign Auto Makers." *Business Week*, August 12, 1967, p. 119
Scott, David. "Fiat's Prestige Sedan." *Automotive Industries*, August 15, 1969, p. 22.
U.S., Congress, Senate. "Report of the Senate Commerce Committee, June 23, 1966, #1301." In *U.S. Code Congressional and Administrative News.* 89th Cong., 2d sess., 1966, pp. 2710–72.
"When Wrecks Help Sell Cars." *Business Week*, December 10, 1955, p. 53.
"Why Safety Is a Delicate Subject." *Iron Age*, April 24, 1958, p. 100.

CASE 18 / AUTOMATIC CHASSIS AND BODY ASSEMBLY

Over the last twenty years, automatic chassis and body assembly has been characterized by diversity in the technology and approaches used in different assembly plants. This diversity reflects the relationship between the flexibility of body design and the degree of automation. Automation becomes less practical when design changes are more frequent. Therefore, the acceptance of automated assembly has been limited, despite potential improvements in productivity and product quality.

Two important components of automated assembly, transfer lines and automatic welding, had been used in the 1920s and 1930s to produce parts of the automobile. Automation of final assembly required the development of auxiliary equipment to integrate these two processes. Auxiliary equipment included work-moving devices and work-holding devices, specialized welding fixtures, and welding "robots." Important developments include Ford's "gate-line" framing in 1953, Volkswagen automation in 1955 and 1963, GM's welding robots in 1968, and the Vega and Econoline assembly plants of GM and Ford in the 1970s. The most sophisticated assembly plants now use self-monitoring robot welders and push-button controls that allow different models to be produced on one line.

Extensive automation has improved productivity and changed the tasks that workers perform. Production at the Vega plant was about seventy-five cars per hour, despite some labor problems, compared to traditional production rates of fifty to sixty cars per hour. Workers monitor machines and perform many tasks that are not automated. For example, about 5 percent of the welds on the Vega are still performed manually, and many of the nonwelding tasks are not fully automated.

Automation has also required more compatibility between product design and the production process. The Vega assembly process was simulated thousands of times on computers before the design of the car was finalized. More than ever before, the car was being designed for a specific production facility. This compatibility results in less design flexibility. Major design changes require expensive changes in almost all of the automated equipment in the assembly plant. A car such as the Volkswagen "Beetle," which has had the same basic design since 1947, is well suited to automation. For vehicles that do not have a standardized design, automation is less rewarding.

CHRONOLOGY OF EVENTS

1920s Early uses of automatic welding.
1930s Early use of automatic transfer lines.
1953 Use of gate-line concept at Ford's Wayne body plant.
1955 Automation of Volkswagen front end assembly.
1964 Production of Mustang underbodies using automatic welding at Ford.
1966 Complete automation of Volkswagen body production.
1966 Gate-line concept and automatic welding with body style flexibility at GM Ste. Therese plant.
1970 Extensive use of automatic welding, robots, and other automatic processes at GM's Lordstown plant for Vega bodies. The most automated assembly line in the United States.
1975 High level of automation, plus design flexibility, at Ford Econoline plant.

REFERENCES

"AM Trends." *American Machinist*, August 10, 1970, p. 59.
Benes, James J. "Automatic Assembly." *Machine Design*, March 20, 1969, p. 193.
"Building the Chevrolet Vega." *Automobile Engineer*, November 1970, p. 456.
"Canadian Car Assembly." *Automobile Engineer*, April 1967, p. 148.
Cary, H. G. "Automatic Welding in Automotive Production." *Welding Journal*, March 1973, p. 155.
Eschelman, R. H. "Automation Plus at Lordstown." *Automotive Industries*, October 1, 1970, p. 40.
"432 Welds a Minute." *Engineering*, March 10, 1967.
Geschelin, Joseph. "Ford Mustangs on the Production Line." *Automotive Industries*, May 1, 1964, p. 49.
———. "Producing Hornet Bodies." *Automotive Industries*, November 15, 1969, p. 68.
———. "Scheduling Problems in L-M Body Plant, Part II." *Automotive Industries*, November 15, 1953, p. 34.
Jefferson, T. B. "Automatic R.W. Line Joins 18 VW 'Beetle' Shells per Minute." *Welding Engineer*, October 1965, p. 43.
Kilbenschlag, Mike. "Robots Invade Detroit." *American Machinist*, May 4, 1970, p. 129.
"Lordstown: Putting Some Myths to Rest." *Iron Age*, May 31, 1973, p. 33.
"MIG Spotwelding Has Finally Arrived." *American Machinist*, June 26, 1972, p. 68.
Mortimer, John. "Gate-Line Assembly Will Boost Car Output." *Engineer*, September 4, 1969, p. 13.
"Production of the Avenger, Part I." *Automobile Engineer*, April 1970, p. 149.
"Robot Stud Welds Caddy Floor Pans." *Welding Engineer*, May 1968, p. 41.
Scott, David. "Gate Line Cuts Cost of Morris Marina Assembly." *Automotive Industries*, January 1, 1972, p. 24.
Weinert, Charles A. "Automatic Assembly of Passenger Car Bodies of VW." *Automotive Industries*, May 1, 1966, p. 54.
Wilburn, Julian E. "Automatic Assembly Increases Profits." *Automation*, April 1966, p. 80.

CASE 19 / ADVANCES IN THE ELECTRICAL SYSTEM: THE TWELVE-VOLT SYSTEM, THE ALTERNATOR, AND ELECTRONIC IGNITION

Electrical advances since 1950 have responded to three trends in American passenger cars: the increasing use of high-compression, high-performance engines; the growing number of accessories that require more electrical power; and the desirability of maintenance-free ignition systems.

High-compression engines, introduced in the late 1940s, required a higher-voltage ignition system to fire spark plugs. Twelve-volt electrical systems had been used earlier in the United States and Europe, but the six-volt system had proved adequate for most cars until the development of high-compression engines. Twelve-volt systems were introduced in 1953 on some Chrysler and GM models. By 1956, all American cars used twelve-volt electrical systems.

The AC generator, or alternator, was offered as an option by Ford in 1958, was standard equipment on Chrysler in 1960, and was standardized by Ford and GM in 1963. The alternator was much more efficient than the DC generator and met an increasing need for more electrical power. Between 1953 and 1963, the electrical load in cars had increased from 340 watts to more than 600 watts. The alternator was also more effective at low engine speeds in congested traffic.

The conventional breaker-point ignition system required periodic maintenance and did not always perform well at high speeds or in cold weather. Electronic ignition systems replaced breaker points with magnetic and transistor devices, eliminating these problems. Development began in the late 1950s by Electric Autolite, Motorola, Delco-Remy, and Joseph Lucas, Ltd. 1963 Pontiacs offered electronic ignitions as optional equipment; other models followed in the 1960s. Between 1972 and 1975 electronic ignition became standard on all American cars.

The greatest impediment to all of these innovations was cost. At the time of their introduction, existing equipment generally performed adequately; more expensive equipment with only minor performance advantages was not immediately accepted. As electrical needs changed, the performance advantages became more important. As the innovations were widely accepted, costs dropped. The electrical system, which had not substantially changed between 1920 and 1950, had universally incorporated these three innovations between 1950 and 1975.

CHRONOLOGY OF EVENTS

1912–20	Twelve-volt starter-generator used on many cars.
Late 1940s	Many European cars use twelve-volt electrical system.
1948	Brattain and Bardeen invent transistors.
1953	Cadillac, Chrysler, Oldsmobile, and Buick introduce twelve-volt systems.
1956	All American new cars have twelve-volt systems.
1958	Alternators are optional equipment on some Ford models.
1960	Electric Autolite and Delco-Remy use transistors to reduce electrical load on breaker points.
1961	Joseph Lucas, Ltd., patents transistorized ignition without breaker points.
1963	Alternators are standard equipment on Ford and GM new cars.
1963	Delcotronic transistorized ignition is optional on Pontiac.
1973	Electronic ignition is standard equipment on all Chrysler Corporation cars.
1975	All American new cars have electronic ignition.

REFERENCES

"Auto Ignition Has No Breaker Points." *Electronics*, February 9, 1962, p. 63.
Balan, I., and Van Halteren, C. J. "Performance of Electronics in the Automobile to Date at Chrysler." Paper presented before the Society of Automotive Engineers, January 8, 1973.

Bickley, B. "Automotive Semiconductor Devices." *Automotive Industries*, August 15, 1966, p. 86.

Bradley, W. F. "Twelve-volt Electrical Systems Predominate on European Cars." *Automotive Industries*, May 1, 1952, p. 110.

Bushor, W. E. "Electronics and the American Automobile." *Electronics*, November 21, 1958, p. 73.

"Detroit Looks for Electrical Breakthroughs." *Steel*, May 28, 1962, p. 55.

"Electronics Advances in Ignition Systems." *Electronics*, March 25, 1960, p. 82.

"Electronics in Tomorrow's Cars." *Electronics*, October 3, 1958, p. 13.

"Generators Yield to Alternators." *Iron Age*, July 12, 1962, p. 91.

Hartzell, H. L. "Ignition Systems for Future High-Compression Engines." *SAE Journal*, November 1951, p. 45.

―――. "Why Twelve Volts?" *Automotive Industries*, November 1, 1952, p. 56.

Hetzler, Lewis, and Kline, Paul. "Engineering C-D Ignition for Modern Engines." Paper presented before the Society of Automotive Engineers, January 9, 1967.

Hogle, R. C., and Mieras, L. F. "Development of Ford Transistorized Ignition System." *Automotive Industries*, February 1, 1964, p. 50.

"How Electrical Needs Are Changing." *Steel*, November 4, 1953, p. 141.

Lawrence, Floyd G. "Automakers Are None Too Enthusiastic about Twelve-volt Ignition System." *Steel*, June 22, 1953, p. 59.

―――. "Why Twelve-volt Ignition?" *Steel*, August 8, 1955, p. 51.

Norris, James. "Design of Delcotronic Transistorized Ignition System." *General Motors Engineering Journal*, 3d Quarter 1963, p. 16.

Peroutky, Donald C. "High Frequency Ignition Needs No Breaker Points." *Automotive Industries*, January 1, 1951, p. 34.

Scott, David. "Lucas Introduces Electronic Ignition System." *Automotive Industries*, August 1, 1961, p. 52.

Shano, Charles L., and Hutton, Arthur G. "Capacitor Discharge Ignition: A Design Approach." Paper presented before the Society of Automotive Engineers, January 9, 1967.

Sharpe, J. W. "Three Steps to Ideal Transistorized Ignition." *SAE Journal*, October 1965, p. 48.

"Transistors." *Encyclopedia Americana*, 1966, 27:8.

Tuttle, H. C. "Twelve-volt Electrical System Will Be on Some 1953 Cars." *Steel*, December 15, 1952, p. 89.

CASE 20 / PROGRAMMABLE CONTROL

Programmable control is the most recent major advance in automatic control of manufacturing processes. Programmable controllers (PC) replace handwired relay control panels in controlling sequential activities on one or a series of machines. Changes in relay panels, necessitated by the need to change machine operations, required rewiring by an electrician. A PC, however, can be reprogrammed by replacing a program chip or by push buttons. Programmable control differs from an earlier development, numerical control, which is the electronic control of operations on one complex machine tool. PCs have been extensively applied to transfer-line operations, where a series of machines are involved.

PCs are solid-state devices similar to minicomputers. They are an operational compromise between relay control and computer control, with advantages over both systems. Unlike most computers, PCs can withstand harsh factory environments and can be programmed by plant personnel without assistance from computer specialists. Compared to relay panels, PCs are easily programmed, take less floor space, can be interfaced with a central computer, are more reliable, and offer significant time-saving economies. An installation at Ford, for example, had estimated time savings of $100,000.

PCs originated in the automobile industry in 1968. GM specified the functions of the device and asked control manufacturers to design it. Digital Equipment Corporation built the first PC, installed at GM's Hydra-Matic transmission plant in 1969. Other companies quickly entered the field, including Modicon, Allen-Bradley, Struthers-Dunn, and Reliance Electric Company. By 1975, several thousand PCs were being used by the auto industry. Although the earliest PCs were more expensive, they now cost from $1,000 to $20,000. Originally, PCs were economical when more than twenty-five to thirty-five relays were involved, but newer devices are designd to replace even smaller relay panels. In the future, PCs are expected to have expanded capabilities, improved cost/performance ratios, and more simplified programming approaches.

CHRONOLOGY OF EVENTS

Late
1960s Minicomputers applied to manufacturing processes.
1971   About three hundred PCs installed, most in the auto industry in the northeast United States.
1972   About 1,600 PCs installed in Canada, European Economic Community, and all industrial sectors of United States.
1973   PCs used in almost all major industries and in the Far East, South America, and Australia.

REFERENCES

Burridge, P. D. "A Cheap Alternative to Computer Control." *Electrical Review*, May 3, 1974, p. 473.
Kish, Steven C. "Programmable Controllers." *Machinery*, June 1972, p. 46.
Maki, Erven I., and Hudson, Christopher A. "Manufacturing Control—Present and Future." *Automation*, April 1974, p. 58.
Pond, James B. "How Computers Unify Manufacturing." *Automotive Industries*, June 1, 1974, p. 32.
"Programmed Controls Spark New Detroit Era." *Iron Age*, February 10, 1972, p. 82.
Rekstad, Gary M. "Lift Off for Programmable Control." *Factory*, January 1973, p. 38.
Shapiro, Sydney F. "A Look at Computer Control and Automation in Automotive Manufacturing." *Computer Design*, October 1973, p. 48.
Ware, William. "Programmable Controller Use Accelerates." *Detroit Engineer*, April 1974, p. 22.
Wilson, Robert A. "Programmable Controllers for the Unsophisticated." *Iron Age*, August 26, 1974, p. 46.

APPENDIX 2 / CHRONOLOGY OF FORD CARS, BODIES, AND ENGINES

CHRONOLOGY OF FORD MOTOR COMPANY PASSENGER CAR PRODUCT-LINE CHANGES, 1903 TO 1975

I. Models and Body Types

This chronology focuses on the changing composition of Ford Motor Company passenger vehicle models and engines. The intent is to highlight rudimentary patterns of consistency and change in body and chassis as they relate to the product line that is marketed each year. Engine specifications are listed with body and chassis models through 1954, and those after 1954 are given in Section II, "Engine Statistics." After 1961, a common corporatewide engine line was adopted so that engines were no longer uniquely associated with models.

Initially, a model designation is applied to a chassis, engine-suspension, power-train combination. The body is specified independently, as it was designed and purchased. The model is the unit definition of the product that is marketed. Later (1930s through 1950s) the model becomes synonymous with the year (model year) as change is introduced annually in a systematic, planned framework. A major model change typically implies systematic change across all components. In the late 1950s and 1960s the engine and transmission are increasingly separated out as standardized components, specified separately as options by the customer. The model that is marketed becomes a particular chassis/body suspension, styling configuration within the broader product line. Change is managed independently within each of these models (T Bird, Fairlane, etc.), and sweeping product improvements are no longer introduced across the product line as they were earlier, as with the Model T, A, V-8, and the 1949 Ford. During later years the focus is on the Mustang, Pinto, and others, and in changes to these models. Finally, standardized bodies as well as engine power-train components are increasingly introduced (as reflected in body family designations in this chronology). The result is to make the model, defined for product-marketing purposes, a styling concept that is built up of standard engineering components and differentiated from other models by the components employed and the appointments.

Data on basic units in each year are organized as follows:

1. For each year all major passenger car models in the Ford Motor Company passenger car line are given (as defined during the era in question):

a. First, each name and/or included name-plate series is given, and where available, the FMC model number.

b. Next, the wheelbase for the model is given in inches (for example, 100″). This was initially standardized for all body models (a function of chassis standardization). The wheelbase tends to reflect frame design choices and changes. Later, wheelbases and frame construction, vary (for example, stretched) with body options (two-door, four-door, station wagon, etc.). In this case the wheelbase for a standard body option defined by the *Automotive Industries* statistical series is reported (usually two- or four-door sedan depending on year).

c. Next, major car aspects uniquely associated with the model are given: (1) In early years this is the engine. The cubic-inch displacement (CID), cylinder and valve configuration. (2) The body appointment and style series available for the model (crestline, customline, etc.). In the 1960s and 1970s an attempt is made to identify distinct body designs. (3) From 1967 on a body family designator (such as Frame 1 = F 1) is developed to indicate the use and adoption of common body designs across model lines. The designator identifies the duration of a basic body design even though alterations in length or weight may have been introduced while it was in production. Changes in designators correspond with basic body design changes as opposed to annual model modifications.

2. The median weight of all major cars in the Ford product line (for example, M-WT 2,195 pounds) is given in each model year (first line, right-hand side of list for each year) to reflect changes in weight of the line. Because the basis for specifying gross weight changes over time these data can be considered only as approximations.

3. Notes on distinctive body features (DBF) and other information are given following the list of models. In early years, when a wide variety of bodies were purchased from outside suppliers and literally dropped over a standard chassis, the body design was largely independent of other body chassis and engine designs (starting heavily with steel-clad bodies in 1925 through the late 1930s). The changing nature of body-type definition reflects this change.

4. Note is made of unitized body construction as the base of the body family designator beginning in the late 1950s. The type is either frame (F) or unit body construction (UBC). This later type of construction is a complete integration of frame and body in one design. The frame per se is eliminated. The unitized Lincoln Zephyr body in the late 1930s was purchased by Ford from a supplier.

Sources

The reported data are obtained from four major sources, as noted below, but have been interpreted by the author and in some instances altered to avoid what appear to be inconsistencies between sources. Such inconsistencies grow out of differences in model-year and calendar-year statistics, differences in international and U.S. products (Canadian operations), differences in terminology between internal FMC designations and industrywide designations, and incomplete data sources.

1. "Suggested Retail Prices, Ford Passenger Cars since 1903." Ford Motor Company, circa 1956. Updated by the Technical and Product Information Staff of the Ford Motor Company.

2. *Automotive Industries.* Available each year from circa 1912, reporting statistics on U.S. and foreign automobile specifications.

3. Information supplied by Ford Motor Company personnel on the history of body design. In particular, the information and cooperation afforded by Michael W. R. Davis, technical and product information manager of Ford, has been invaluable in identifying body changes and commonalities.

4. Records of FMC operations available in the Ford Archives, Greenfield Village, particularly the branch assembly plant accessions. (Pertinent largely to periods 1913 to 1940 for the Ford line.)

5. *Official Used Car Guide*, National Automobile Dealers Association (various years).

Chronology of Ford Body Types and Models, 1903–1974

1903	Model:	A 72″ WB	WT 1,250	100.5 CID, 8-hp 2-cyl. horizontal opposing engine	
	DBF:	Runabout, Tonneau			
1904	Models:	B 92″ WB	WT 1,710	318 CID, 20 hp, IL* 4	M-WT 1,505
		C 72″ WB	WT 1,300	100.5 CID 10 hp, 2 cyl.	
	DBF:	Runabout, Touring Car			
1905†	Models:	B 92″ WB			M-WT 1,550
		F 84″ WB	WT 1,400	127 CID, 12 hp, 2 cyl.	
1906	Models:	N 84″	WT 1,050	149 CID, 15 hp, IL 4	M-WT 1,300
		R 84″	WT 1,050		
		S 84″	WT 1,100		
		K 114″	WT 2,000	453 CID, 40 hp, IL 6	
	DBF:	Runabout, Roadster, Touring; Common chassis used for Models N, R, and S. Cylinder block cast in pairs of cylinders.			
1907	Models:	N 84″			M-WT 1,400
		R 84″			
		S 84″			
		K 114″			
	DBF:	Roadster, Touring, Runabout			
1908	Models:	N 84″			M-WT 1,300
		R 84″			
		S 84″			
		T 100″	WT 1,100	177 CID, (22.5 SAE), 20 hp, 4 cyl.	
	DBF:	Touring, Town Car, Roadster, Coupe, Landaulet, Runabout			
1909	Models:	R 84″			M-WT 1,100
		S 84″			
		T 100″			
	DBF:	Runabout, Roadster, Touring, Tourabout, Coupe, Landaulet, Town			
1910	Models:	T 100″			M-WT 1,200
	DBF:	Roadster, Tourabout, Touring, Coupe, Town, Landaulet			
1911	Models:	T 100″			M-WT 1,287
	DBF:	Torpedo, Touring, Town, Runabout, Coupe			
1912	Models:	T 100″			M-WT 1,375
	DBF:	Torpedo, Touring, Town, Runabout, Coupe, Delivery Wagon (hereafter DW)			

* IL stands for in-line cylinder configuration.

† Engine specifications are omitted in years when no change was reported from prior year.

1913	Models:	T 100″	M-WT 1,405
	DBF:	Torpedo, Touring, Town, Runabout, Coupe, DW	
1914	Models:	T 100″	M-WT 1,435
	DBF:	Torpedo, Touring, Town, Runabout, Coupe, Sedan (2 dr.), DW	
1915	Models:	T 100″	M-WT 1,465
	DBF:	Touring, Town, Runabout, Coupe, Sedan (2 dr.), DW, Truck (hereafter TK)	
1916	Models:	T 100″	M-WT 1,515
	DBF:	Touring, Town, Runabout, Coupe, Sedan (2 dr.), DW, TK	
1917	Models:	T 100″	M-WT 1,565
	DBF:	Touring, Town, Runabout, Coupe, Sedan (2 dr.), DW, TK	
1918	Models:	T 100″	M-WT 1,567
	DBF:	Touring, Town, Roadster, Runabout, Coupe, Sedan, DW, TK (demountable rims, starter options)	
1920	Models:	T 100″	M-WT 1,628
	DBF:	Touring, Town, Roadster, Runabout, Coupe, Sedan, DW, TK (rims and starter options)	
1921	Models:	T 100″	M-WT 1,628
	DBF:	Touring, Town, Runabout, Roadster, Coupe, Sedan, DW, TK	
1922	Models:	T 100″	M-WT 1,680
		Lincoln 136″ 358 CID, 90 hp [36.45 SAE], 8 cyl., L head	
	DBF:	Touring, Town, Runabout, Roadster, Coupe, Sedan (2 dr. and 4 dr.), DW, TK (Lincoln acquired)	
1923	Models:	T 100″	M-WT 1,705
		Lincoln 136″	
	DBF:	Touring, Town, Runabout, Roadster, Coupe, Sedan (2 dr. and 4 dr.), DW, TK (starter, rims, pneumatic tires standard on some models)	
1924	Models:	T 100″	M-WT 1,730
		Lincoln 136″	
	DBF:	Touring, Town, Runabout, Roadster, Coupe, Sedan (2 dr. and 4 dr.), DW, TK	
1925	Models:	T 100″	M-WT 1,820
		Lincoln 136″	
	DBF:	Touring, Town, Runabout, Roadster, Coupe, Sedan (2 dr. and 4 dr.), DW, TK (starter and rim options on some bodies)	
		In August 1925, Ford announced the most pronounced changes in the Model T body since it was first introduced: steel bodies for open models, chassis lowered, color options offered with matching upholstery, body lengthened 3½ inches. Chassis was not greatly changed, however.	
1926	Models:	T 100″ 177 CID, IL 4	M-WT 1,861
		Lincoln 136″ 358 CID, 8 cyl.	
	DBF:	Touring, Town, Runabout, Roadster, Coupe, Sedan (2 dr. and 4 dr.), DW, TK (starter and rims standard on all passenger vehicles)	
1927	Models:	A 103.5″ WB 200 CID, 40 hp, 4 cyl., L head	M-WT 2,180
		Lincoln 123″ 358 CID, 90 hp, V-8, L head	
	DBF:	Phaeton, Town, Roadster, Coupe, Sedan (2 dr. and 4 dr.), DW, TK (rumble seat option)	

1928 Models: A 103.5"   M-WT 2,245
Lincoln 136"   385 CID, 100 hp, V-8, L head
- DBF: Phaeton, Roadster, Coupe, Sedan 2 dr. (Tudor), Sedan 4 dr. (Fordor), Town Sedan, Cabriolet, Town Car, Station Wagon (hereafter SW), DW, Taxi (rumble seat option)

1929 Models: A 103.5"   M-WT 2,312
Lincoln 136"
- DBF: Phaeton, Roadster, Coupe, Tudor, Fordor, Town Sedan, Cabriolet, Town Car, Taxi, SW, DW, TK (rumble seat option)

1930 Models: A 103.5"   M-WT 2,315
Lincoln 136"
- DBF: Phaeton, Roadster, Coupe, Tudor, Fordor, Town Sedan, Cabriolet, Town Car, Taxi, Ambulance, Victoria, SW, DW, TK (rumble seat option, multiple window option, and deluxe options available on some styles)

1931 Models: A 103.5"   M-WT 2,316
Lincoln 136"
- DBF: Phaeton, Roadster, Coupe, Tudor, Fordor, Victoria, Cabriolet, SW, DW, Ambulance, Convertible (deluxe and standard options from this year through 1940s)

1932 Models: Ford 18 106"   221 CID, 65 hp, V-8, L head   M-WT 2,335
B 106"   200 CID, 50 hp, 4 cyl., L head
Lincoln 136"   447.9 CID, 150 hp, V-12, L head
- DBF: Phaeton, Roadster, Coupe, Cabriolet, Victoria, Tudor, Fordor, Convertible, SW, DW, TK (well fender, colored glass, rumble seat options)

1933 Models: Ford 40 112"   221 CID, V-8, L head; 200 CID, IL 4 M-WT 2,553
Lincoln 136"   381.7 CID, 125 hp, V-12, L head
Lincoln 145"   447.9 CID, 150 hp, V-12, L head
- DBF: Phaeton, Roadster, Coupe, Cabriolet, Victoria, Tudor, Fordor, SW, DW, TK (window, rumble seat options) (eight basic body styles). V-8 engine modified to eliminate faults. Aluminum head introduced. A new X-type frame introduced to stiffen car.

1934 Models: Ford (40) 112"   221 CID, V-8, 200 CID, IL 4   M-WT 2,573
Lincoln 136" and 145"
- DBF: Phaeton, Roadster, Coupe, Cabriolet, Victoria, Tudor, Fordor SW, Sedan delivery (hereafter SD) (window, rumble seat options)

1935 Models: Ford (48) 112"   221 CID, V-8   M-WT 2,801
Lincoln (K) 136" and 145"   414 CID, V-12, 150 hp
- DBF: Phaeton, Roadster, Coupe, Cabriolet, Victoria, Tudor, Fordor Convertible, SW, SD (rumble seat and window options)

From about 1935 on, light trucks have distinctive separate styling, mechanics, and models except for "sedan delivery."

1936 Models: Ford (68) 112"   221 CID, V-8   M-WT 2,783
Lincoln (K) 136" and 145"   414 CID, V-12
Lincoln Zephyr (901) 122"   (267.3 CID, V-12, 110 hp) unit construction body
- DBF: Phaeton, Roadster, Coupe, Cabriolet, Tudor, Fordor,

Convertible, SD (rumble seat options). Zephyr added with new semiunit construction body supplied by vendor and has headlights in fenders.

1937 Models: Ford (74 and 78) 112"   136 CID, 2.6" bore, V-8,   M-WT 2,568
60 hp, and 221 CID,
2¹⁄₁₆" bore, V-8, 85 hp
Lincoln (K) 136" and 145"   414 CID, 150 hp, V-12
Lincoln Zephyr (HB) 122"   267.3 CID, 110 hp,
V-12

DBF: Zephyr body, Tudor, Fordor, Coupe, Phaeton, Roadster, Cabriolet, Touring Sedan, Convertible, SW, SD (rumble seat) Engine option offered in Ford V-8 with aluminum piston in one and iron in the other. New body introduced this year with a rationalized appointment series; standard and deluxe options. Ford and Lincoln integrate headlights into fenders.

1938 Models: Ford (81A and 82A) 112"   136 CID, V-8, and   M-WT 2,619
221 CID, V-8
Lincoln (K) 136" and 145"   414 CID, V-12
Lincoln 86 H Zephyr 125"   267.3 CID, V-12

DBF: Zephyr body, Phaeton, Tudor, Fordor, Coupe, Convertible, SW, SD. "Standard" and "Delux" implemented with distinctive front-end styling. Standard retains 1937 front sheet metal while Delux is new; pattern continues through 1940 model.

1939 Models: Ford (922A and 91A) 112"   136 CID, V-8 and   M-WT 2,679
221 CID, V-8
Mercury 116"   239 CID, V-8   New car with
unique body
and engine
Lincoln (K) 136" and 145"   414 CID, V-12
Lincoln Zephyr 125"   267.3 CID, V-12 Sedan

DBF: Tudor, Fordor, Coupe, SW, Convertible, Sedan Delivery. Two distinct body styles for Ford. Hydraulic brakes adopted on all models.

1940 Models: Ford (022A and 01A) 112"   136 CID, V-8, and   M-WT 2,778
221 CID, V-8
Mercury (09A) 116"   239 CID, V-8, 95 hp
Lincoln (K) 136" and 145"   414 CID, V-12
Lincoln Zephyr/Continental (06H) 125"   292 CID,
V-12,
120 hp

DBF: Tudor, Fordor, Coupe, Convertible, SW, DTK, TK, (three levels of appointments introduced; in Ford Special, Delux and Super Delux on many body styles). New torsion bar stabilizer on 85-hp car.

1941 Models: Ford (11A and 1GA) 114"   221 CID, V-8, and
226 CID, IL 6, 90
hp Small V-8
dropped
Mercury (19A) 118"   239 CID, V-8
Lincoln Custom (168H) 138"   292 CID, V-12,
120 hp
Lincoln Zephyr/Continental (16H) 125"   292 CID,
V-12

DBF: New bodies introduced in Ford, Mercury, and Lincoln Custom. Running boards completely absorbed in body. Models continued essentially unchanged until

1949 models. 1942 models produced in limited quantities before WW II shutdown. All standard Lincoln bodies used unit construction. Improved X frame on Fords, with box center section, 100 percent stiffer than prior years.

1942   Models: Produced in limited quantities—new front end, sheet metal, instrument panel changes, last year of Lincoln custom.

1945   Models: Ford (69A and 6GA) 114″   239.4 CID, V-8   M-WT 3,199
                                    100 hp, and 226
                                    CID, L head, IL 6, 90 hp

              Mercury (69M) 118″   239.4 CID, 100 hp, V-8
              Lincoln and Continental (66H) 125″   292 CID, 130 hp, V-12

      DBF: Coupe, Tudor, Fordor, Convertible, SW, SD (Delux, Super Delux, and engine choice options)

1947   Models: Ford (79A and 7GA) 114″   239.4 CID, V-8, and   M-WT 3,277 226 CID, IL 6
              Mercury (79M) 118″   239.4 CID, V-8
              Lincoln (76H) 125″   292 CID, V-12

      DBF: Coupe, Tudor, Fordor, Convertible, SW, SD (Delux and Super Delux options, heavy truck lines introduced)

1948   Models: Ford (89A and 87HA) 114″   239.4 CID, V-8, and   M-WT 3,277 226 CID, IL 6
              Mercury (89M) 118″   239.4 CID V-8, 100 hp
              Lincoln (876H) 125″   292 CID, V-12

      DBF: Coupe, Tudor, Fordor, Convertible, SW, DTK, TK, (Delux and Custom Delux options)

1949   Models: Ford (8BA and 8HA) 114″   239.4 CID, V-8, and   M-WT 3,195 226 CID, IL 6
              Mercury (9CM) 118″   255.4 CID, V-8, 110 hp
              Lincoln (9EL) 121″   336.7 CID, V-8, 152 hp
              Lincoln (9EH) 125″   336.7 CID, V-8, 152 hp

      DBF: 1949 models incorporated major structural and styling design changes across all lines, with simple lines, less chrome, rear and front deck, and new transmission. Appointment options available in Delux, Custom Delux classes. V-12 engine dropped. Independent front coil springs replace transverse springs in front and longitudinal springs adopted in rear. Hotchkiss drive replaces torque tube. Bendix brakes used. Chassis uses box section frame with strong side rails. Two pinion differential replaces four. Car is lighter and weight redistributed.

1950   Models: Ford (OBA and OHA) 114″   239.4 CID, V-8, and   M-WT 3,217 226 CID, IL 6
              Mercury (OCM) 118″   255.4 CID, V-8
               Lincoln (OEL) 121″   336.7 CID, V-8
               Lincoln (OEH) 125″   336.7 CID, V-8

      DBF: Same (Delux, Custom Delux options) Special "crestliner" sports tudor model introduced as predecessor of two-door "hardtop" (or pillarless) model.

1951   Models: Ford (1BA, 7 1HA) 114″   239.4 CID, V-8, and   M-WT 3,255 226 CID, IL 6
              Mercury (1CM) 118″   255.4 CID, V-8

| | Lincoln (1EL) 121" | 336.7 CID, 154 hp, V-8, L head | |
| | Lincoln (1EH) 125" | 336.7 CID, 154 hp, V-8, L head | |

DBF: Coupe, Tudor, Fordor, Convertible, SW. Appointment classes include Delux, Custom, and Custom Delux. Automatic transmissions introduced as option for Ford and Mercury. Ford introduces two-door hardtop "Victoria" model.

1952 Models:
Ford 114"   215.3 CID, 101 hp, ILHV 6, and 239.4 CID, V-8   M-WT 3,312
Mercury 118"   255.4 CID, V-8, L head
Lincoln 121"   317.5 CID, 160 hp, V-8 OHV
Lincoln 125"   317.5 CID, 160 hp, V-8 OHV

DBF: New 1952 model offered new body shell across Ford, Lincoln, and Mercury lines to introduce wide curved windshield, suspend pedals, etc.; generally to improve and perfect radical body change introduced in 1949. All-steel station wagon introduced, and sedan delivery model returns. A major change in emphasis in appointment options is introduced by offering three series of Fords with distinct differences in appointments: Mainline, Customline, and Crestline. New 215.3 overhead-valve 6-cyl. engine added in Ford line and new 317.5 CID overhead-valve (OHV) V-8 engine added for Lincoln. The first major change in V-8 design since 1932.

1953 Models:
Ford 115"   215.3 CID, IOHV 6, and 239.4 CID, V-8, L head   M-WT 3,293
Mercury 118"   255.4 CID, V-8, L head
Lincoln 123"   317.5 CID, OHV, V-8

DBF: New commercial vehicle bodies introduced emphasizing comfort. Last of 1932-type V-8 engines, with flat heads in Ford passenger cars this year. Body types Sedan, Sunliner Convertible, Hardtop Coupe, Victoria, SW Coupe.

1954 Models:
Ford 115.5"   223 CID, IL 6, and 239.4 CID, OHV, V-8   M-WT 3,353
Mercury 118"   256 CID, OHV, V-8
Lincoln 123"   317.5 CID, OHV, V-8

DBF: Same as 1953
New overhead-valve engines added: the 239 CID, OHV, V-8 engine. For Fords, the 256 CID V-8 engine for Mercury, the 6-cylinder engine grows to 223 CID.

1955 Models:
Ford 115.5"
Thunderbird 102"   First new car since Mercury in 1939; beginning of model proliferation.
Mercury 119"
Lincoln 123"

DBF: Appointment options available by lines; Mainline, Customline, Fairlane for Ford; Montclair, Monterey for Mercury. Body types include: Sedan, Coupe, SW, Hardtop (with transparent top), Convertible. Proliferation of engine options started this year making the upward inflection in the so-called horsepower race. Since engine options are too numerous to include, a separate attachment showing engine specifications is at the end of the chronology.

1956 Models: Ford 115.5"   Mainline, Customline, Fairlane—   M-WT 3,230
F 1 frame

T Bird 102"
Mercury 119"
Lincoln 73 126"   285 hp, V-8
Continental Mark II 126"

DBF: Four basic body families in use. The Ford family (designated here F 1) supporting Mainline, Customline, and Fairlane (top of line) appointment series; Mercury (a derivative of the Ford body) supporting Custom, Monterey, and Montclair appointment series; Lincoln (a distinctly different body) supporting the 73 and Continental appointment series and T Bird sports body. The Ford family reportedly accounted for some 97 percent of output volume. A variety of separate Ford and Mercury engines available as options.

1957 Models: Ford Custom 116"   Body F 1   M-WT 3,347
Ford Fairlane 118"   New frame body for top Ford line—F 2

T Bird 102"   Last year for two-seat, frame, sports body

Mercury 122"   New frame body—F 3, Monterey, Montclair, Turnpike

Lincoln 126"   Capri, Premiere
Continental 126"

DBF: 1957 models distinguished by introduction of different wheelbase Ford bodies in same year's line. All body types are of frame construction (there are generally five families of bodies: Ford F 1 and F 2, Mercury, Lincoln, and T Bird). New "Ranchero" model introduced as pickup truck based on two-door wagon.

1958 Models: Ford Custom 116"   F 1   M-WT 3,476
Ford Fairlane 118"   F 2
Edsel Ranger 118"   Ranger and Pacer on F 2 body
Edsel Corsair 124"   Corsair and Citation on Mercury F 3 body

Mercury Monterey 122"   Monterey and Monclair F 3 body

Mercury Parklane 125"   F 3 body
Lincoln 131"   New unit construction body UBC 2
T Bird 113"   New unit construction UBC 1

DBF: Introduction of unit construction with distinct divisional product-line concepts, reinforce family of bodies concept. The short Ford 116" wheelbase was dropped following this year. Four-passenger replaces prior two-passenger T Bird. Continental dropped as distinct line until 1968.

1959 Models: Ford Custom 118"   Custom, Fairlane, and Galaxie   M-WT 3,687
F 2 frame
Edsel 120"   Ranger and Corsair—F 2 frame
Mercury 126"   Monterey, Montclair—F 3
Mercury Parklane 128"   Frame F 3
Lincoln 131"   Premiere and Continental MK III—Series UBC 2

T Bird 113"   UBC 1

DBF: Engines standardized across product lines (as reflected in engine attachment). Distinctive engines for particular car lines discontinued, and Mercury engines are finally dropped in the 1961 model year. Body appointment features vary largely by body family except as noted from this year on. Body types: Sedan, Hardtop (retractable option), Convertible, SW.

1960 Models:
Ford 119″	Fairlane and Galaxie—Frame F 2	M-WT 3,246
Edsel 120″	Discontinued after short six-week production	
Comet 114″	Introduction of new model with new body "Stretched" UBC 3	
Falcon 109.5″	Introduction of new model with new UBC 3	
T Bird 113″	UBC 1	
Mercury 126″	Monterey, Montclair, Parklane F 3 body	
Lincoln 131″	Lincoln, including Premiere, Continental UBC 2	

DBF: The FMC body line includes five families, the two frames (Ford and Mercury) bodies and the three UBCs, the large Lincoln, T Bird, and the compact car body. New body introduced—UBC 3. Lincoln, Mercury and Ford production facilities consolidated this year. Last year for unique Mercury bodies. Falcon/Comet offered in 2 and 4 door sedan and SW.

1961 Models:
Ford 119″	Fairlane, Galaxie, and 500 series F 2	M-WT 3,265
Falcon 109.5″	UBC 3	
Comet 114″	UBC 3 derivative	
Mercury 120″	Meteor, Monterey—Frame F 2 derivative	
T Bird 113″	Introduction of new body—UBC 4	
Lincoln 123″	Introduction of new body—UBC 5	

DBF: Ford and Mercury put back on same basic body.

1962 Models:
Ford 119″	Galaxie F 2 body	M-WT 2,991
Fairlane 115.5″	New midsize unit construction body UBC 6	
Falcon 109.5″	UBC 3	
T Bird 113″	UBC 4	
Comet 114″	UBC 3 derivative	
Meteor 116.5″	New UBC medium car for Mercury UBC 6	
Mercury 120″	Frame F 2 derivative	
Lincoln 123″	UBC 5	

DBF: New midsize unit construction body introduced—UBC 6 for Fairlane and Meteor. Effectively the original F 1 and F 3 frame bodies, and unit construction bodies UBC 1 and 2 have been dropped from the line.

1963 Models:
Ford 119″	Galaxie 500, 500XL, F 2 body	M-WT 2,997
Mercury 120″	Monterey, Montclair, Parklane—F 2 body	
Falcon 109.5″	UBC 3	
Fairlane 115.5″	UBC 6	
T Bird 113.2″	UBC 4	
Lincoln 123″	UBC 5	

Comet* 109.5"/114"   UBC 3 derivative
Meteor 116.5"   UBC 6 derivative

DBF: * SW is 109.5", Sedan is 114"

1964   Models: Ford 119"   Galaxie, Custom, 500XL F 2 body   M-WT 3,114
Mercury 120"   Monterey, Montclair, Parklane—
            F 2 body
Falcon 109.5"   UBC 3
Comet* 109.5"/114"   UBC 3 derivative
T Bird 113.2"   UBC 4
Fairlane 115.5"   UBC 6
Lincoln 126"   UBC 5 derivative, longer wheelbase

DBF: Meteor discontinued
        * Sedan 114", SW 109.5"

1965   Models: Ford 119" (119" SW)   Custom, Galaxie [500   M-WT 3,432
                    LTD, XL] New major
                    chassis introduction—
                    F 4

Mercury 123" (119" SW)   Monterey, Montclair,
                    Parklane, new major
                    chassis introduction—
                    F 4 derivative

Fairlane 116"   UBC 6 derivative
Mustang 108"   New UBC car with new body
            UBC 7
Falcon 109.5"   UBC 3
Comet 114" (109.5 SW)   UBC 3 derivative
T Bird 113"   UBC 4
Lincoln 126"   UBC 5

DBF: Major model change year. New chassis for Ford and
        Mercury introducing perimeter frame (providing
        some advantages of unit body construction) with
        rear coil springs, designated F 4. The Mustang body
        design relied on some Falcon parts but was essen-
        tially a new body—UBC 7.

1966   Models: Ford 119"   Custom, Galaxie (500, 500 XL, LTD)   M-WT 3,115
                    F 4
Mercury 123"   Monterey, Montclair, Parklane—
            F 4 derivated or stretched
Fairlane 116"   New UBC body introduced UBC 8
Falcon (111"/113" SW)   New UBC body intro-
                    duced UBC 8

Mustang 108"   UBC 7
Comet (116"/113" SW)   New UBC body intro-
                    duced UBC 8

T Bird 113"   UBC 4
Lincoln 126"   UBC 5

DBF: A new intermediate class of UBC body introduced for
        Fairlane, Comet, Falcon. Dual wheelbases for
        Comet reflect short and long version for two door
        and four door as was also the case with 1957–58
        Ford.

1967   Models: Ford 119"   Custom, Galaxie [500, XL, LTD]—   M-WT 3,180
                    F 4 body
Mercury 123" (119" SW)   Monterey, Montclair,
                    Parklane Broughman,
                    Marquis—F 4 body
Mercury 119"   Colony Park, Commuter Wagons
            use F 4 body

Fairlane 116"/113" SW   UBC 8
Comet 116"/113" SW   UBC 8
Cougar 111"   New model, derivative of Mustang
           using basic UBC 7 body
Falcon 111"/113" SW   UBC 8 derivative
Mustang 108"   UBC 7
T Bird 115" (117" 4 door)   Introduced new frame
           construction F 5;
           dropped UBC
Lincoln 126"   UBC 5

DBF: Transition from unit construction for larger cars
      begins this model year.

1968   Models: Ford 119"   Custom, Galaxie (500, XL, LTD)   M-WT 3,429
                F 4 body
            Mercury 123"   Monterey, Monclair, Parklane F 4
                body
            Fairlane/Torino 116"/113" SW   Torino, Fairlane
                500, UBC 8
            Comet/Montego 116"/113" SW   UBC 8
            Falcon 111"/113" SW   UBC 8 derivative
            Cougar 111.1"   UBC 7 derivative
            Mustang 108"   UBC 7
            T Bird 115"/117"   Frame body F 5
            Lincoln 126"   UBC 5

DBF: Name plate changes. Ford Fairlane becomes Torino
      and Mercury Comet becomes Montego. Longer T
      Bird is for Landau version.

1969   Models: Ford 121"   Custom, Galaxie (500, XL) F 4   M-WT 3,221
            Mercury 124"   Monterey, Marquis, F 4 derivative
            Mercury 121"   Marauder, Ford frame F 4 der-
                ivative
            Falcon 111"/113"   UBC 8
            Torino/Fairlane 116"/113"   UBC 8
            Comet/Montego 116"/113"   UBC 8
            Cougar 111"   UBC 7 derivative
            T Bird 115"/117"   Frame F 5
            Lincoln Cont. 126"   Last Lincoln of unit body con-
                struction UBC 5
            Continental MK III 117"   Introduced on T Bird F 5
                frame body derivative
            Mustang 108"   UBC 7

DBF: Falcon/Torino/Montego station wagon share 113"
      wheelbase and body. Mustang/Cougar redesigned
      bodies with same basic dimensions. New larger Ford
      body with longer wheelbase.

1970   Models: Ford 121"   Custom, XL LTD, frame body F 4   M-WT 3,198
            Mercury 124"   Monterey, Marquis, frame body
                stretched F 4
            Lincoln Continental 127"   Introduced frame con-
                struction, stretched
                F 4 derivative
            Lincoln MK III 117"   Frame construction, F 5
                derivative
            Maverick 103"   Introduce new car and body UBC 9
            Falcon 111"/113"   UBC 8 and derivative (phased
                out December 1969)
            Mustang 108"   UBC 7

Torino 117″/114″   Fairlane, Broughman, and Cobra
                     Redesigned body but still
                     UBC 8 derivative
Montego 117″/114″   Redesigned body but still
                     UBC 8 derivative
Cougar 111″   UBC 7 derivative
T Bird 115″/117″   Frame F 5 derivative

DBF: Falcon replaced with Maverick. Body allocations are:
         (1) Frame body F 4 for Ford, Lincoln, Mercury;
         (2) Frame body F 5 for T Bird and Continental
         MK III; (3) UBC 7 for Mustang/Cougar; (4)
         UBC 8 derivative for Torino/Montego; and (5)
         UBC 9 for Maverick.

1971 Models: Ford 121″   Frame construction body F 4   M-WT 3,074
                 Mercury 124″   Frame construction body F 4
                 Lincoln Continental 127″   Stretched F 4 derivative
                 Comet 103″/110″   Comet reintroduced using UBC 9
                                     (some differences)
                 MK III 117″   Frame F 5 derivative (last F 5 body)
                 Pinto 94″ (4 cyl.)   Introduce new car and UBC
                                        body, UBC 10
                 Maverick 103″/110″   UBC 9
                 Torino 117″/114″   UBC 8 derivative
                 Mustang II 109″   UBC 7 derivative
                 Montego 117″/114″   UBC 8 derivative
                 Cougar 112″   UBC derivative
                 T Bird 114.7″/117.2″   Frame F 5 derivative

DBF: The new Pinto was an unusual introduction in that
         engine, transmission, and steering gear parts were
         first used and manufactured in Europe (England and
         Germany). In a real sense, the Pinto was a car that
         was standardized internationally. The first use of
         4-cylinder engines at Ford since the 1930s. The
         larger 2.0-liter OHC engine was designed at Dear-
         born, initially produced in Ford's plant in Cologne,
         Germany, for European models and also sold to
         other major European car producers, then used in
         the Pinto. The smaller 4-cylinder 1.6-liter engine
         was a Kent product (Ford of Britain).

1972 Models: Ford 121″   Custom, Galaxie (LTD) F 4 frame   M-WT 3,115
                 Mercury 124″ (121″ SW)   Monterey, Marquis
                                            Frame F 4
                 Continental MK IV 120″   Introduce new frame
                                            construction F 6
                                            stretched
                 Lincoln 127″   Frame construction stretched F 4
                                  derivative
                 Torino 114″/118″   Introduce new frame construc-
                                      tion F 6
                 T Bird 120″   Introduce new frame construction
                                 F 6 stretched
                 Maverick 103″/110″   UBC 9
                 Comet 103″/110″   UBC 9
                 Mustang 109″   UBC 7 derivative
                 Montego 114″/118″   New frame construction F 6
                 Pinto 94″   UBC 10
                 Cougar 112″   UBC 7 derivative

DBF: Major change toward frame construction over unit construction with introduction of new F 6 frame replacing UBC in Torino and Montego. 114″ WB is for two-door hardtop; 118″ is four-door hardtop and sedan and four-door SW; stretched shell and frame used for 120″ WB, T Bird and Continental MK IV.

1973   Models: Ford 121″   Custom 500, Galaxie LTD F 4
Mercury 124″ (121″ SW)   Monterey, Marquis, Brougham F 4
Lincoln MK IV 120″   F 6 stretched
T Bird 120″   F 6 stretched
Continental 127″   Stretched F 4 derivative
Torino 114″/118″   2 door/4 door F 6
Montego 114″/118″   2 door/4 door F 6
Pinto 94″   UBC 10
Maverick 103″/110″   Coupe/Sedan UBC 9
Mustang 109″   UBC 7 derivative, last year
Cougar 112″   UBC 7 derivative, last year
Comet 103″/110″   UBC 9

DBF: New exterior sheet metal for Ford/Mercury.

1974   Models: In the 1973/74 period there are four families that are derivative of prior evolutionary changes and new introductions.

Large frame family—F 4   Ford, Mercury, Lincoln large car frame family: Monterey, Marquis, Galaxie, and others.

Stretched F-6 frame family   Lincoln MK IV and T Bird, stretched frames—derivatives of F-6

Intermediate frame family—F 6   Intermediate Ford and Mercury derivatives: Torino, Montego, Cougar

Compact UBC family—UBC 9   Intermediate unit construction family: Maverick, Comet

Small UBC family—UBC 10   Small car unit construction family: Pinto

—UBC 11   Mustang II, redesigned body based on UBC 10

1975   Models: Same as 1974 models except for a new body UBC 12 for Granada and Monarch and the Bobcat added as a 1975½ year model using UBC 11 body.

II. ENGINE STATISTICS, SELECTED MAJOR EARLY ENGINES—BEFORE 1955

(A more complete listing of engines is given with bodies from 1903 to 1954 in the Body Chronology)

Year	Car Model	Cylinder and Configura- tion	Cubic- Inch Displace- ment (CID)	Com- pression Ratio	Brake Horsepower (BHP) at stated RPM (00s)	Bore and Stroke (in inches)
1903	Ford A	OP 2	100.5		8	4 x 4
1904	B	IL 4	318		20	4.5 x 5
	C	2	100.5		10	4 x4
	F	2	127		12	4.5 x 4
1906	N	4	149		15	3.75 x 3.375
	J	IL 6	453		40	4.5 x 3¾
1908–27	Ford T	IL LH 4	177	3.6 to 1	20 @ 16	3.75 x 4
1922	Lincoln	8	358		90 @ 28	3.375 x 5
1928	Lincoln	V LH 8	385		100	
1927–32	A	IL LH 4	200.5	4.24 to 1	40 @ 22	3.875 x 4.5
1932	B	IL LH 4	200.5	4.60 to 1	50 @ 28	3.875 x 4.5
1932	18	V LH 8	221	5.5 to 1	65 @ 34	3.06 x 3.75
1932	Lincoln	V LH 12	447.9		150 @ 34	3.25 x 4.5
1935	Lincoln	V LH 12	414	6.38	150 @ 34	3⅛ x 4½
1936	Lincoln Zephyr	V LH 12	267.3		110 @ 39	2¾ x 3¾
1937	Ford	V LH 8	136	6.6	60 @ 36	2.6 x 3.2
1939	Mercury	V LH 8	239	6.15	95 @ 38	3³⁄₁₆ x 3¾
1941	Ford	IL LH 6	226	6.7	90 @ 33	3.3 x 4.4
1949	Lincoln	V LH 8	336.7	7.0	152 @ 36	3.5 x 4⅜
1952	Lincoln	VOH 8	317.5		160	
1952	Ford	IL OH 6	215		101 @ 35	3.56 x 3.6

Abbreviations: Overhead valves: OH or OHV, Valves in block: L head or LH, Overhead cam: OHC, "In" line cylinder configuration: IL, "V" Configuration cylinders: V. Hence, VOH 6 designates a 6-cylinder engine with overhead valves in a V configuration, and OP designates opposing cylinder configuration.

III. FORD MOTOR COMPANY FULL PASSENGER ENGINE LINE, 1955–1975

Year	Car	Cylinder and Con- figuration	Cubic- Inch Displace- ment (CID)	Brake Horse- power (BHP)	RPM (00)
1955	Ford Mainline, Customline, Fairlane	IL OH 6	223	120	40
	Ford Mainline, Customline, Fairlane	VOH 8	272	162	44
	T Bird, Mercury	VOH 8	292	188	44
	Lincoln	VOH 8	341	225	44
1956	Ford Mainline, Customline, Fairlane	IL OH 6	223	137	42
	Ford Mainline, Customline	VOH 8	272	173	44
	T Bird, Fairlane	VOH 8	292	200	46

Year	Car	Cylinder and Configuration	Cubic-Inch Displacement (CID)	Brake Horsepower (BHP)	RPM (00)
	T Bird, Mercury	VOH 8	312	210	46
	Lincoln, Continental	VOH 8	368	285	46
1957	Ford Custom, Fairlane,	IL OH 6	223	144	42
	Custom	VOH 8	272	190	45
	T Bird, Fairlane	VOH 8	292	206	45
	Mercury	VOH 8	312	255	45
	Lincoln, Continental	VOH 8	368	300	48
1958	Ford Custom, Fairlane	IL OH 6	223	145	42
	Custom, Fairlane	VOH 8	292	205	45
	Fairlane 500, 51A, 57A, 58B, 63A, 64B	VOH 8	332	265	46
	T Bird	VOH 8	352	300	46
	Edsel Ranger, Pacer	VOH 8	361	303	46
	Mercury, Monterey, Montclair	VOH 8	383	312	46
	Edsel Corsair, Citation	VOH 8	410	345	46
	Lincoln, Continental, Mercury Park Lane	VOH 8	430	360	46
1959	Ford Custom, Fairlane, Edsel Ranger	IL OH 6	223	145	40
	Ford Custom, Fairlane, Edsel Ranger	VOH 8	292	200	44
	Edsel Corsair	VOH 8	332	225	44
	Mercury Monterey	VOH 8	312	210	44
	T Bird	VOH 8	352	300	46
	Mercury Montclair	VOH 8	383	322	46
	Lincoln, Continental, Mercury Park Lane	VOH 8	430	345	44
1960	Ford Falcon, Comet	IL OH 6	144.3	90	42
	Ford Fairlane, Galaxie	IL OH 6	223	145	40
	Ford Fairlane, Galaxie	VOH 8	292	185	42
	Mercury Monterey	VOH 8	312	205	40
	T Bird	VOH 8	352	300	46
	Lincoln, Continental, Mercury Montclair, Mercury Park Lane	VOH 8	430	310	41
1961	Ford Falcon, Comet	IL OH6	144.3	85	42
	Ford Fairlane, Galaxie, Mercury Meteor	IL OH 6	223	135	40
	Ford Fairlane, Galaxie, Mercury Meteor, Mercury Monterey	VOH 8	292	175	42
	T Bird	VOH 8	390	300	46
	Lincoln Continental	VOH 8	430	300	41
1962	Ford Falcon, Mercury Comet	IL OH 6	144.3	85	42
	Ford Falcon, Mercury Comet, Mercury Meteor, Ford Fairlane	IL OH 6	170	101	44
	Mercury Meteor, Ford Fairlane	VOH 8	221	145	44
	Ford Galaxie, Mercury Monterey	IL OH 6	223	138	42
	Ford Galaxie, Mercury Monterey	VOH 8	292	170	42
	Ford Galaxie*, Mercury Monterey*	VOH 8	352	220	43
	T Bird, Ford Galaxie*, Mercury Monterey*	VOH 8	390	300	46
	Ford Galaxie*, Mercury Monterey*	VOH 8	406	385	58
	Lincoln Continental	VOH 8	430	300	41

Year	Car	Cylinder and Configuration	Cubic-Inch Displacement (CID)	Brake Horsepower (BHP)	RPM (00)
1963	Ford Falcon, Mercury Comet	IL OH 6	144.3	85	42
	Ford Falcon*, Fairlane, Mercury Comet*, Mercury Meteor	IL OH 6	170	101	44
	Ford Fairlane, Mercury Meteor	VOH 8	221	145	44
	Ford 300, Galaxie 500	IV OH 6	223	138	42
	Ford Fairlane*, Ford 300, Galaxie 500, Mercury Meteor	VOH 8	260	164	44
	Ford 500 XL, Ford 300*, Galaxie 500*	VOH 8	352	220	43
	T Bird, Mercury Monterey, Ford 300*, Galaxie 500*, 500X.*	VOH 8	390	300	46
	Lincoln Continental	VOH 8	430	320	46
1964	Ford Falcon, Futura	IL OH 6	144.3	85	42
	Ford Falcon Futura (Convertible), Fairlane, Mercury Comet 202, 404	IL OH 6	170	101	44
	Ford Falcon, Fairlane, Mercury Comet 202, 404, Caliente	IL OH 6	200	116	44
	Ford Custom, Galaxie 500	IL OH 6	223	138	42
	Ford Falcon Sprint, Fairlane, Mercury Comet 202, 404, Caliente	VOH 8	260	164	44
	Ford Fairlane, Custom, Galaxie 500, Mercury Comet, Cyclone	VOH 8	289	195	44
	Ford Custom, Galaxie	VOH 8	352	250	44
	T Bird, Ford Custom, Galaxie, Mercury Monterey, Montclair, Park Lane	VOH 8	390	300	46
	Lincoln Continental	VOH 8	430	320	46
1965	Ford Falcon, Futura	IL OH 6	170	105	44
	Ford Falcon, Futura, Mustang, Fairlane, Mercury Comet 202, 204, Caliente, Cyclone	IL OH 6	200	120	44
	Ford Custom 500, Galaxie	IL OH 6	240	150	40
	Ford Falcon, Futura, Mustang, Fairlane, Galaxie, 500 LTD, Mercury Comet 202, 404, Caliente, Cyclone	VOH 8	289	200	44
	Ford Custom, 500, Galaxie 500	VOH 8	352	250	44
	T Bird Landau, Mercury Monterey, Montclair, Park Lane, Ford Custom, 500, Galaxie	VOH 8	390	300	46
	Ford Custom, 500, Galaxie, Mercury Monterey, Montclair, Park Lane	VOH 8	427	425	60
	Lincoln Continental	VOH 8	430	320	46
1966	Ford Falcon, Futura, Ford Falcon, Futura, Mustang, Fairlane	IL OH 6	170	105	44
	Mercury Comet, 202, Capri, Caliente, Cyclone	IL OH 6	200	120	44
	Ford Custom, 500, Galaxie 500, XL, LTD 7-Litre	IL OH 6	240	150	44
	Ford Custom, 500, Galaxie, Mercury Comet 202, Capri, Caliente, Cyclone	VOH 8	289	200	44
	Ford Custom, 500, Galaxie	VOH 8	352	250	44
	T Bird, Ford Fairlane, Ford Custom,				

Year	Car	Cylinder and Configuration	Cubic-Inch Displacement (CID)	Brake Horsepower (BHP)	RPM (00)
	Galaxie, Mercury Monterey, Montclair, Comet, Cyclone	VOH 8	390	265	44
	Mercury Park Lane	VOH 8	410	330	46
	Ford Custom, 500, Galaxie	VOH 8	427	410	56
	T Bird, Ford Custom, 500, Galaxie, Mercury S-55	VOH 8	428	345	46
	Lincoln Continental	VOH 8	462	340	46
1967	Ford Falcon	IL OH 6	170	105	44
	Ford Falcon Station Wagon, Futura	IL OH 6	200	120	44
	Mustang, Fairlane, 500, XL, Mercury Comet 202, Capri, Caliente, Station Wagon	IL OH 6	240	135	40
	Ford Taxi, Custom Galaxie Station Wagon	VOH 8	289	200	44
	Ford Custom, 500, Galaxie, Station Wagon, Mercury Station Wagon, Cougar, T Bird, Mercury Monterey, Montclair, Commuter, Colony Park, Cyclone GT	VOH 8	390	315	46
	Mercury Park Lane, Brougham, Marquis	VOH 8	410	330	46
	Mercury S-55	VOH 8	428	345	46
	Lincoln Continental	VOH 8	462	340	46
1968	Ford Falcon	IL OH 6	170	100	40
	Ford Falcon Station Wagon, Mustang, Fairlane, Torino, Mercury Comet, Montego	IL OH 6	200	115	38
	Ford Falcon Standard, Deluxe, Mustang	VOH 8	289	195	46
	Ford Fairlane, Torino, Custom, Galaxie, Mercury Cyclone, Montego, MX Brougham, Cougar, XR-7	VOH 8	302	210	46
	T Bird, Mercury Monterey, Montclair Commuter, Colony Park, Park lane Brougham, Marquis	VOH 8	390	315	46
	Park Lane, S-55	VOH 8	428	340	46
	Lincoln Continental	VOH 8	462	340	46
1969	Ford Falcon	IL OH 6	170	100	40
	Ford Futura, Mustang	IL OH 6	200	115	38
	Ford Custom, Galaxie	IL OH 6	240	150	40
	Ford Mustang E, Fairlane, Torino, Mercury Comet, Montego, Montego MX Brougham	IL OH 6	250	155	40
	Ford Torino, Mercury Cyclone	VOH 8	302	220	46
	Ford Mustang Mach I, Mercury Cougar XR-7	VOH 8	351	250	46
	Mercury Marauder, Monterey, Monterey Custom	VOH 8	390	265	44
	Ford Cobra, Mercury Cyclone, CJ	VOH 8	428	335	52
	T Bird, Landau, Mercury Marquis, Marauder X-100	VOH 8	429	320	44
	Lincoln Continental, Mark III	VOH 8	460	365	46

Year	Car	Cylinder and Configuration	Cubic-Inch Displacement (CID)	Brake Horsepower (BHP)	RPM (00)
1970†	Ford Maverick	IL OH 6	170	105	42
	Ford Falcon, Futura, Mustang	IL OH 6	200	120	40
	Ford Custom 500, Galaxie 500	IL OH 6	240	150	40
	Ford Fairlane 500, Torino, Brougham, Mercury Montego, MX, Brougham	IL OH 6	250	155	40
	Ford Torino GT, Mercury Cougar, XR-7	VOH 8	302	220	46
	Ford Mustang Mach I, Ford XL, Brougham, Mercury Cyclone GT, Cougar Eliminator	VOH 8	351	250	46
	Mercury Monterey, Custom, Marauder, Marquis, Brougham	VOH 8	390	265	44
	T Bird, Torino, Cobra, Mercury Cyclone, Spoiler	VOH 8	429	360	46
	Lincoln Continental, Mark III	VOH 8	460	365	46
1971	Ford Pinto‡	IL OHC 4	97.6	75	50
	Ford Maverick, Mercury Comet	IL OH 6	170	100	42
	Ford	IL OH 6	240	140	40
	Ford Mustang, Torino, Mercury Montego	IL OH 6	250	145	40
	Ford Mustang	VOH 8	302	210	46
	Ford, Torino, Mercury Cougar, Montego, Mercury	VOH 8	351	240	46
	Mercury	VOH 8	400	260	44
	T Bird, Mercury	VOH 8	429	320	44
	Lincoln, Mark III	VOH 8	460	365	46
1972	Ford Pinto	IL OH 4	97.6	54	46
	Ford Maverick, Mercury Comet	IL OH 6	170	82	44
	Ford Custom, Galaxie	IL OH 6	240	103	38
	Ford Torino, Mustang, Mercury Montego	IL OH 6	250	95	36
	Ford Custom, Galaxie, Torino, Mustang, Maverick, Mercury Montego, Comet	VOH 8	302	140	40
	Ford LTD, Mercury Monterey, Montego, Cougar	VOH 8	351	153	38
	T Bird, Mercury Marquis	VOH 8	429	212	44
	Lincoln Continental, Mark IV	VOH 8	460	212	44
1973	Ford Pinto	IL OH 4	97.6	54	46
	Ford Maverick, Mercury Comet	IL OH 6	200	84	38
	Ford Torino, Gran Torino, Mustang, Granada	IL OH 6	250	92	32
	Ford Torino, Gran Torino, Maverick Mach I, Mercury Montego, MX, Brougham, Comet	VOH 8	302	137	42
	Ford Custom, Galaxie, LTD, Mercury Monterey, Custom, Marquis, Brougham, Cougar	VOH 8	429	208	44
	T Bird	VOH 8	429	208	44
	Lincoln, Mark IV	VOH 8	460	219	44

Year	Car	Cylinder and Con-figuration	Cubic-Inch Displace-ment (CID)	Brake Horse-power (BHP)	RPM (00)
1974	Ford Pinto	IL OHC 4	122	80	54
	Ford Mustang	IL OHC 4	140	88	50
	Ford Maverick, Mercury Comet	IL OH 6	200	84	38
	Ford Torino, Mercury Comet, Montego, MX, Brougham	VOH 8	302	140	38
	Ford, Custom, Galaxie, LTD, Mercury Cougar, Montego, MX, Brougham	VOH 8	351	162	40
	Mercury Monterey, Monterey Custom	VOH 8	400	170	34
	T Bird, Mercury Marquis, Marquis, Brougham, Lincoln, Mark IV	VOH 8	460	195	38
1975	Ford Pinto, Mustang II	IL OHC 4	140	83	48
	Ford Mustang II	VOH 6**	170.8	97	44
	Ford Maverick, Granada, Mercury Comet, Monarch	IL OH 6	200	—	—
	Ford Granada Ghia	IL OH 6	250	72	29
	Ford Maverick, Mustang II, Granada, Mercury Comet, Monarch	VOH 8	302	122	38
	Ford Torino, LTD, Mercury Cougar, Montego	VOH 8	351	148	38
	Mercury Marquis	VOH 8	400	158	38
	T Bird, Mercury Marquis Brougham, Grand Marquis, Lincoln, Mark IV	VOH 8	460	194	38

SOURCE: *Automotive Industries*, Statistical Issue, Respective years.

* Optional.

† California Law on advertising engine rating caused change in BHP rating specifications as of this year.

‡ Produced in Germany but designed in the United States.

** European engine.

APPENDIX 3 / DATA SOURCES FOR EQUIPMENT AND PROCESS CHARACTERISTICS (TABLES 5.4, 5.7, 6.5, 6.8)

This appendix provides references used to determine process characteristics and technological changes as discussed in Chapters 5 and 6. A special key is provided for Tables 5.4 and 6.5, indicating the particular equipment characteristics that are referenced.

REFERENCE KEY TO TABLE 5.4

Engine Equipment Reference Sources
(a: transfer span, b: grouped operation, c: automation level)

1910–12
a   None noted [1] [48] [51].*
b   Baush, twenty-four-spindle drilling machine [46].
c   Ingersol milling machine, continuous operation while operator loads and unloads. [1].

1913–14
a   No change (moving assembly and conveyor only) [51].
b   Foote-Burt drilling machine, forty-five holes at once from four directions [51].
c   Ford camshaft shaping machine, master contour cam control provides simultaneous operation on all cams [51].

1924–26
a   No change (increased mechanized movement, no automated transfer) [18] [25] [14].
b   Drill machine makes forty-eight holes at once in four directions, twelve cylinder blocks group milled all at once by one machine [20] [53].
c   No change [20] [54] [14].

1927–28
a   No change (continued increase in movement by conveyor, no automated transfer) [23] [21] [9].
b   Foote-Burt drilling and tapping machine, performs thirty-four simultaneous operations [9].
c   No change [9].

1932–36
a   First known transfer—Ford designed battery of four spindle vertical drills, rough bores the cylinder using a hydraulically operated indexing fixture that rotates the casting and at the same time gives it a lengthwise travel from one operation

239

to the next. It was designed to accommodate offset on left and right V-8 cylinder bank [15, p. 812].
b   Five-way machine puts eighty-three holes in cylinder block [15].
c   No change.

1935–36
a   Tunnel-type, full automatic milling machine, mills, drills, and remills, implying a sequence of three or four stations [16].
b   No change.
c   Norton automatic cam grinder, sequentially moves and grinds each cam. The grinding wheel is automatically trued, compensating for wheel wear. Operator only loads and unloads, cycle is automatic [16].

1947–48
a   Excello three-way eight-station, milling, drilling, and tapping transfer machine package. No evidence of feedback measurement [3] [4].
b   Thirty-two spindle drilling machine [3] [4] [17].
c   No change [3] [4] [28] [17].

1952 (Cleveland Engine Plant)
a   The longest path of automated transfer was estimated as 150 stations in terms of equivalent stand-alone machine tools [56, p. 365].
b   The maximum number of operations at any one station, as reported, is twelve [30] [39].
c   Peak automation level for Cleveland Engine Plant is given as level 10 by J. R. Bright for 1954–55 conditions [52]. Automatic air-gauge inspection is provided at numerous points in transfer line to determine out-of-tolerance blocks [41] [42].

1970–72 (Pinto Engine Plant in Cologne and Lima, Ohio, were both equipped by U.S. machine-tool companies and designed along similar lines)
a   Transfer lines extended through into assembly and operating on a twenty-four-second cycle. Assembly insertions were automated, for example, in insertion of valve keepers and joining of cylinder head and block [38].
b   No change.
c   Gauges automatically classify cylinder by deviation. Cylinder classification numbers are scanned by closed-circuit TV cameras and are reproduced on a TV monitor screen. A linked numerical-control tape system orders matching pistons from stock for insertion into the block later. A diamond honing machine for cylinder finishing incorporates a gauge that provides feedback and correction during operation [38].

REFERENCE KEY TO TABLE 6.5

Assembly Equipment Reference Sources
(a: transfer span, b: grouped operations, c: automation level)

1914
a   None noted, introduction of moving assembly line [51] [13] [18] [54].
b   Few mechanized hand tools [54] [13].
c   Level 4, presses and welding apparatus employed [51 [13].

   * A brief description of the equipment and its special feature is noted, followed by references to the sources that were searched to determine equipment characterizations. Complete citations follow in the reference list. "None noted" means that no automatic transfer was evident in the literature, while "No change" means no change was apparent since the earlier reported period.

1927
a None noted, extensive moving conveyors—no automatic transfer [9].
b Small, single-purpose hand tools, all multiple operations are centralized.
c Level 4, power tool, hand controlled.
  Frame assembly is placed in Southwark compressed air press and rivet fixture, twelve rivets one at a time [9].

1930–32
a None noted, extensive moving conveyors; no automatic transfer [5] [6] [15] [25] [29].
b Small single-purpose hand tools; no noted multiple operations [5] [6].
c Level 4, welding press introduced but operator hand positions weld head sequentially to various locations to make multiple welds [5] [25].
"In the first operation . . . a jig, the dash, toeboard and windshield strainer are cold-riveted together with pneumatic hammers . . . a standard spot welder is used to make two welds beside each rivet" [5, p. 1021].
Tire-inflating machine uses six-station merry-go-round to "automatically" inflate tires, fed by two operators (only inflation is automatic) [25].

1936–38
a None noted; extensive moving conveyors; no automatic transfer [16] [40] [45].
b Small, single-purpose hand tools [16].
c No change [16].

1953–55
a None noted [31] [35] [39] [41] [43].
b Underbody section prepared in a clearing, welding press fitted with 144 guns [31].
c Level 8, tire travels about four feet during its cycle carrying the tire to a station where it is automatically filled with air. Here it passes over three limit switches. The first is for low pressure, the second turns on the high pressure, and the third unloads the assembly to the conveyor [43].
  Master gauging fixture in use for car body tolerance quality control [35].

1964
a None noted [36] [49].
b No change [36].
c Level 9 [36].
  A completely self-contained door-fitting and hinging fixture automatically aligns the door. Alignment in all directions is produced by means of gauges as well as power cylinders in the fixture [35, p. 50].

1970†
a Underbody build-up on Pinto; two-station welding presses.
b Welding presses, 190 welds estimated.
c No change [38].

1974‡
a Underbody build-up and integration through mechanized transfer in six stages incorporating stationary welding presses.
b Welds on underbody performed in three-stage sequence with part clamped in press, while welding head bank sequences through three stages with approximately thirty welds per sequence.
c No change.
  (Estimate from plant tour to Wayne Assembly Plant, October 1974).

1975‡
a Econoline plant has approximately twenty in-line transfers in body build-up [38].
b No change [38].
c No change [38].

  † According to interview data, the first transfer line in body construction at Ford was in 1965 in truck body manufacturing and involved two stages.
  ‡ Based on plant visit.

REFERENCES

Articles and Industry Publications
1. Abell, O. J. "Making the Ford Motor Car." *Iron Age* 89, no. 23 (June 6, 1912): 1383–92.
2. "Assembly Line." *Iron Age*, June 3, 1968, p. 100.
3. Baird, D. G. "Ford Reconverts." *Mill and Factory*, August 1945, pp. 89–92.
4. ———. "Ford Streamlines Operations in Motor Building." *Mill and Factory*, March 1947, pp. 100–104.
5. Chase, H. "Ford Body Assembly." *American Machinist*, June 26, 1930, pp. 1021–23.
6. ———. "One Ford a Minute." *American Machinist*, July 10, 1930, pp. 41–43.
7. Denham, Athel F., and Dibble, L. G. "Mechanical Details of New Ford." *Automotive Industries* 57, no. 23 (November 26, 1927): 781–785.
8. Ezell, J. V. "Assembly Plant Power Tools." *Automotive Industries*, October 15, 1970, pp. 53–57.
9. Faurote, Fay Leone. "Equipment Makes Possible the Ford Model A." *American Machinist*, a series of articles subtitled and dated as follows:
   "Preparing For Ford Production," April 21, 1928.
   "Cylinder Block and Head Operations," April 26, 1928.
   "Fabricating the Frame," May 3, 1928.
   "Operations on the Aluminum Pistons," May 10, 1928.
   "A Gasoline Tank that Serves as a Cowl," May 17, 1928.
   "Transmission Case," May 31, 1928.
   "Crankshaft and Camshaft," June 28, 1928.
   "Rear Axle," July 5, 1928.
   "Differential, Steering Gear and Wheels," July 12, 1928.
   "Assembly of the Motor," July 26, 1928.
   "Final Assembly," August 18, 1928.
10. ———. "Ford Shop Changes Estimated at $25,000,000." *Iron Age*, April 19, 1928, pp. 1080–83.
11. "The Ford Petrol Cars." *Automotor Journal*, June 1, 1907, pp. 741–98.
12. "Ford Light Touring Car for 1909." *The Automobile*, September 24, 1908, p. 435.
13. "Ford Service System." *The Automobile*, February 13, 1913, p. 470.
14. "Ford Changes Announced." *Automotive Industries*, August 27, 1925, p. 89.
15. "Ford Builds a V-8." *American Machinist*, July 6, 1932, p. 805.
16. "Ford Production Methods." *Mill and Factory*, January 1936 (entire issue), pp. 1–588.
17. "Ford Retools Cylinder Block Line." *Automotive Industries*, February 1, 1948, p. 38.
18. Ford Motor Company. *Ford Factory Facts*. 1st ed. (Detroit: Ford Motor Co., 1912), p. 65.
19. Ford Motor Company, *Factory Facts from Ford* (Dearborn, Mich., 1923).
20. ———. 1924, p. 147.
21. ———. 1925, p. 63
22. ———. 1926, p. 63.
23. ———. 1927, p. 63.
24. ———. 1929, p. 63.
25. Geschelin, Joseph. "Ingenious Equipment Speeds Up Export Plant." *Automotive Industries*, August 13, 1932.
26. ———. "Latest Body Assembly Techniques." *Automotive Industries*, September 15, 1947, p. 28.
27. ———. "Revolutionary Automation at Ford." *Automotive Industries*, November 15, 1948, p. 24.

28. ———. "Engine Plant Operation by Automation." *Automotive Industries*, May 1, 1952, p. 36.
29. ———. "Many Automatic Machines in Ford's New Engine Plant." *Automotive Industries*, July 1, 1952, p. 44.
30. ———. "Scheduling Problems in L-M Body Plant." *Automotive Industries*, November 15, 1953, p. 34.
31. ———. "Latest Machines and Methods at Ford's Dearborn Engine Plant." *Automotive Industries*, March 1, 1954, p. 26.
32. ———. "Automation Applied to Engine Assembly." *Automotive Industries*, May 1, 1954, p. 66.
33. ———. "Full Automation for Piston Pins." *Automotive Industries*, June 1, 1954, p. 48.
34. ———. "Flexible Controls for Body and Conveyor and Painting Systems." August 1, 1955, p. 48.
35. ———. "Ford Mustangs on the Production Line." *Automotive Industries*, May 1, 1964, p. 51.
36. Hoffmann, P. "Building the Pinto Engine." *American Machinist*, November 1970, p. 75.
37. LeGrand, Rupert. "How Ford Automates Production Lines." *American Machinist*, March 17, 1952, p. 135.
38. Knighton, C. L. "Manufacturing the Third Generation Econoline." Paper presented to the Society of Automotive Engineers, 1975 Congress and Exposition, Detroit, Michigan, February 24–28, 1975.
39. "Lincoln Zephyr." *American Machinist*, May 4, 1938, p. 362.
40. MacNew, Thomas. "Latest Tooling for Making Mercury Engine Cylinder Heads." *Automotive Industries*, April 1, 1954, p. 289.
41. ———. "Automatic Inspection Incorporated in Cylinder Block Automation." *Automotive Industries*, June 1, 1954, p. 53.
42. ———. "Ford Assembly Plant Has Separate Truck and Car Lines." *Automotive Industries*, December 15, 1955, p. 64.
43. "Mechanized Spot Welding at Ford." *American Machinist*, December 28, 1970, p. 33.
44. "New Lincoln Zephyr." *Automotive Industries*, November 2, 1935, p. 592.
45. Owen, C. B. "Organization and Equipment of an Automobile Factory." *Machinery*, March 1909, p. 493.
46. Slauson, H. W. "Efficient System for the Rapid Assembly of Motor Cars." *Machinery*, October 1909, p. 114.
47. Walsh, C. E. "Automobile Machine Tools." *Iron Age*, March 12, 1903, p. 10.
48. Wick, C. "Automated Production of Car-Frame Side Rails." *Machinery*, January 1965, p. 120.
49. Williams, D. N. "NEP Devaluation Speeds Pinto Engine Naturalization." *Iron Age*, January 20, 1972, p. 27.

Books and Government Documents
50. Arnold, H. L., and Faurote, F. L. *Ford Methods and Ford Shops*. New York: Engineering Magazine Co., 1915.
51. Bright, J. R. *Automation and Management*. Boston: Division of Research, Harvard University, Graduate School of Business, 1958.
52. Crandall, R. W. "Vertical Integration in the United States Automobile Industry." Ph.D. dissertation, Northwestern University, 1968.
53. Nevins, Allan. *Ford: The Time, The Man, The Company*. New York: Charles Scribner, 1954.
54. ———. *Ford: Expansion and Challenge*. New York: Scribner, 1957.
55. ———. *Ford: Decline and Rebirth*. New York: Scribner, 1963.
56. Sorensen, Charles E. *My Forty Years with Ford*. New York: Norton, 1956.

57. U.S., Congress, Senate, *Federal Trade Commission Report on Motor Vehicle Industry*, 76th Cong., 1st sess., House Document 4-68. Washington, D.C.: U.S. Government Printing Office, June 1939.
58. U.S., Congress, Senate, *Hearings before the Committee on Small Business, on Planning, Regulation and Competition: Automobile Industry*, 90th Cong., 2d sess., July 10–23, 1968. Washington, D.C.: U.S. Government Printing Office, 1968.

APPENDIX 4 / ASSEMBLY PLANT UTILIZATION AND CAR ALLOCATION DATA

INDICES SHOWING THE ALLOCATION OF MODELS TO ASSEMBLY PLANTS

The allocation of vehicles to assembly plants at Ford has changed significantly over time. Initially the allocation was obvious. There was only one plant. Then many were introduced, reaching a peak of thirty-three reported in operation at one time in the late 1920s and early 1930s. Each was a replication of the other in equipment and the product they produced. They were regional plants, positioned in most major cities as an important part of the company's local marketing, service, and training activities and to take full advantage of the freight savings that could be achieved through bulk shipment. Today there are only fifteen plants for cars in the United States to serve a much larger peak-year volume; they have been pulled away from extreme locations like Seattle, Boston, and Miami to more central locations; they are no longer tied to regional marketing activities; and they tend to be much more product-specific, that is, they tend to specialize in producing certain cars in the line. The role of these plants has obviously changed greatly. The data and analysis included here are intended to summarize more extensive primary data on model allocation to assembly plants in a way that will reflect principal components of this change.

Present data focus on two aspects of these plants. The first concerns the specialization of the plants to particular cars, called *plant specialization*. A highly specialized plant would be one that produced one type of car rather than many different types in the corporatewide product lines. The second concerns the extent to which the plants that produce one type of car are replicated in various geographical areas, for example, a Cougar plant in four different regions. This tendency will be referred to as *capacity replication*. Trends in three measures will be shown in regard to plant specialization. These are: the average number of different wheelbases in a given year produced per assembly plant, the average number of cars per assembly plant, and the percentage of the plants that produced only one car. The computation of these statistics is relatively straight forward, as illustrated in Exhibit 3.

The plant replication measure represents the extent to which available assembly capacity is allocated to provide production of the same product in different locations. More specifically, if r_i is the number of different plants in which the production of car, i, is replicated ($i = 1 \ldots I$); c_i is the amount of plant capacity devoted to product i, in fractional assembly plant equivalents, and C is total capacity in numbers of assembly plants, then the average replication of capacity, R, is defined as

$$R = \frac{1}{C} \sum_{i=1}^{I} r_i c_i.$$

This provides a measure of the average number of times the process capability to produce the same car is replicated at different locations. The average is taken over *capacity not number of car models* because the latter measure would bias results toward expensive, low-volume cars. For example, as illustrated in Exhibit 3, thirty-three plants produced three basic vehicles in 1930.

The Ford car and truck were produced in thirty-two, the Lincoln in only one, with respective unit volumes of 1,155,162, 272,897, and 3,515. A product-weighted replication measure would indicate twenty-one replications. As shown in Exhibit 3, the present capacity weighted measure yields an average of 31.3 plants/vehicles, much more representative of assembly plant characteristics.

Definition of Indices

The definition of the measures and the data they summarize are described below. Exhibit 1 lists the indices as computed for selected years. Exhibit 2 explains the method of computation with illustrative data for two selected years, 1930 and 1972. Finally, the computation of indices is illustrated for these two years in Exhibit 3. In these data the focus is on main-line passenger vehicles in the Ford Motor Company line. No attempt has been made to represent the full detail of the entire line. Tractors and name-plate variations of the same car are not considered. All commercial vehicles produced in assembly plants that also produce passenger vehicles are included in the common category of commercial vehicles.

1. Average Number of Different Wheelbases per Plant
This is the weighted average of the number of models with different wheelbases that are produced in the same plant. The average is taken over all plants.
2. Average Number of Different Models per Plant
This is the average of the number of models produced in each plant, weighted by the number of plants.
3. Number of Assembly Plants
This is the number of active assembly plants producing the car models that are counted in (1) and (2). This excludes the Wayne truck plant, Louisville truck plant, the assembly plants that were shut down during the depression of the 1930s, Canadian plants prior to the U.S.-Canada auto pact, and the Highland Park tractor plant. The number of U.S. only and U.S. Canadian assembly plants are shown starting in 1968 (16/18) since these plants add flexibility.
4. Average Capacity Replication, R, as defined above.
5. Percent of Plants Producing One Car Model.

EXHIBIT 1. Aggregate Indices on the Allocation of Models to Plants

	1* Ave. No. Different W.B. Per Plant	2† No. Different Cars In Assy. Plant	3‡ No. of Active Passenger Car Plants	4 Ave. Capacity Replication: No. Plants Producing Same Car	5 Percent of Plants Producing 1 Car Only
1903	1	1	1	1	100
1906	2	4	1	1	0
1910	1	1	1	1	100
1918	1	1	27	27	100
1925	1	1	33	31.1	100
1930	1.97	1.97	33	31.1	3
1933	2.0	2.0	9	7.2	0
1937	2.06	2.06	18	16.1	0
1939			17		0
1947			15		
1949	2.0	2.0	17.0	13.4	6
1950	1.94	1.94	18	12.9	11
1951	1.94	1.94	18	12.9	11
1953	1.89	1.89	19	12.5	10
1961	1.93	1.93	15	6.5	27
1966	2.12	2.37	16	5.8	12
1968	2.05	2.11	16/19	5.3	15
1972	1.89	2.05	15/18	4.95	35
1974 (before introduction of 1975 models)	1.6	1.75	15/18	4.7	40

* Wheelbase: W.B.

† All commercial vehicles are counted as one additional wheelbase and model in the line from 1930 and on; therefore the model count will differ from other model lists (Bronco and Econoline are excluded).

‡ Canadian plants included in 1968 and later years (US/US and Canada). The number reflects plants principally producing cars and therefore understates the number of Ford assembly plants in later periods.

EXHIBIT 2. Sample Data Showing the Allocation of Models to Assembly Plants in 1930 and 1972

1930 Assembly Plant Model Allocations

Ford Vehicles
Ford Model A: (including body styles: Phaeton, Roadster, Coupe, Victoria, Tudor Sedan, Fordor Sedan, Town Car, Cabriolet) Wheelbase 103.5″
Commercial Vehicles: (including Panel Delivery, Commercial Chassis, and Truck Chassis) Wheelbase 103.5″ and larger

Assembly Plants
During the period January 1 to December 31, 1930, the body types identified above in both the Ford and commercial vehicle lines were produced in volumes ranging from 56 units to 40,000 units per body type per assembly plant in the following Ford assembly plants.

1. Atlanta	4. Chester, Pa.	7. Cleveland	10. Denver
2. Buffalo	5. Chicago	8. Columbus	11. Des Moines
3. Charlotte, N.C.	6. Cincinnati	9. Dallas	12. Edgewater, N.J.

EXHIBIT 2. (Continued)

13. Houston	18. Louisville	23. Oklahoma City	28. San Francisco
14. Indianapolis	19. Memphis	24. Omaha	29. Seattle
15. Jacksonville	20. Milwaukee	25. Pittsburgh	30. Somerville, Mass.
16. Kansas City	21. New Orleans	26. Portland	31. Twin Cities
17. Long Beach, Calif.	22. Norfolk	27. St. Louis	32. Dearborn (Rouge)

Lincoln

During 1930 the Lincoln, 136" wheelbase, was produced only at the Lincoln facility in Detroit in volumes of approximately 3,500 units.

SOURCE: Ford Archives Production Records, 1930. Branch Assembly Plant Accession, Henry Ford Museum, Greenfield Village, Dearborn, Michigan.

1972 Assembly Plant Model Allocations (Wheelbases given in inches)

	Comet (103/110)	Pinto (94)	T Bird (120)	Mercury (121/124)	Ford (121)	Mustang (109)	Torino (114/118)	Montego (114/118)	Maverick (103/110)	Truck Various
Atlanta, Ga.							X			
Chicago, Ill.					X					
Dearborn Cougar (112")	X					X		X		
Highland Park (tractor and postal trucks not included)										
Kansas City, Mo.	X								X	X
Lorain, Ohio Econoline (van)						X	X			
Los Angeles		X			X					
Louisville, Ky. (2 plants-incl.)					X					X
Mahwah, N.J. (1 included)					X					X
Metuchen, N.J.		X								
Norfolk					X					
Oakville, Ontario (2 plants) Meteor				X	X		X			X
San Jose, Calif.		X								X
St. Louis, Mo.				X						
St. Paul					X					
St. Thomas, Ont.		X								X
Wayne, Mich. (truck bronco, not included)									X	
Wayne, Mich.					X					X
Wixom, Mich.—MK IV (121") Lincoln Cont. (127")		X								

SOURCES: Ford Motor Company, *Ford Facts and Figures* 1972, and *Automotive Industries*, Statistical Issue, 1972.

EXHIBIT 3. Sample Calculations of Indices 3, 4, and 6 for 1930 and 1972

Index 3 Wheelbases Per Plant

1972 No. Wheelbases Per Plant	No. Plants	Weighted Ave.		*1930* No. Wheelbases Per Plant	No. Plants	Weighted Ave.
1	5	(5/18 x 1)	.278	1	1	.031
2	11	(11/18 x 2)	1.222	2	32	1.94
3	1		.167			
4	1		.222			
Ave. No. Wheelbases/Plant	(18)		1.89		(33)	1.97

Index 4 Models Per Plant

1972 Models Per Plant	No. Plants	Weighted Ave.		*1930* Models Per Plant	No. Plants	Weighted Ave.
1	5	(5/18 x 1)	.278	1	1	.031
2	8	(8/18 x 2)	.889	2	32	1.94
3	4		.667			
4	4		.222			
Ave. No. Models/Plant	(18)		2.05		(33)	1.97

Index 6 Plants Per Model

1972 Replications Per Vehicle (No. Plants Producing)	Models	Devoted Fractional Plant Capacity		Fractional Capacity	Plants Capacity Weighted	*1930* Replications Per Vehicle (No. Plants Producing)	Models	Devoted Fractional Plant Capacity		Fractional Capacity	Plants Capacity Weighted
	Comet	¼ + ⅓	=	.583	1.17	32	Ford	½ × 32	= 16		512
	Pinto	1 + ½ + ½	= 2.		6.0	32	Commercial Vehicle	½ × 32	= 16		512
	T Bird			.833	1.67	1	Lincoln	1 × 1	= 1		1
	Mercury			1.5	3.0				33		1025
	Ford			5.	40.0						
	Mustang			.25	.25						
	Torino			1.66	5.0						
	Montego			.583	1.17						
	Maverick			.833	1.67						
	Cougar			.58	.58						
	MK IV Lincoln			.33	0.33						
	Continental			.33	0.33						
	Truck			3.5	28.0						
				18.	89.2						

$R = 1025/33 = 31.1$
(Different production locations per vehicle)

R, degree of capacity replication = 89.2/18 = 4.95 ave. number of different production locations per vehicle

NOTES

CHAPTER 1

1. U.S., Congress, Senate, *Hearings before the Committee on Small Business, Planning, Regulation and Competition: Automobile Industry*, 90th Cong., 2d sess., July 10–23, 1968 (Washington, D.C.: U.S. Government Printing Office, 1968), p. 256.

2. Joseph A. Schumpeter, *Capitalism, Socialism and Democracy* (New York: Harper and Row, 1946).

3. M. Brown and A. Conrad, *The Theory and Empirical Analysis of Production*, ed. M. Brown (New York: Columbia University Press, 1967), pp. 341–71. Interesting reviews of this research are contained in Jesse Markham, "Concentration: A Stimulus or Retardation to Innovation," in *Industrial Concentration: The New Learning*, ed. Goldschmid et al. (Boston: Little, Brown and Co., 1974); and F. M. Scherer, *Industrial Market Structure and Economic Performance* (Chicago: Rand McNally and Co., 1970).

4. See, for example, John L. Enos, *Petroleum Progress and Profits* (Cambridge, Mass.: M.I.T. Press, 1967), and W. R. MacLaurin, *Invention and Innovation in the Radio Industry* (New York: Macmillan Co., 1949).

5. Tom Burns and G. M. Stalker, *The Management of Innovation* (London: Tavistock, 1961).

6. John Jewkes et al., *The Sources of Invention* (London: Macmillan and Co., 1960).

7. Illinois Institute of Technology, "Technology in Retrospect and Critical Events in Science" (Report for the National Science Foundation [NSF C535], December 15, 1968).

8. Roderick W. Clarke, "Innovation in Liquid Propelled Rocket Engines" (United States Air Force Office of Research Analysis [ORA-680006], Holloman Air Force Base, N.M., March 1968).

9. Kenneth E. Knight, "A Study of Technological Innovation: The Evolution of Digital Computers" (Ph.D. dissertation, Carnegie Institute of Technology, 1963).

10. James R. Bright, *Automation and Management* (Boston: Division of Research, Graduate School of Business Administration, Harvard University, 1958).

11. Alan R. Fusfeld, "The Technology Progress Function: A New Technique for Forecasting," *Technological Forecasting and Social Change* 1 (1970).

12. Richard S. Rosenbloom, "Technological Innovation in Firms and Industries: An Assessment of the State of the Art," in *Technological Innovation: A Critical Review of Current Knowledge*, ed. Patrick Kelly and Melvin Kranzberg et al. (San Francisco: San Francisco Press, 1978), pp. 215–30.

13. Louis T. Wells, Jr., ed., *The Product Life Cycle in International Trade* (Boston: Division of Research, Graduate School of Business, Harvard University, 1972).

14. R. W. Conway and A. Schultz, Jr., "The Manufacturing Progress Function," *Journal of Industrial Engineering* 10, no. 1 (January–February 1959): 39–53.

15. Richard Bender, *A Crack in the Rear View Mirror: A View of Industrialized Building* (New York: Van Nostrand, 1973).

CHAPTER 2

1. James J. Flink, *America Adopts the Automobile, 1895–1910* (Cambridge, Mass.: M.I.T. Press, 1970), p. 25.

2. Allan Nevins and Frank E. Hill, *Ford: The Times, the Man, the Company* (New York: Charles Scribners, 1954), chap. 10.

3. Ralph C. Epstein, *The Automobile Industry: Its Economic and Commercial Development* (Chicago: A. W. Shaw and Co., 1928), p. 188.

4. U.S., Congress, Senate, *Hearings before the Committee on Small Business, Planning, Regulation and Competition: Automobile Industry*, 90th Cong., 2d sess., July 10–23, 1968 (Washington, D.C.: U.S. Government Printing Office, 1968) p. 353.

5. U.S. Department of Commerce, *Technological Innovation: Its Environment and Management* (Washington, D.C.: U.S. Government Printing Office, 1968), p. 16.

6. U.S., Congress, Senate, *Hearings before the Committee on Small Business, Planning, Regulation and Competition*, July 19, 1968, p. 395.

7. Nevins and Hill, *Ford: Times, Man, Company*, p. 133.

8. Ibid., chap. 7.

9. Automobile Manufacturers Association, *Automobiles of America* (Detroit: Wayne State University Press, 1970), p. 23.

10. Nevins and Hill, *Ford: Times, Man, Company*.

11. U.S. Federal Trade Commission, *Report on the Motor Vehicle Industry to the 75th Cong., 3d sess., House Document 468* (Washington, D.C.: U.S. Government Printing Office, 1939), p. 911.

12. Ibid., pp. 911–15.

13. Charles E. Sorensen, *My Forty Years with Ford* (New York: W. W. Norton and Co., 1956), p. 102.

14. Nevins and Hill, *Ford: Man, Times, Company*.

15. Epstein, *Automobile Industry*, p. 110.

16. U.S. FTC, *Report on the Motor Vehicle Industry*, p. 917.

17. William T. Hogan, S.J., *Economic History of the Iron and Steel Industry in the United States*, 5 vols. (Lexington, Mass.: D. C. Heath, 1971), 3:1009.

18. Epstein, *Automobile Industry*, p. 49.

19. AMA, *Automobiles of America*, p. 25.

20. Nevins and Hill, *Ford: Man, Times, Company*, pp. 497–508.

21. H. L. Arnold and F. L. Faurote, *Ford Methods and Ford Shops* (New York: Engineering Magazine Co., 1915), pp. 130–58.

22. Keith Sward, *The Legend of Henry Ford* (New York: Rinehart and Co., 1948), p. 20.

23. Hogan, *Economic History of the Iron and Steel Industry*, 3:1011.

24. James R. Bright, *Automation and Management* (Boston: Division of Research, Graduate School of Business, Harvard University, 1958).

25. Allan Nevins and Frank E. Hill, *Ford: Decline and Rebirth* (New York: Charles Scribners, 1962), pp. 117–19.

26. Flink, *America Adopts the Automobile*, pp. 255–80.

27. Nevins and Hill, *Ford: Man, Times, Company*, p. 282.

28. Ibid., p. 348.

29. Ibid., p. 349.

30. Sorensen, *Forty Years with Ford*, pp. 98–99.

31. Ibid., p. 235.

32. Alfred P. Sloan, *My Years with General Motors* (New York: Macfadden-Bartell Corp., 1963), p. 4.

33. Ibid., pp. 63, 66, 69.

34. Ibid., p. 80.

35. Ibid., p. 92.

36. Nevins and Hill, *Ford: Decline and Rebirth*, pp. 320–45.

37. U.S. FTC, *Report on the Motor Vehicle Industry*, pp. 349, 619.

38. Nevins and Hill, *Ford: Decline and Rebirth*, pp. 351–74.

39. Lawrence J. White, *The Automobile Industry since 1945* (Cambridge, Mass.: Harvard University Press, 1971), p. 207.

40. Ibid., pp. 177–88.

41. William J. Abernathy and Phillip L. Townsend, "Technology, Productivity and Process Change," *Technological Forecasting and Social Change* 7 (1975): 379–96; James Utterback and William J. Abernathy, "A Dynamic Model of Process and Product Innovation," *Omega* 3, no. 6 (1975): 639–56.

CHAPTER 3

1. Jan Horbye, "A Half Hour History of Unit Bodies," *Special-Interest Autos* (August–October 1973): 24–29; Roger Huntington, "Pioneer without Profit: Edward G. Budd Built the First All-Steel Auto Bodies," *Fortune* 15, no. 2 (February 1937): 82–89.

2. Such a composite picture of process advances in various countries can be constructed from sources like the following: David Scott, "Advanced Production Methods for Daimler-Benz Cars," *Automotive Industries* 120, no. 12 (June 15, 1959): 76–78, and 121, no. 2 (July 15, 1959): 87–128; "American Methods Fitted to German Conditions at Volkswagen," ibid., 113, no. 4 (April 15, 1955): 54–57; and "Japanese Auto Maker Pushes Automation," *Steel* (August 9, 1965): 112–18.

3. For several variations of this same argument see John L. Enos, *Petroleum Progress and Profits* (Cambridge, Mass.: M.I.T. Press, 1967); and R. E. Miller, *Innovation, Organization and Environment* (Sherbrooke, Quebec: University of Sherbrooke, 1971).

4. See, for example, Lawrence J. White, *The Automobile Industry since 1945* (Cambridge, Mass.: Harvard University Press, 1971); and U.S., Congress, Senate, *Hearings before the Committee on Small Business, Planning, Regulation and Competition: Automobile Industry*, July 10–23, 1968 (Washington, D.C.: U.S. Government Printing Office, 1968).

5. Jacob Schmookler, *Invention and Economic Growth* (Cambridge, Mass.: Harvard University Press, 1966).

6. "Modernization Miracles," *Mill and Factory* (Special edition, "Ford Production Methods") 18 no. 1 (January 1936): 87–111.

7. William T. Hogan, S.J., *Economic History of the Iron and Steel Industry in the United States*, 5 vols. (Lexington, Mass.: D. C. Heath, 1971), 3:1305–15.

CHAPTER 4

1. This chapter is based in large part on two papers: William J. Abernathy and James M. Utterback, "Innovation and the Evolving Structure of the Firm" (Harvard Business School Working Paper HBS 75-18, June 1975), and an earlier paper, William J. Abernathy and Phillip L. Townsend, "Technology, Productivity and Process Change," *Technological Forecasting and Social Change* 7 (August 1975): 379–96.

2. Samuel Hollander, *The Sources of Increased Efficiency* (Cambridge, Mass.: M.I.T. Press, 1965).

3. John L. Enos, *Petroleum Progress and Profits* (Cambridge, Mass.: M.I.T. Press, 1967).

4. Kenneth E. Knight, "A Study of Technological Innovation: The Evolution of Digital Computers" (Ph.D. dissertation, Carnegie Institute of Technology, 1963).

5. William T. Hogan, S.J., *Economic History of the Iron and Steel Industry in the United States*, 5 vols. (Lexington, Mass.: D. C. Heath, 1971), 5:1845–49.

6. Rodrick W. Clarke, "Innovation in Liquid Propelled Rocket Engines" (Ph.D. dissertation, Stanford University, Graduate School of Business, 1968); also published as United States Air Force Office of Research Report (ORA-680006) (Holloman Air Force Base, N.M., March 1968).

7. Raymond Vernon, "The Location of Economic Activity," in *Economic Analy-*

sis and the Multinational Enterprise, ed. J. H. Dunning (London: George Allen and Unwin, 1974).

8. Richard Normann, "Organizational Innovativeness: Product Variation and Reorientation," *Administrative Science Quarterly* 16, no. 2 (June 1971): 203–15.

9. James M. Utterback, "The Process of Innovation: A Study of the Origination and Development of Ideas for New Scientific Instruments," *IEEE Transactions on Engineering Management* EM-18, no. 4 (November 1971): 124–30.

10. Max Hall, ed., *Made in New York* (Cambridge, Mass.: Harvard University Press, 1959).

11. W. H. C. Simmonds, "Toward an Analytical Classification of Industry," *Technological Forecasting and Social Change* 4, no. 4, (April 1973): 375–85.

12. Kenneth E. Knight, "A Study of Technological Innovation: The Evolution of Digital Computers" (Ph.D. dissertation, Carnegie Institute of Technology, 1963).

13. Eric von Hippel, "The Dominant Role of Users in the Scientific Instrument Innovation Process" (M.I.T. Sloan School of Management Working Paper 75-764, January 1975).

14. Robert O. Schlaifer and S. D. Heron, *Development of Aircraft Engines and Fuels* (Cambridge, Mass.: Harvard University Press, 1950).

15. John E. Tilton, *International Diffusion of Technology: The Case of Semiconductors* (Washington, D.C.: Brookings Institution, 1971), pp. 73–87.

16. Ibid., pp. 15–18.

17. Ibid., p. 60.

18. Almarin Phillips, *Technology and Market Structure: A Study of the Aircraft Industry* (Lexington, Mass.: Heath Lexington Books, 1971), pp. 90–91.

19. R. Miller and D. Sawers, *The Technical Development of Modern Aviation* (New York: Praeger, 1970), pp. 98–127.

20. Ibid., p. 128.

21. James R. Bright, *Automation and Management* (Boston: Division of Research, Graduate School of Business Administration, Harvard University, 1958), pp. 22–30.

22. *First Quarter and Stockholders Meeting Report,* Texas Instruments, Inc. (Dallas, Texas, April 18, 1973), p. 8.

23. Robert D. Buzzell and Robert E. Nourse, *Product Innovation in Food Processing: 1954–1964* (Boston: Division of Research, Graduate School of Business Administration, Harvard University, 1967).

24. Donald H. Peters, "The Development of Frozen Orange Juice Concentrate," *Research Management* 11, no. 1 (1968): 45–60.

25. E. M. Tauber, "How Market Research Discourages Major Innovation," *Business Horizons* 17, no. 3 (June 1974): 22–26.

26. Charles E. Sorenson, *My Forty Years with Ford* (New York: W. W. Norton and Co., 1956), pp. 84–112.

27. Hogan, *History of the Iron and Steel Industry,* 5:1851.

28. Alfred P. Sloan, *My Years with General Motors* (Garden City, N.Y.: Doubleday, 1964), pp. 340–75.

29. Allan Nevins and Frank E. Hill, *Ford: Expansion and Challenge, 1915–1933* (New York: Charles Scribners, 1957), pp. 409–36.

30. James M. Utterback and William J. Abernathy, "A Dynamic Model of Process and Product Innovation by Firms," *Omega* 3, no. 6 (1975): 639–56.

31. William J. Abernathy and Kenneth Wayne, "Limits of the Learning Curve," *Harvard Business Review* 52, no. 5 (September–October 1974): 109–19, and private communication with a manager in RCA.

32. R. W. Conway and A. Schultz, Jr., "The Manufacturing Progress Function," *Journal of Industrial Engineering* 10, no. 1 (January–February 1959): 39–53.

33. Nicholas Baloff, "Start-ups in Machine-Intensive Production Systems," *Journal of Industrial Engineering* 17 (January 1966): 25–32.

34. Christopher Freeman, "Research and Development in Electronic Capital Goods," *National Institute Economic Review* 34 (November 1965): 40–64, and

D. C. Mueller and J. E. Tilton, "R&D Cost as a Barrier to Entry," *Canadian Journal of Economics* 2, no. 4 (November 1969): 570–79.

35. Abernathy and Wayne, "Limits to the Learning Curve," pp. 109–19.

36. David L. Marples, "The Decisions of Engineering Design," *IEEE Transactions on Engineering Management* EM-8, no. 2 (June 1961): 55–71, and D. Ramstrom and E. Rhenman, "A Method of Describing the Development of an Engineering Project," *IEEE Transactions on Engineering Management* EM-12, no. 3 (September 1965): 79–86.

37. D. S. Frischmuth and T. J. Allen, "A Model for the Description of Technical Problem Solving," *IEEE Transactions on Engineering Management* EM-16, no. 2 (May 1969): 58–64.

38. Clarke, "Innovation in Liquid Propelled Rocket Engines."

39. Center for Policy Alternatives, *National Support for Science and Technology: An Evaluation of Foreign Experiences—Final Report* (Cambridge, Mass.: M.I.T. Press, 1975), chap. 6.

40. Buzzell and Nourse, *Product Innovation.*

41. Peter R. Richardson, "The Acquisition of New Process Technology by Firms in the Canadian Mineral Industries" (Ph.D. dissertation, University of Western Ontario, 1975).

42. William J. Abernathy, "Some Issues Concerning the Effectiveness of Parallel Strategies in R&D Projects and Procurement," *IEEE Transactions on Engineering Management* EM-18, no. 2 (August 1971): 80–89.

43. Jesse W. Markham, "Concentration: A Stimulus or Retardation to Innovation," *Industrial Concentration: The New Learning,* ed. Goldschmid et al. (Boston: Little, Brown and Co., 1974).

44. Jay Galbraith, *Designing Complex Organizations* (Reading, Mass.: Addison-Wesley, 1973), pp. 14–15.

45. James M. Utterback and Elmer H. Burack, "Identification of Technological Opportunities and Threats by Firms," *Technology Forecasting and Social Change* 8 (1975): 7–21.

46. Elmer H. Burack, "Industrial Management in Advanced Production Systems: Some Theoretical Concepts and Preliminary Findings," *Administrative Science Quarterly* 12, no. 4 (December 1967): 479–500.

47. Wickham Skinner, "The Focused Factory," *Harvard Business Review* 52, no. 3 (May–June 1974): 113–21.

48. Burack, "Industrial Management in Advanced Production Systems," p. 484.

49. Joan Woodward, *Industrial Organization: Theory and Practice* (London: Oxford University Press, 1965), and Edward Harvey, "Technology and the Structure of Organizations," *American Sociological Review,* 3, no. 2 (April 1968): 247–59.

50. Richard H. Hall, *Organizations: Structure and Process* (Englewood Cliffs, N.J.: Prentice-Hall, 1972), p. 119.

51. Burack, "Industrial Management in Advanced Production Systems," p. 489.

52. Tom Burns and G. M. Stalker, *The Management of Innovation* (London: Tavistock, 1961).

53. Jerald Hage and Michael Aiken, "Program Change and Organizational Properties: A Comparative Analysis," *American Journal of Sociology* 72, no. 5 (March 1967): 503–19.

54. George J. Stigler, *The Organization of Industry* (Homewood, Ill.: Richard D. Irwin, 1968).

55. Ibid., pp. 135–37.

56. Bright, *Automation and Management,* pp. 79–86.

57. Harvey, "Technology and the Structure of Organizations."

58. D. J. Hickson et al., "Operations Technology and Organization Structure: An Empirical Reappraisal," *Administrative Science Quarterly* 14, no. 3 (September 1969): 378–97.

59. Charles Perrow, "Hospitals: Technology, Structure and Goals," *Handbook of Organizations,* ed. J. G. March (New York: Rand McNally and Co., 1965).

60. Robert Stobaugh, "The Neotechnical Account of International Trade: The Case of Petrochemicals," in *The Product Life Cycle in International Trade*, ed. L. T. Wells, Jr. (Boston: Division of Research, Graduate School of Business Administration, Harvard University, 1972), pp. 83–103.

61. William J. Abernathy, C. K. Prahalad, and Alan Sheldon, *The Management of Health Care: A Technology Perspective* (Cambridge, Mass.: Ballinger Publishing Co., 1974).

62. Galbraith, *Designing Complex Organizations*.

63. Abernathy and Wayne, "Limits of the Learning Curve."

CHAPTER 5

1. Allan Nevins and Frank E. Hill, *Ford: Decline and Rebirth* (New York: Charles Scribner, 1962), p. 365.

2. U.S., Congress, Senate, *Hearings before the Committee on Small Business, Planning, Regulation and Competition: Automobile Industry*, 90th Cong., 2d sess., July 10–23, 1968 (Washington, D.C.: U.S. Government Printing Office, 1968).

3. Charles E. Sorensen, *My Forty Years with Ford* (New York: W. W. Norton and Co., 1956).

4. Keith Sward, *The Legend of Henry Ford* (New York: Rinehart and Co., 1948), p. 20.

5. Allan Nevins and Frank E. Hill, *Ford: The Man, the Times, the Company* (New York: Charles Scribners, 1954).

6. Sward, *Legend of Henry Ford*, p. 32.

7. H. L. Arnold and F. L. Faurote, *Ford Methods and Ford Shops* (New York: Engineering Magazine Co., 1915), p. 38.

8. Sward, *Legend of Henry Ford*, p. 33.

9. Sorensen, *Forty Years with Ford*, p. 126.

10. Arnold and Faurote, *Ford Methods and Ford Shops*, p. 33.

11. Sorensen, *Forty Years with Ford*, p. 102.

12. Ibid.

13. Sward, *Legend of Henry Ford*, p. 23.

14. Sorensen, *Forty Years with Ford*, p. 128.

15. Ibid., p. 24.

16. Nevins and Hill, *Ford: Man, Times, Company*, p. 456.

17. Sorensen, *Forty Years with Ford*, p. 127.

18. James R. Bright, *Automation and Management* (Boston: Division of Research, Graduate School of Business Administration, Harvard University, 1958), p. 45.

19. Sorensen, *Forty Years with Ford*, p. 129.

20. "Ford Production Methods," *Mill and Factory* (special edition on Ford), (January 1936): 527.

21. Bright, *Automation and Management*, p. 86.

22. Nevins and Hill, *Ford: Decline and Rebirth*, p. 367.

23. Rupert Le Grand, "How Ford Automates Production Lines," *American Machinist* 96, no. 6 (March 17, 1952): 135–58.

24. F. L. Faurote, "Ford Shop Changes Estimated at $25,000,000," *Iron Age* 121, no. 16 (April 19, 1928): 1080, 1083.

25. "Ford Builds a V-8," *American Machinist* 76, no. 26 (July 6, 1932): 805–17.

26. Bright, *Automation and Management*, p. 171.

27. Sward, *Legend of Henry Ford*, pp. 15–40.

28. Arnold and Faurote, *Ford Methods and Ford Shops*, pp. 97, 128.

29. Ibid., pp. 128–59.

30. Nevins and Hill, *Ford: Man, Times, Company*, pp. 354–86.

31. Arnold and Faurote, *Ford Methods and Ford Shops*, pp. 113–27.

32. "Ford Builds a V-8."

33. Bright, *Automation and Management*, p. 180.

34. Peter Hoffman, "Building the Pinto Engine," *American Machinist* 114 (November 1970): 75–77.

35. F. L. Faurote, "Equipment Makes Possible the Ford Model A: Crankshaft and Camshaft," *American Machinist* 68, no. 26 (June 28, 1928): 1034–39.

36. See "Ford Production Methods," pp. 130–40; Arnold and Faurote, *Ford Methods and Ford Shops*, pp. 10–86; and Nevins and Hill, *Ford: Decline and Rebirth*.

37. *The Ford Industries* (Detroit: Ford Motor Company, 1924), p. 89.

38. "Ford Production Methods," pp. 429, 438.

CHAPTER 6

1. D. N. Williams and W. G. Patton, "Crystal Gazing: Manufacturing's Future," *Iron Age* 208, no. 1 (July 1, 1971): 44–45.

2. Allan Nevins and Frank E. Hill, *Ford: The Times, the Man, the Company* (New York: Charles Scribners, 1954), pp. 252–83.

3. Ibid., p. 282.

4. Ibid., p. 64.

5. The list of "Ford firsts" has been compiled from a variety of Ford Motor Company documents. In particular the internal publication titled *Ford Factory Facts* in years 1912 through 1917 and *Ford Motor Company Facts and Figures* for years 1950, 1951, 1953, 1966, 1967, 1968, 1969, 1970, 1971, and 1973, as filed in Ford Archives, Henry Ford Museum, Greenfield Village, Dearborn, Michigan, have provided a primary source of these facts.

6. William T. Hogan, S.J., *Economic History of the Iron and Steel Industry in the United States*, 5 vols. (Lexington, Mass.: D. C. Heath, 1971), 3:1300–1318.

7. H. L. Arnold and F. L. Faurote, *Ford Methods and Ford Shops* (New York: Engineering Magazine Co, 1915).

8. "Historic Events at the Rouge Plant, The Ford Motor Company" (photostatic copy of a chronology, 1902–41, PW 475, Ford Archives, Henry Ford Museum, Greenfield Village, Dearborn, Michigan, no date).

9. Nevins and Hill, *Ford: Man, Times, Company*, p. 380.

10. Keith Sward, *The Legend of Henry Ford* (New York: Rinehart and Co., 1948), p. 32.

11. Charles E. Sorensen, *My Forty Years with Ford* (New York: W. W. Norton and Co., 1956), pp. 99–105.

12. Two sources describe early overseas operations: Allan Nevins and Frank Hill, *Ford: Expansion and Challenge* (New York: Charles Scribners, 1957), pp. 355–78, and *The Ford Industries* (Detroit: Ford Motor Company, 1924), pp. 135–47.

13. As described in interviews with Ford Motor Company managers, 1974.

14. "Ford Production Methods," *Mill and Factory* (special edition on Ford), (January 1936): 515–87.

15. Ibid., p. 190.

16. F. L. Faurote, "Equipment Makes Possible the Ford Model A: Final Assembly," *American Machinist* 69, no. 7 (August 16, 1928): 269–75.

17. Thomas MacNew, "Ford Assembly Plant," *Automotive Industries* 113, no. 12 (December 15, 1955): 61; and Joseph Geschlin, "Ford Mustangs on the Production Line," *Automotive Industries* 130, no. 9 (May 1, 1964): 50–51.

18. Joseph Geschelin, "Scheduling in L-M Plants," *Automotive Industries* (November 15, 1953): 35.

19. The contrasting conditions are described in two articles: F. L. Faurote, "Preparing for Ford Production," *American Machinist* 68 no. 18 (April 19, 1928): 635–39; and "Large/Small Switch at Wayne," *Automotive Industries* 150, no. 5 (March 1, 1974): 19–23.

20. "Large/Small Switch at Wayne," p. 20.

21. Charles A. Weinert, "Automatic Assembly of Passenger Car Bodies at VW," *Automotive Industries* 130, no. 9 (May 1, 1964): 54–56.

22. N. D. Williams, "G. M. Opens Up on the Vega 2300," *Iron Age* 206, no. 6 (August 6, 1970): 45–46.

23. David Scott, "Advanced Production Methods for Daimler-Benz Cars," *Automotive Industries* 120, no. 12 (June 15, 1959): 76–78; and 121, no. 2 (July 15, 1959): 87–128; "Japanese Auto Maker Pushes Automation," *Steel*, August 19, 1965, p. 112.

24. Nevins and Hill, *Ford: Expansion and Challenge*, p. 466.

CHAPTER 7

1. Almarin Phillips, *Technology and Market Structure: A Study of the Aircraft Industry* (Lexington, Mass.: Heath Lexington Books, 1971).

2. John E. Tilton, *International Diffusion of Technology: The Case of Semiconductors* (Washington, D.C.: Brookings Institution, 1971).

3. A composite picture of originating sources for process advances in various countries can be constructed from sources like the following: David Scott, "Advanced Production Methods for Daimler-Benz Cars," *Automotive Industries* 120, no. 12 (June 15, 1959): 76–78; and 121, no. 2 (July 15, 1959): 87–128; "American Methods Fitted to German Conditions at Volkswagen," *Automotive Industries* 114, no. 4 (April 15, 1955): 54–57; and "Japanese Auto Maker Pushes Automation," *Steel*, August 19, 1965, pp. 112–18.

4. James Utterback and William J. Abernathy, "A Dynamic Model of Process and Product Innovation," *Omega* 3 no. 6 (1975): 639–56.

5. George J. Stigler, *The Organization of Industry* (Homewood, Ill.: Richard D. Irwin, 1968).

6. Nicholas Baloff, "Start-Ups in Machine-Intensive Production Systems," *Journal of Industrial Engineering* 17 (January 1966): 25–32.

7. William J. Abernathy and Phillip L. Townsend, "Technology, Productivity and Process Change," *Technological Forecasting and Social Change* 7 (1975): 379–96.

8. Jesse Markham, "Concentration: A Stimulus or Retardation to Innovation," in *Industrial Concentration: The New Learning*, ed. Goldschmid et al., (Boston: Little, Brown and Co., 1974), p. 267.

9. R. R. Nelson, "The Allocation of Research and Development Resources: Some Problems of Public Policy," in *Defense, Science and Public Policy*, ed. Edwin Mansfield (New York: W. W. Norton and Co., 1968), pp. 192–209.

INDEX

The Johns Hopkins University Press

This book was composed in Linotype Times Roman text and
Permanent Bold display type by Maryland Linotype Composition
Company from a design by Susan Bishop. It was printed on 50-lb.
Publishers Eggshell Wove paper and bound in Joanna Arrestox cloth
by Universal Lithographers, Inc.

Library of Congress Cataloging in Publication Data

Abernathy, William J.
    The productivity dilemma.

    Includes bibliographical references and index.
    1.   Automobile industry and trade—United States.   2.   Labor
productivity—United States.   3.   Technological innovation—
United States.   I.   Title.

HD9710.U52A56   338.4'7'62920973   78–1034
ISBN 0–8018–2081–2